Yeast

10 lb rye meal 10 lb malt meal ½ lb Yeast
cook in water too 212 F leave set 8 or 10 hours
then cool to 80 F – put in yeast

Mash

leaved set about 3 days until it settle
down then cook it off

Old Moore shiner

Vassel Owens

GOOD SPIRITS

Gene Logsdon

GOOD SPIRITS

A New Look at Ol' Demon Alcohol

CHELSEA GREEN PUBLISHING COMPANY

White River Junction, Vermont · Totnes, England

Book design by Christopher Kuntze.
No part of this book may be transmitted or reproduced in any form by
any means without permission in writing from the publisher.

The author and publisher certify that the information contained in this
book is accurate and reliable to the best of our knowledge. All instruc-
tional material is subject to any and all applicable local, state, and federal
laws of the United States of America, or of any other jurisdiction in
which this book shall be sold or used. The author and Chelsea Green
Publishing Company disclaim all liability that may be incurred with the
use of this information.

PRINTED IN THE UNITED STATES OF AMERICA

03 02 01 00 99   I 2 3 4 5

First printing September 1999.

Printed on acid-free, recycled paper.

"Sloe Gin," from *Opened Ground: Selected Poems 1966–1996*
by Seamus Heaney. Copyright 1998 by Seamus Heaney. Reprinted by
permission of Farrar, Straus and Giroux, LLC.

Library of Congress Cataloging-in-Publication Data
Logsdon, Gene.
    Good Spirits : a new look at ol' demon alcohol / Gene Logsdon.
        p.   cm.
    Includes bibliographical references and index.
    ISBN 1-890132-43-8 (cl) ISBN I-890132-66-7 (pbk)
    1. Brewing.   2. Distillation.   3. Alcoholic beverages—Social
aspects—United States.   4. Distilling, Illicit—United States.
    I. Title.
    TP570.L64   1999   99-38559
    641.2'5'0973—dc21   CIP

Chelsea Green Publishing Company
P.O. Box 428
White River Junction, Vermont 05001
(800) 639-4099   www.chelseagreen.com

Dedicated to my wife, Carol; her father and mother, Vassel and Helen Downs; and the other members of her family who have helped me with this book: Keith and Lois Downs, Morrison and Christine Downs, Demetria Downs, Nelson and Betty (Downs) Bentley, John and Ninia Downs, Paul and Anne Downs, James and Fran Downs, Jean (Downs) Ott, Bill and Joan Downs, and Ron and Deborah (Downs) Hauss.
They have also helped me learn
how to enjoy life better.

SLOE GIN

The clear weather of juniper
Darkened into winter.
She fed gin to sloes
And sealed the glass container.

When I unscrewed it
I smelled the disturbed
Tart stillness of a bush
Rising through the pantry.

When I poured it
It had a cutting edge
And flamed
Like Betelgeuse.

I drink to you
In smoke-mirled, blue-black,
Polished sloes, bitter
And dependable.

—SEAMUS HEANEY

CONTENTS

FOREWORD

Civilization began with a drink. When human beings ceased to be nomadic hunter-gatherers and settled down to farm the land, their first crop was grain and their first recipe, beer. Distill that, and you have whiskey.

Jesus turned water into wine (or beer, some of us would argue). Monks still make wine and beer in Europe, and former abbey sites produce Scotch whisky. The belief that alcoholic drinks are ungodly is a phenomenon of modern times.

In the industrial age, we have largely forgotten the farmhouse origins of beer and whiskey, though they never ceased to be agricultural products. Curiously, we never forgot that wine and brandy grow from the soil. As we enter the post-industrial epoch, we are rediscovering the true qualities of fruit-based drinks such as wine and "hard" cider, brandy, and applejack, along with grain products like small-batch whiskeys and micro-brewed beers.

The blander the global brands of drink become, the greater the gap that opens to accommodate the small and beautiful. *Good Spirits* brings a pastoral truth to the exploration of civilized drink. It is a practical manual, but it is also a captivating memoir, a valuable social history and an eloquent manifesto.

More power to its elbow.

Michael Jackson,
author of numerous books, including *Ultimate Beer*
and *The Complete Guide to Single Malt Scotch.*

PREFACE

I got started on this book primarily to honor three people I greatly admire, but I had to wait until they died so they would not get into trouble.

As a last resort during hard times, these three men and their wives met their farm payments by making and selling good moonshine whiskey. They were all of outstanding, law-abiding character in every other way, and I find them every bit as noble in defense of their freedom as the minutemen at Lexington. (The minutemen, by the way, were well fortified with rum when they made their stand against the English tax on alcohol.) If my honoring the memory of these farmers makes me an outlaw too, I don't mind in the least. A bad law is a bad law, and Prohibition, which we have not shed completely to this day, was a bad law.

It is difficult for the rich and the pious, in their holier-than-thou righteousness, to appreciate what heroism it took for these families to risk everything they owned to hold on to their farms. If caught, they would not only have gone to jail (one of them did, in fact) but, by one of the worst laws in our "democracy," they could have had their farms confiscated. Just as dreadful in their eyes was the shame that would have been heaped upon them by local society if they were found out.

The first of these men was Vassel Downs, my father-in-law, about whom I write extensively in the second chapter. To me he was a great man. When I think of him, I remember first the silo he and his sons built on their dairy farm. It was 30 feet tall and 12 feet in diameter if I remember correctly, and every bit of concrete in it was mixed by hand and hoisted by rope and pulley up the silo wall, a three-gallon bucketful at a time, and dumped into the form.

Every step of the way, iron reinforcing rod was hoisted up and planted in the wet concrete. When Vassel did something, he did it right. The grit and tenacity that would drive a man to build a silo this way (the only way he could afford to) is unimaginable in modern America.

When the bulldozers came to usher in the subdivision society, the developer thought he would just topple the old silo over and haul the pieces away. Vassel laughed. The developer stared at him, not understanding. Forward came the mighty bulldozer. Rumble, rumble. The silo did not budge. Another dozer was called in and cables were attached from the top of the silo to the two powerful machines. The cables snapped, and Vassel, by now seated in the shade of a nearby tree to enjoy what he knew was going to be a good show, laughed again. He had made that silo back when people had a notion of a permanent society, a permanent way of life foreign to bulldozers. The developer tried again. And again. And again. He could not believe in the ultimate limitations of bulldozers. The only thing that fell was the supply of new cable in the marketplace. Vassel threw his old hat in the air in glee.

Finally, after a long day with men and air hammers and acetylene torches, enough of the foundation was cut away so that the silo would topple over, given yet another bulldozer and a couple hundred feet of more cable. But when the old structure fell, it did not bust into pieces as the developer thought it would. It fell like a giant oak tree, one big solid trunk. Thunk! It took several days to pound it apart with air hammers, sledges, and torches. Vassel, in the shade, just kept on grinning. When the silo was finally cleared away, he put his hat on and walked back to the house, a satisfied smirk still on his face. But I was sure I saw two tiny tears slip down his cheeks.

The second moonshiner I honor lived not far from where I grew up. He is the inspiration for the short story that appears in this book as chapter 4. This story is partly fictional, so I will not reveal the name of the man or his family out of fear that the fictional parts will be ascribed to them as true. But in its essential message (and in many of the details), the story *is* true, and it describes, to the best of my ability, the indomitable human spirit in the face of stupid laws, unjust repression, and almost insurmountable economic conditions.

The third man was Karl Kuerner, who is probably one of the most famous men in the world, although not exactly by name or deed (see chapter 3). Karl operated a little farm right over the hill from Andrew Wyeth's boyhood home and lifetime studio, and he was the subject of many internationally renowned paintings by the famous artist. I got to know him while writing a book about Wyeth's work, and learned a precious lesson. What compels great artists to paint what they do are great subjects. Karl Kuerner fought in the first world war on the Germans' side and told me, sadly, that he had to kill many Americans or be killed himself. Deprived of ancestral lands after the war (he and his wife had both been shepherds), he came to this country unable to speak English and with little more than the shirt on his back. Against unbelievable odds, he and Anna established an old-fashioned farm so striking in its parsimonious but effective operation that Andrew Wyeth was moved to paint it many times. The farm is now preserved as an international shrine to the work of Andrew Wyeth and also, though only old farmers understand, to the subsistent genius of traditional farming.

Desperate in the early days to pay for the farm, Karl turned to moonshining right in the big kitchen fireplace. Out on a delivery one night, he was arrested and taken to jail. Anna and the children, who are my age and told me this story, spent the night in terror. They had no phone, no way to find out what had happened, but they suspected the worse. Yet the redoubtable Karl was released next day. He probably paid off the sheriff with moonshine. That ended his kitchen distillery business. Thereafter he stuck to cider.

If in my own small world I could become acquainted almost entirely by happenstance with three farmers who used whiskey to get out of debt, how many more there must have been—perhaps still are. I note that in *Our Fathers' Fields* (University of South Carolina Press), an excellent new book about the history of a southern farm, author James Kibler devotes a chapter to the story of how the owners made moonshine to keep from losing the farm. It amuses me that in this day and age, when the Secretary of Agriculture so unctuously lectures farmers about how they must "add value" to their crops before selling them if they want to stay in farming, no bureaucrat ever acknowledges that the law forbids farmers from choosing the most effective way to do that: turning grain and fruit into liquor.

My father once told me that he had tried a little wine making (or perhaps it was beer, I forget which) during Prohibition, when he was young and reckless. It didn't help pay for any farm. In fact he never did get his farm paid for. But sometimes I think he enjoyed life more than the financially successful. He and a friend, Cocky Neumeister, pursued their illegal activity above the bakery operated by Cocky's family, so Dad said, but soon quit for fear of getting caught. Much, much later, after discussing religion with me one day, Cocky had the nerve to tell my father that I was a danger to society. Yet he meant it as a compliment.

I remember a little ritual Cocky and Dad established as older men. About once a week, they would meet at Bolish's saloon just across the main street (Sandusky Ave.) from the bakery in our town of Upper Sandusky. Dad would bring along a pound of butter from the farm. Cocky would come sauntering across the street at the appointed hour with a loaf of warm, freshly baked bread tucked under each arm and a bread knife in his back pocket. They would sit at one of the euchre tables in back of the saloon and order big, frosty steins of the local Friemann lager on tap. Imagine an era when every small town had its own brewery and bakery. Then Cocky would slice the two loaves lengthwise down the middle, and pull out and discard the gooey inner dough. They would coat the insides of the thick, boat-shaped half-loaves of crust with a quarter pound of butter each. As the butter melted, they would lean back in their chairs and crunch away in utter bliss, washing down the bread with long, soothing gulps of draft beer.

Can life get any better than that, even if the farm ain't paid for, yet?

ACKNOWLEDGMENTS

My thanks to all the folks at Chelsea Green who helped with this book, especially Stephen Morris and Jim Schley for their encouragement, and Ben Watson and Deb Dwyer for sensitive and wise editing. My gratitude also goes to my wife's family for their immense help, especially Mrs. Joan Downs and Mrs. Deborah Hauss for arranging meetings with master distillers I probably would not have been able to see on my own. Thanks to Booker Noe at Jim Beam Distillery and Dave Scheurich at Labrot and Graham Distillery for taking the time to explain the finer points of good liquor to me, and to Wendell Berry, Wes Jackson, Marty Bender, Steve Bonney, John Gallman, David Beam, Richard Gilbert, Andy Wineberg, Mike Wineberg, Vern Ader, Steve Semken, Philip Omdahl, my uncle Robert Logsdon, and my brother Giles for sharing valuable information and insights. Last but not least, my thanks to Jill Logsdon, my daughter-in-law, for her amazing ability as a researcher, cruising the information highway for me.

INTRODUCTION

Toward a Sane Use of Alcohol

N THE SUBJECT of alcohol, hypocrisy is the standard-bearer of public opinion in America. As I did research for this book, I seized upon every opportunity in conversation with friends, associates, and new acquaintances to bring up the subject of alcohol. Invariably, people I could draw out would "suddenly" remember the family member who made liquor illegally in the past or who still does, a fact they were ashamed of rather than proud to admit, as I think they should be. I think that kind of shame is the main reason we do not come to grips effectively with the problem of drunkenness. When I worked at *Farm Journal* magazine in Philadelphia—and this was in the 1960s, not the 1920s—the fact that farmers drank spirits to about the same degree as the rest of the population was never admitted officially. Editorial policy dictated a huge and preposterous lie: that farmers did not drink alcohol. I listened to the editors—who were farmers themselves or born and raised on farms—defend this policy even when they were themselves a little tipsy. "We have a large circulation in the South, in the Bible Belt," they would say piously as an explanation. "Can't offend those people." But, I would persist, it was in this so-called Bible Belt that Hadacol, the popular patent medicine of the 1950s, had its biggest sales and moonshine its largest concentration of devotees. The reaction I got from statements like that was almost always an embarrassed silence accompanied by righteous staring at the ceiling. Even the recipes published in the magazine dared not include any spirits to enhance taste, even when, in the cooking, alcohol would be oxidized or distilled out of the food. Beer batter fish? Forget it. Wine in a fish chowder? No way. I pointed out that the pig slop (soaked grains) being advocated as good hog feed was a fermented product. It even smelled like beer. More staring at the ceiling.

Social disapproval of alcohol encourages heavy weekend binge drinking, in my opinion. Fewer people would drink so compulsively if they did not think of spirits as a sort of forbidden fruit that magically dissolves their problems when they give themselves over to it with abandon. Full of bottled-up emotion from work-related stress or personal discontent, they look to the weekend for release but overdrink and end up feeling even more depressed.

On the other hand, the home brewer or vintner, with a cellar full of alcoholic beverages, approaches drinking in a more relaxed way, and views the fruit of his or her labor with immense individual pride. With more than one could ever drink racked away in the cellar, there is no challenge to "drink the damn place dry," as the old saloon refrain puts it. Instead, he (and often, she) sips in quiet satisfaction. Conversely, the weekend binge-drinker guzzles in intense frustration, and the guiltier he feels about it, the more he guzzles. Getting plastered becomes a sort of ritual rarely encountered among wine drinkers in France or vodka drinkers in Russia or scotch drinkers in Scotland, all of whom (even children, I am told) drink with and between meals, for the most part becoming slightly happy or fortified every day rather than miserably drunk and life-threatening once a week.

Television and movies are no help. According to Hollywood, every time people go into a house (often an elegant million-dollar palace), the first act is to pour a drink. If someone is under stress, he or she gulps down the drink, or maybe two. No lover of good liquors I know makes a habit of downing a shot of whiskey in one gulp, much less two shots in two gulps. That is to proper whiskey drinking what swallowing a tablespoonful of salt would be to sprinkling it very lightly on potatoes. It's just insane, and quite possibly deadly.

More evil is done in the name of good than in any other fashion, because the goal of persuading people to act morally invites the idea that the end justifies the means. So the fervent teetotalers believe that stamping out drunkenness (a good goal, if totally preposterous) justifies any means, especially persecuting people who make their own booze and don't contribute to the bureaucratic and business wealth by paying taxes on it. Over half the price of distilled liquors at retail is taxes. Booker Noe, the grandson of Jim Beam, says that if you count all the taxes, they add 90 percent to the manufacturing cost of whiskey. Taxing liquor oppressively is okay because it's considered a "sin" tax, Americans say. The rich, of course, can afford to pay. Let the poor drink rotgut. However, the repressive laws against making liquor and the extremely high taxes on the store-bought product have actually encouraged the proliferation of cheap spirits so low in quality that maybe they have to be gulped down, simply to avoid the taste.

If you look at all the bad things this repression of rights has led to, such as Mafia power, our lack of will to change the law seems itself culpable. The Bureau of Alcohol, Tobacco and Firearms (ATF) and its bureaucratic forebears have for over two centuries violated human rights with the most incredible arrogance. In *Mountain People in a Flat Land* (Ohio University Press, 1998), Carl E. Feather recounts the story of how revenue agents put the wife of a moonshiner in jail to force him out of hiding. As Feather points out: "[Virgil] surrendered to the authorities to redeem his wife, unaware of the windfall he might have won had he recognized that his wife's civil rights had been violated."

Federal law forbids *any* home distillation of liquors, even for home consumption, which is something most people don't even realize. Though not often enforced anymore, the law prescribes not only heavy fines and jail terms for anyone caught making moonshine illegally, but also seizure of all personal property found at the still site, as well as "all right, title and interest" the distiller might have in the real property upon which the still sits. At a time when everyone is allowed to make beer and wine, such heavy punishment for making whiskey is ridiculous.

In every instance where regulations have been relaxed in the making of alcoholic spirits (encouraging the creation of small-scale microbreweries and family farm wineries), economic benefit has immediately followed for government, consumers, and the spirits business alike. Left free to experiment openly without fear of government reprisal, small, entrepreneurial brewers and vintners are improving the quality and variety of wines and beers both in terms of health and taste. We have even reached the point where nutritionists are more likely to agree on the healthfulness of moderate alcoholic beverage consumption than on the healthfulness of dairy products!

How much better off would we all be if government adopted a more positive attitude toward alcohol? Could we not at least be able to make a small amount of distilled spirits for home consumption? And would it not be better to encourage small commercial distillery operations instead of hunting down moonshiners or blanketing the law-abiding home distiller with red tape and prohibitively expensive permit fees? Government should encourage the formation of alcohol cooperatives and let them sell their spirits in somewhat the same way dairy cooperatives sell milk. As with milk, the product of the individual farmstead stills could be hauled by truck to central locations, where the cooperative would ensure quality control, age the spirits properly in warehouses, and then sell the product in the name of the producers. Actual total tax receipts, with lower, more affordable taxes, would probably be as high in net value as they are now, especially if you take into account the income taxes these small distillers would be paying on their profitable businesses.

As for permit fees, think of the outcry that would be generated if government decided to make people pay a permit fee for the privilege of growing sweet corn. Where did the notion come from that it is okay for government to exact fees for producing *any* food or drink?

If a more permissive policy were adopted, improvements might follow that would make home-distilled liquors as good as the best products now available commercially. France is famous for its wines and brandies not so much because of its climate but because individual families have been able century after century to develop good spirits without heavy intervention by government. A more permissive policy in the United States might also make distilling alcohol for fuel more economical (it is not generally considered to be so now). I am told that a couple of those big old buildings at Beltsville, Maryland, the heart of the research facilities of the U.S. Department of Agriculture, were originally intended for fermentation research. It seems to me that research of that kind would surely have meant important and faster advances in producing fuel and other products from renewable resources. If the design of home distillation stills had been researched and encouraged all these years the way home stills were perfected over centuries in Europe, we might today have more efficient ways to produce alcohol, too. We would certainly have small motors that could burn alcohol for fuel with great efficiency (see Chapter 11). But fermentation science did not long remain a major goal at Beltsville. A certain elite in America just couldn't quite stand to see the government doing research that might aid and abet the improvement and use of alcoholic spirits and at the same time possibly help small farms and businesses.

Appalachia, home of the moonshiner, could be a prosperous region today instead of the poverty-stricken zone it now is. Hundreds of thousands of more people could be living on small farms profitably making spirits of all kinds instead of being forced into cities where they brew riots instead of beer. Microbreweries and family farm wineries are showing the way. But we're still a long way from seeing microdistilleries dotting the American landscape, creating jobs and opportunity as well as better alcohol.

Inevitably, in writing this book, I will be accused of aiding and abetting drunkenness and therefore encouraging the general decline of society. I think it was Aristotle who first suggested this notion, and he didn't have drunk driving to lend strength to his argument. It is a hard theory to refute. Since society is always in decline somewhere, at least by some standards, and since some people insist on drinking intoxicating beverages to excess, a case can surely be made that booze causes the decline of civilization. But one might argue with equal forcefulness, and be equally as wrong, that the decline of civilization causes excessive drinking. Watching the antics of human beings today, especially in our declining seats of power, even Carry Nation, the famed temperance leader, might be driven to drinking.

Far from encouraging drunkenness, I hope with this book to reduce its incidence, or at least neutralize some of its negative social effects. Rather than trying to stop people from drinking, which the Eighteenth Amendment to the Constitution proved only makes them drink more, I hope to show how the use of alcohol can, in moderation and in high quality, be safe, enjoyable, and perhaps even healthful. Made at home, alcoholic beverages can save the frugal household money, too. Incidental to doing this, the home producer of spirits will inevitably do more drinking at home or in home neighborhoods, thereby cutting down on the incidence of drinking and driving. Perhaps that contention is naive, but we've tried the alternatives, without much success.

Understanding fermentation processes better, a household can also learn to produce fermented foods from which the alcohol oxidizes during processing. Making cereals and breads from fermented grain, fermenting dairy products, and fermenting fruits and vegetables are cost-efficient ways to use and preserve healthful food. And, at the very least, no one should shy away from using alcoholic beverages in cooking, since such beverages enhance the flavor of many foods, and the alcohol mostly oxidizes during cooking.

In the face of the fact that Americans are drinking millions of gallons of booze annually, it seems to me ludicrous to oppose intoxicating liquors altogether. Even a cursory study of history will convince the open mind that human beings *will* drink alcohol, no matter what. For instance, there are thousands of people who do not particularly like the taste of whiskey but who nonetheless love to drink it. What they like is not the liquor itself, but the *idea* of liquor. Remember that not even the most powerful country in the world, the United States, could make Prohibition work: the government might as well have tried to prohibit sex. All that the Eighteenth Amendment accomplished was to generate some of the worst crime and worst acts of repression this country has ever experienced, at least up until that time. Then it was necessary to waste all that money and effort in order to repeal Prohibition with the Twenty-first Amendment. The Mafia flourished while thousands of small farmers, who knew how to make good spirits, sank into poverty. Appalachia went on welfare, and has been a terrible drain on the national treasury ever since. Furthermore, by discouraging small farm distilleries, wineries, and breweries with heavy taxation and repressive laws, even after Prohibition, government assured the wealthiest classes a near monopoly of the market for alcoholic spirits. The best liquors became too expensive for lower-middle-class people to enjoy. The poor were left to drink rotgut.

Such repression could happen in a democratic society only because it was coupled with religious fervor of the best intentions. Religious fervor always has the best intentions. Even though Christianity cherishes the tradition that Christ changed water into wine at a wedding and, at the Last Supper, referred to wine as his blood; even though wine is used ceremonially in many Christian churches; even though throughout the Bible there is as much support for alcoholic spirits ("wine maketh the heart rejoice") as there is condemnation of drunkenness, fundamental Christianity has made a near fetish, at least in public, of opposing drinking alcohol. In fact, this opposition to alcohol has become as characteristic a part of American culture as drinking itself.

But that opposition appears to be of relatively recent origin in Christianity, similar to its ambivalence about the naked human body. Michelangelo painted nudes on the walls and ceilings of the Sistine Chapel without raising great outcries of offended sensibilities. But a century or so later, pinch-minded moralists had loincloths and other adventitious strips of clothing painted over the genitals of figures in these Christian masterpieces. A parallel hypocrisy beset alcohol. Monks in Germany, near Munich, a name that derives from the German word for monk, made beer, and monks in ancient Gaul discovered how to use hops to give their "beor" some kick. A Benedictine, Dom Perignon, perfected champagne and was also the first known vintner to use cork to stopper his bottles. Franciscan missionaries brought wine and brandy making to California. To this day, the finest liqueurs are either made by monks or come originally from monastery recipes. When alchemists first learned how to distill spirits, they called it *aqua vitae*, "the water of life," and far from considering it the work of the devil, they thought the discovery was divinely inspired.

Statistics indicate that there are ten and a half million alcoholics in this country, and while that is ten and a half million too many, it represents only a small fraction of the populace. There are eight million more heavy drinkers who, by definition, may not be true alcoholics, but who consistently prove themselves incapable of drinking sensibly. There are still others who, even when drinking modestly, tend to drunkenness. As we say in our neighborhood, they can get drunk just by being hit in the ass with a rotten apple. For all these people, abstinence from alcohol would be by far the wisest choice. But if the statistics are reasonably accurate, something less than 10 percent of the populace has a serious drinking problem. More than that, I'm sure, have a serious problem controlling their weight, but do we therefore decide to outlaw homemade fattening food?

Let it be said once more. True alcoholics dare not drink intoxicating beverages, just as some people dare not eat foods that they are seriously allergic to. In fact, some people get so sick when they overdrink that they are forced to moderation. If the gene or DNA strand that causes this phenomenon could be transferred into drunkards, what a better world would result.

Most humans seem to be naturally moderate about drinking and rarely imbibe too much and never to the point of disgusting stupor or obstreperousness. Statistics indicate that bar drinking is actually on the decrease (I don't believe it) compared to home drinking, but if true, this is a good trend. It means that more people are seeing the wisdom of drinking at home at the end of the day when they no longer have to drive anywhere. At home, the kind of group excitation that so often leads to unplanned and unwanted intoxication is avoided.

I do not wish to suggest, however, that bars and other public drinking places are bad—you can overdrink at home too. Bars can be wonderful places of sociable get-togethers, where we share not only a drink but our thoughts.

I would even argue that a moderate amount of alcohol is good for most people. Alcohol inspires humans to speak what is inside them, almost always a psychologically healthful exercise. Charles Allen Smart, in his delightful 1938 best-seller, *RFD* (out in a new edition from Ohio University Press), put it this way: "I don't think that any of us can afford to look at nature and at the major facts of the human situation while dead sober. Then they seem serious, irrational, and rather dreadful. When one looks at them in a very mild state of intoxication, they seem equally irrational, but more strange and amusing than horrible. I suspect, furthermore, that the slightly drunken view is the true one, more true simply because perceived with greater sympathy."

In some people who are rather dull when sober, a drink or two will bring out a surprising acuity or cleverness. Ben Franklin, who was death on drunkenness but not on drinking, wrote at length about the effects of alcohol on the human brain: " 'Tis true drink does not improve our faculties, but it enables us to use them, and therefore I conclude that much study and experience and a little liquor are of absolute necessity for some tempers in order to make them accomplished orators. [Some people] discover an excellent judgment when inspired with a glass or two of claret, but pass for fools among those . . . who never saw them the better for drink. And here it will not be improper to observe that the moderate use of liquor and a well-placed and well-regulated anger often produce this same effect, and some who cannot ordinarily talk but in broken sentences and false grammar, do in the heat of passion express themselves with as much eloquence as warmth."

I can find no more fitting way to conclude my argument than to quote Tom Stevenson from *The New Sotheby's Wine Encyclopedia* (DK Publishing, 1997). After pointing out how "grossly misleading" is the American health warning on wine labels, he lists the good health effects from wine that science has demonstrated: that compared to nondrinkers and heavy drinkers, moderate drinkers are sharper-minded when asked to perform cognitive skills, are less prone to stress, high blood pressure, heart attack, cerebral thrombosis, rheumatoid arthritis, late-onset diabetes, Leukoaraiosis (associated with mental dysfunction, vascular dementia, Alzheimer's type dementia, and cerebrovascular disease), postmenopausal osteoporosis, and gallstones. Furthermore, he goes on, drinkers of wine (and this would certainly be true for all alcoholic beverages) have greater protection against food-borne bacteria such as salmonella, *E. coli*, and shigella and an 85 percent greater resistance against one of five strains of the common cold virus. What's more, moderate drinkers are likely to live two to five years longer than nondrinkers. Concludes Stevenson: "What amazes me is that a country regarded by the rest of the world as litigation-mad has a wine industry that does not have the conviction to stand up for itself. Why not hire the largest firm of first-rate lawyers in the country and sue the Surgeon General, BATF, and the U.S. Government for $50 billion?" Atta boy, Tom.

GOOD SPIRITS

CHAPTER 1

The American History
You Were Never Taught

S OME FERMENTATION and distillation of spirits has been a case study in the repression of truth and human rights from the very beginning of U.S. history. Alcoholic beverages have tremendously affected our history, but literary and educational guardians of morality have always dutifully hidden this fact while "educating the masses."

The American Revolution was triggered by rum, but there is little chance of finding that fact in grade-school or high-school textbooks—the source of the only "history" most Americans are ever taught. The colonists were upset by the English tax on tea, of course, but it was the tax on rum (the Molasses Act) and other alcoholic beverages that really galled them. They chose to throw tea into the ocean to show their displeasure because who would want to waste good rum? The colonial economy literally ran on rum. Traders shipped molasses from Jamaica, distilled it into rum in New England, traded rum for slaves in Africa, and traded slaves for more molasses, meanwhile taking a margin of profit on each trade (and, of course, rolling their eyes heavenward as they told each other what good Christians they were).

Many of the key events of our history began in taverns and bars. Thomas Jefferson wrote the first draft of the Declaration of Independence in the Indian Queen Tavern near Philadelphia. The participants in the famous "Tea Party" of 1773 only worked up the courage to toss crates of tea into the harbor after first tossing back a few drinks in their favorite Boston alehouses. Likewise, the minutemen made their famous stand at Lexington after discussing the issue at length in the Buckman Tavern. When the British army ordered them to disperse, the minutemen, by then well fortified with rum, decided they weren't in a hurry to go anywhere. Shots rang out, and, as we say, the rest is history.

Despite the colonists' anger at British liquor taxes, one of the first things that George Washington and Alexander Hamilton did in the new "democracy" was to slap an onerous tax on spirits, thereby ruining the pioneer farmers' best chance of making profits on their frontier farms. With the war "for independence" still a vivid memory, western Pennsylvanians rebelled against the new republic. The revolt was so serious that Washington, who was making whiskey himself at Mount Vernon, sent troops to quell the uprising in 1794. This event barely gets a footnote in the laundered history taught in schools. Can't have children knowing that the Father of Our Country was a whiskey distiller screwing his citizens just as England had done. The farmers' rebellion against the hated "Hamilton's tax," as it was called, occurred not just because whiskey was an efficient way to turn grain into cash to haul to market (which the history books invariably give as the reason for the revolt, if they give any at all). The crucial issue was that there was very little money on the frontier at that time, and what was in circulation was, literally, "not worth a Continental." The pioneers therefore used whiskey as a form of currency, because alcoholic beverages were something nearly everyone had or wanted to have. Benjamin Franklin had amused himself in 1737 by putting together a dictionary of 230 words or phrases that were euphemisms for drinking or drunkenness, none of them "borrowed from foreign languages, neither are they collected from the writings of the learned, but rather wholly from the modern tavern conversation of tipplers," as he wrote. America liked its liquor, and not without reason: life was tough, especially for the working poor on the frontier. As Charles Allen

Smart writes in his book *RFD:* "Our experience has been that here on the farm we need a stiff drink much less frequently than elsewhere, but that when we need one, we really need it. On such occasions it is more important than food." Can't let talk like that reach our impressionable young people in school.

When Hamilton demanded the whiskey tax in cash, he was asking the impossible and imposing a worse hardship on people than what England had done. There was no cash in western Pennsylvania. Whiskey was cash. If Hamilton had demanded payment of the tax in kind, in liquor, the farmers could have complied, but that would have meant competition for Washington's distillery. Although Aaron Burr was hardly an American hero, his killing of Hamilton in a duel in 1804 was an event not mourned on the frontier.

But Washington, who to his credit eventually pardoned the captured leaders of the Whiskey Rebellion, went on enforcing the tax. He also kept on making liquor at Mount Vernon. In 1799 the Father of Our Country netted a little over a thousand dollars from the sale of liquor, an amount equivalent to about $150,000 in 1999 dollars. Do you remember being taught that in school? Furthermore, I recently read an article (can't remember where) revealing that, to gain election to Virginia's House of Burgesses in 1758, canny George gave local voters 160 gallons of booze, over a quart and a half for every voter.

John Adams, the next president, was, if possible, an even bigger hypocrite. He continued to enforce the tax and support the arguments in favor of it, even though, as the owner of New England rum distilleries before the war, he had ignored the English taxes he was supposed to pay.

The point is that there is no more effective way to raise money than by taxing alcoholic beverages, because consumption was, and is, so universal. The rich can afford the taxes, so they don't really mind, and the righteous abstainers think that making poor people suffer financially for their drinking is fit punishment. So life will ever be.

Only with the third U.S. president, Thomas Jefferson, did the first inklings of the freedom promised by the Constitution begin to take hold. Jefferson abolished the taxes on spirits except during the War of 1812, and until the Civil War, Americans could make alcoholic beverages to their hearts' content without being beholden to revenue agents. Lo and behold, the country did not disintegrate into vice and corruption as the pious Puritan tradition predicted. In fact, historians often refer to this period as the Golden Age of Expansion and Invention.

In 1750 there were sixty-three rum distilleries in Massachusetts alone. Some thirty distilleries flourished in Newport, Rhode Island. The colonists were consuming 12 million gallons of rum a year, 8 gallons for every man, woman, and child, says Oscar Getz in his book *Whiskey* (New York, David McKay Co., 1978). That's in addition to lots of beer and hard cider. This passion for intoxicating drink flourished in spite of repressive laws and regulations. In 1699 in Maryland (a Catholic, not a Puritan, colony, and so conceivably more lenient in the drinking department), one of many similar laws stated: "No inhabitant of this Province shall sell without License, any Syder, Qwince drink, or other strong Liquor to be drunk in his or her house upon penalty of one thousand pounds of Tobacco [!] for every conviction, half to the King, half to the informer." One of many typical Puritan "blue laws" in New England stated that "none be suffered to retale wine or strong water, or suffer the same to be druncke in their houses, except it be at some inne or victualing house and there only to strangers at their first coming, not exceeding the value of two pence a person, and that no beer be sold in any such place to exceed two pence the Winchester quart."

These regulations were largely ignored, of course, but they were in place so that any bluenose with a personal vendetta against a neighbor could nail him by reporting violations of the spirits laws.

After the Whiskey Rebellion was crushed in western Pennsylvania, farmers who knew a thing or two about spirits, especially the Scotch-Irish, moved on to Kentucky. Pennsylvania's loss was

Kentucky's gain, and today almost all the legal bourbon in the world is made in Kentucky. Bourbon, though it has a French name, is the only alcoholic beverage (along with Tennessee whiskey, which is very similar to it) that is truly and uniquely American. A vast county in Kentucky, later subdivided, was first known as Bourbon County, honoring the Bourbon king of France who helped America gain its "freedom," and it was there that the Scotch-Irish, taking advantage of excellent limestone water and soil rich enough to grow good corn, and the absence (at first) of tax collectors, started making whiskey in earnest. They used recipes and methods brought from Scotland and Ireland, but substituted corn for most of the rye or other small grain. Without the constant harassment and burden of dodging revenue agents, the early distillers made rapid advancements in both the mechanical methods of distillation and the quality of their spirits. Farmers who did not care to make whiskey were at the same time learning to convert corn to pork and drive the hogs to market, thereby gaining some efficiency of production similar to the conversion of corn to whiskey for transport. But soon clever farmer-distillers realized that the spent corn mash (distillers dried grains, as it became known later) fattened hogs nearly as efficiently as corn straight from the field, and distilling (and brewing beer) proceeded concomitantly with the practice of finishing hogs in pens on the spent mash. Robert West Howard, in his history of American agriculture, *Two Billion Acre Farm* (Doubleday, 1945), gives credit to the early distilleries for pioneering corn-fed pork production, which he calls "one of the most important discoveries in all the history of American agriculture." If you can find this observation in any primary or secondary school textbook, or any college history textbook for that matter, I will buy you a pork roast dinner at the sumptuous restaurant of your choice and a glass of bourbon to wash it down with.

Even in the earliest days of western settlement, intoxicating beverages were everywhere available, as they had been in colonial times. In 1803, the year Ohio became a state, Thomas Rodney, a frontier judge, related in his *A Journey through the West* (Ohio University Press, 1998) that when dining in Wheeling, West Virginia, he enjoyed excellent Madeira and Lisbon wines plus peach brandy. His flatboat journey down the Ohio and Mississippi Rivers was properly outfitted with a barrel of whiskey. He also carried wine and gin, the latter used apparently more for medicine than pleasure.

Abraham Lincoln opened a saloon in Illinois country in 1833. His father had sold the home farm in Kentucky for ten barrels of whiskey and twenty dollars cash. According to information in the Barton Museum of Whiskey History, in Bardstown, Kentucky, Abe in his tavern sold French brandy, peach brandy, apple brandy, Holland gin, domestic gin, wine, rum, and whiskey.

Americans were resourceful in finding something to ferment when the usual fruits or grains were not available. Metheglin, for example, was a fermented drink somewhat like mead in that usually it was made from honey. According to a 1701 book published in London, *The Whole Duty of a Woman*, metheglin was made by first boiling spices (not specifically named) in a bit of water and then pouring the spices into the honey to be fermented. Water was added until the honey mix would float an egg. Yeast was then introduced to start fermentation, since honey won't ferment very much on its own. Shortly thereafter, the potion was drinkable. That's why metheglin was cheap—no aging necessary. However, honey was not a readily available commodity in early America, although metheglin was common in the taverns. Frontiersmen had found a substitute, reports Harriette Simpson Arnow in her *Seedtime on the Cumberland* (University of Nebraska Press, 1995). They used the sweet pulp inside honey locust pods. This pulp tastes quite good (I know from experience), but one would have to be really hankering for intoxicating drink to extract enough of it from the pods to make even a gallon of metheglin. There is hardly half a teaspoon of sweet pulp in a pod, and how it might be separated from the pod except by tedious handwork is difficult to imagine. I assume frontiersmen learned how to cook the pods to free the sweet pulp.

Where corn was not locally available, especially in the South, Arnow says a beer was made from wild persimmons or from molasses and bran.

As population increased and towns grew, breweries and distilleries thrived, especially in the corn-growing Midwest. Wineries too flourished where soil and climate were favorable for fruit growing. Hops for beer was a common crop even in northern Ohio and still grows wild in profusion along fencerows in the vicinity of the old hop farms. In my hometown of Upper Sandusky, which has always prided itself in taking a public stance of disapproval when alcoholic beverages are being discussed, there was a distillery before the Civil War called Guckenheimer Brothers—this in a town of less than three thousand people at the time. Later the Guckenheimers moved to Pennsylvania and became famous for their whiskey. A fairly large vineyard grew next to their distillery in Upper Sandusky, so they probably made brandy too. Across the street from the distillery a brewery opened at about the same time. By 1902 the brewery advertised its beer as "put up for *family* use" (my emphasis). The last owner of the brewery, John Freimann, was still going strong in the 1930s and early 1940s, when I was a boy. He weathered Prohibition with a thriving ice business. Late in the thirties, in the afternoons when he was bottling off a batch of lager, Mr. Freimann would set out pitchers and mugs and serve free beer to all who came by. Now that's what I call the good old days. If Freimann could have lasted fifty more years, his business would have been called a microbrewery.

Taxation of spirits did return, of course, beginning about the time of the Civil War, for the usual declared reason: to pay for the war. Consumption of legal whiskey slowed its surge upward for a few years because the tax encouraged the beginning of the bootlegging business and ignited a veritable war between moonshiners and their government that lasted from the 1870s to the 1950s. But even without counting the unknown millions of gallons of bootleg being consumed, the legal market took off again after the financial panic of 1873. In the years immediately preceding Prohibition, the consumption of legal beer, wine, and whiskey had reached over 22 gallons per person annually—over 2 *billion* gallons. No one knows how many more millions of gallons of moonshine were also being consumed annually, not to mention the millions that distillers found ways to pipe off secretly to avoid inspection by government "gaugers" and so not pay tax on.

In human behavior, every action generates an equal and opposite reaction, as philosophers like to say. So while America guzzled, temperance and prohibition groups began to organize and gain in strength, especially among women, who so often led lives of suffering from being married to drunkards. But even when temperance and prohibition groups were able to stop the legal sale of spirits in many local areas and sometimes in whole states, such as Kansas, the consumption of alcoholic beverages continued to grow. Carry Nation could wreck saloons in Kansas and get away with it because saloons were supposed to be illegal in Kansas. And Nation had good reason for her anger. Her first husband was drunk when she married him, died drunk, and was drunk most of the time in between. Her second husband was a financial failure. Her life was in most ways miserable. It is no wonder that she heard voices telling her to destroy saloons. She might have been better off if her voices told her to have a glass of whiskey every night. But smashing barrels of whiskey was not original with her. Some fifty years earlier, women in Massachusetts, angry because their husbands were drinking up their wages and making their homes hellholes of abuse, retaliated the same way: took the hatchet to the barrel.

Carry Nation did not "carry" the nation even in her heyday. According to a story the anti-Prohibitionists loved to tell, Carry hauled a hapless drunk before her audience one night, doused his eye with a shot of booze, and, while the poor fellow bellowed in pain, said, "That's what alcohol does to your body." Later, the drunk reappeared on stage with a box of cornflakes. He grabbed a handful and ground them into Carry's eye. As she shrieked in pain, the fellow turned to the audience and shouted, "Now *that's* what Corn Crackies do to your body!"

But the message of Prohibition was powerful. Even after repeal, my aunt taught me to sing "Ten Nights in a Bar Room." I remember the first stanza well.

> *Father, dear Father, come home with me now,*
> *The clock in the steeple strikes one.*
> *You said you were coming right home from the shop,*
> *As soon as your day's work was done.*
> *Our fire is gone out, our house is all dark.*
> *And mother's been watching since tea.*
> *With poor brother Benny so sick in her arms,*
> *And no one to help her but me.*

The song affected me powerfully at age eight (and can still bring tears to my eyes). I knew, and know, of circumstances that those lines accurately described. I thought vaguely then the same thought I think very strongly now: if mother and father and maybe aunts and uncles and brothers and sisters had concocted spirits at home *together* and had drunk them *together* in the evening, with even a sip for sick Benny, how much happier would such homes have been. And drinking homebrew, they would not have spent their paychecks to make bureaucrats and big distilleries rich.

Prohibition was a total failure. The focus of bootleg history has always been on Appalachian moonshiners, but in the first nine months of Prohibition, rumrunners brought 900,000 gallons of booze across Lake Erie from Canada. A fortune in good scotch lies on the floor of the lake, dumped when Coast Guard launches endeavored to stop the trade.

The most concrete result of the Eighteenth Amendment was not temperance but serious crime. By the time of its repeal in 1933, historians reckon that Prohibition cost $11 *billion* in lost federal revenue (remember, this is 1930s dollars, not 1990s dollars) and no one knows how many billions in state and local taxes; plus $310 million for law enforcement, which of course was mostly in vain. Nor does this count the billions lost by farmers with excess grain and fruit to sell and nowhere to sell it. Nor will we ever know how many billions were lost because small marginal farmers could not make cash from distilling liquor anymore and so ended up farmless and on welfare. It was generally conceded by some economists and most politicians of both parties running for office in 1932 that Prohibition was a prime cause of the Great Depression. Franklin Roosevelt won the greatest landslide victory in history by promising that the first thing he would do would be to call a special session of Congress and abolish Prohibition. (The Republicans were against Prohibition too, but were shilly-shallying around the issue as usual.)

Yet the end of Prohibition did not mean, as one might logically expect, that citizens were free to make spirits and enjoy the fruits of their labors unfettered by repressive government regulation. It seems that the government, perhaps to please the strong Prohibition sentiments still very much alive in the country, decided to crack down harder on illegal beer, wine, and whiskey than ever before. By 1956 there were 14,000 "revenooers" out hunting down moonshiners. The government destroyed 14,499 stills that year; that is about one still per agent, perhaps the most inefficient law enforcement operation in history. The total cost was reckoned at something like ten thousand dollars per still destroyed, not adding in the loss of income on the part of the moonshiners and the cost of keeping them in jail. All to no avail.

Changes in drinking habits plus the migration of country people to city factories lessened the number of stills smashed after 1956. The government decided there was less moonshining after that, perhaps because it was loath to waste so much money trying to stop it. Yet *The Moonshiner's Manual*, written by one "Michael Barleycorn," in 1975, claimed that one-fifth of the whiskey consumed in this country at that time was still moonshine.

A copy of a letter in my possession tells as well as many pages of history just how hypocritically and stupidly the law against moonshining was enforced. It is signed "Miss Jenny Fenkhart," age eighty, from Mississippi. She wrote it to *Wines and Vines* magazine in 1942, about the expiration of her subscription. Verbatim:

Dear Sir:

> *I am not able to renew the subscription at present, the Sheriff raided me, took all my wine and I am before the court, what I will do don't know yet. Wayne County Mississippi is dry and as the Sheriff says, not allowed to have wines for oneself. It taken all my cash to hire an Attorney. So after that I have to see how I get out of it. What the Federal Alcohol Law says about wines? I am in doubt, but you know better? Would like to see your view on it or the Law.*
>
> *The whysky bootleggers are after me as my wines hurt their whiskey, but I was not catched selling wine but the bootleggers are after me to put me out of business as people say around here they never have a better wines yet. And I had a show to do good business as soon as the wines were of age but the sheriff took all about 250–300 gallons fermenting and first racking as I bought some California from Mobile dealers and that was the cause the Bootleggers were after Sheriff to stop me as I could show them what wine can do. I pretended for my own use but the Sheriff says too much for own use. I said it takes two years to make a good wine, but no use to argue with Prohibitionist or grafters. The Sheriff has 6 brothers-in-law who are bootleggers and they live 2 miles from me up the road and other bootleggers near me.*
>
> *As soon as I am able to renew I will do so but at present I am in debt to the attorney and have to pay him but the trial comes up today before a jury and I won't until the trial is passed and the attorney paid as I have no income now.*

Today we are stuck with one of the most ludicrous situations imaginable in law. Progress has inched along to the point where citizens can make a little beer or wine at home without getting thrown in jail, but oh heavens no, not whiskey. It appears that getting drunk on beer or wine is somehow less evil in the eyes of the law than getting drunk on whiskey, brandy, vodka, gin, rum, or tequila. The only explanation that seems appropriate to me is that society as a whole is not sane even when (especially when) it is sober. Whatever the case, the undeniable lesson of history is that humans *will* drink whether they can afford it or not, come hell or high water or the ATF. They *will* drink, even if they have to put the stuff in a medicine bottle and call it "bitters." They *will* drink even if, under harassment by the government, they turn to making fast and furtive alcohol that is poisonous enough to kill them.

The lunacy of the alcohol regulations reached its peak in the 1970s, when lots of people wanted to make their own ethanol for tractor and car fuel. Ethanol, understand, is drinking alcohol, have no doubts about it. Commercial ethanol "refineries" are nothing but heavily subsidized distilleries that have to add something to the fuel to make it undrinkable or lots of it would never get to the gas pump. So the government had a ticklish situation. People were coming to get the proper permits to make ethanol, not rigging up illegal moonshine stills. (Most of them did not even know the two processes were one and the same.) Because we were supposed to be having a fuel shortage at the time, it was not politically smart to oppose them. So farm entrepreneurs faced a veritable ocean of red tape and fees to get a permit for distilling ethanol from corn, while at the same time the government was giving huge piles of money to big business for ethanol refineries. Is it any wonder that so many people got discouraged? At least on this front, there's been some progress. Today, in order to produce small amounts of ethanol (properly cut with wood alcohol so you can't drink it), you need not pay a fee at all, just as long as you let the gendarmes know exactly what you are doing and fill out a bunch of forms. (See Chapter 11 for a full explanation of getting permission to make small amounts of ethanol.)

Meanwhile, in 1997 the plush magazine *Wine Enthusiast* carried advertisements for whiskey stills, with of course the caveat that the stills are to look at, not to use. Oh sure.

Could it be that common sense will yet prevail?

CHAPTER 2

My Father-in-Law, "The Old Moonshiner"

IT MAY SEEM that including a chapter on the distillation of alcohol before chapters on fermentation, which must precede distillation, is putting the cart before the horse, or the whiskey barrel before the fermenting beer vat. But the chapters that follow, dealing with the necessary partnership of fermentation and distillation, must presume some prior knowledge not only of the former, which is relatively well known, but of the latter, which is relatively unknown. *Homo sippiens* is an alcohol-loving animal, but most of us—myself included, until I sipped my way through myriad bottles of "research"—are rather alcohol-illiterate, no matter how fond we might be of drinking the stuff.

My father-in-law, whom we all called Granddaddy, is gone now, so I can't get him in trouble by relating his story. He decided during Prohibition and the Depression that he was going to make spirits despite the law. Mind you, in every other respect he was the most law-abiding and highly moral person I ever had the pleasure of knowing. So he became a moonshiner, and gathering from the way he signed his name, "The old moonshiner, Vassel Downs," on the parchment on which he left his directions for making whiskey, he was proud of it. Since his moonshine was well respected in those days by all accounts that I can gather, he had to have been, as he was in all his other work, an artisan skilled in, and respectful of, the details. I assume he also received some direction from his father-in-law, John Wesley Kurtz (known as Papa), who was a master distiller at Jim Beam, but Granddaddy never said. Moonshining was rarely discussed in the Downs family in earlier days and when I persisted in hearing about it, the subject was treated by some members as a shameful skeleton in the family closet. But eventually everyone came to be as openly proud of "the old moonshiner" as I was. He was my hero. He understood "value-added" agriculture long before that phrase had been coined. He even told me that moonshine paid for his farm.

But before I tell how he made whiskey, I need to put down some detailed background about the process. Granddaddy understood it, and taught me some of it, but I doubt he could have written it down clearly enough for a modern audience that knows little about the tradition in which he grew up. Granddaddy took for granted knowledge that has been lost to most of us.

First, consider how biologically efficient is the fermentation/distillation process. The spirits industry is one in which there should be no waste management problem. When the juice from a bushel of apples is fermented into about two and a half gallons of cider or distilled into a half gallon of applejack brandy, the pomace remaining will make great vinegar or certain kinds of brandy or can be used for animal feed. Cows and sheep love it. (Don't give them too much at once, though.) Commercial cider mills in fact sell pomace to dairy farms. Or the pomace can be turned into a formidable amount of heat by way of composting, after which the compost makes a good fertilizer. Greenhouses in Austria are sometimes heated with grape pomace compost. Or, if you have a fencerow you'd like to plant to apple trees for wildlife and livestock food, dribble the pomace, which is full of apple seeds, over the area you want seeded, and some of the apple seeds will sprout and grow. The acidic nature of the juice in the pomace enhances sprouting.

This natural efficiency can be seen even better in beer and whiskey making. The mash left after a bushel of grain has fermented into three gallons of beer or distilled into two and a half gallons of whiskey can be fed to animals. Granddaddy used to laugh about how his cows once got into the spent whiskey mash and came to the barn drunk that night. Actually, distillers grain, as the spent mash is called after it is dried and no longer intoxicating, can make nutritious human food too. Distillers have made cookies and other pastries out of it to prove the point. The mash contains at least half the nutrients found in the original corn—nearly all the proteins—and may actually be almost as nutritious because the grain has been rendered more digestible. Furthermore, in a commercial operation, carbon dioxide, a by-product of both fermentation and distillation, can be collected and sold, as can the acetates and aldehydes that are separated from the ethyl alcohol during distillation.

In other words, fermentation and distillation allow you to drink your cake and have it, too, which suggests a sort of victory over the "law" of entropy. That's a heady concept to be suggesting in the same breath with talk about cider and beer. But consider: the first law of thermodynamics states that energy in the universe is constant. The second law states that while the amount of energy is constant, it can change or be changed from one form to another indefinitely. A comforting thought, science has always said. We could go on using energy forever, and it wouldn't diminish. Then some smart-ass came along and argued that, while it is true that energy is never lost but only changed in form, it can't be used over and over again indefinitely without a loss. Burn a match and you can recover the sulfur and ash and other gases that originally made up the match. But you can't remake and reburn that match *and get the same net amount of work or energy out of it.* The unrecoverable energy is an example of entropy, and it means (fill my beer mug again, please) that we are doomed to a slow but inexorable extinction. (A good stout ale will be fine this time around.)

Far be it from me to differ with brilliant scientists who understand this entropical doom descending upon us, but allow me in rebuttal to trumpet the miracle of fermentation. No doubt entropy comes into play here somewhere, but if I raise a bushel of corn, brew from it with water 3 gallons of good beer, feed the mash to livestock, eat the livestock while drinking my beer, collect and use the carbon dioxide given off in the process, and use the manure (mine and the livestock's) to grow another bushel of corn, how much should I really worry about entropy?

Interestingly, the first articulation of the entropy "law" came from a German physicist, Rudolf Clausius, in the mid 1800s, a few years before Louis Pasteur first understood, and declared to a somewhat doubting scientific community, the correct principles of fermentation. Had Louis and Rudolf gotten together over a good glass of German lager or French Bordeaux, we might today have a much happier scientific view of the future.

Fermentation that results in alcoholic beverages is the anaerobic (without air) conversion of sugars and carbon dioxide into alcohol. The conversion is the work of yeasts and the enzymes they excrete as they "eat" the starches and sugars. Yeasts are everywhere, their supply in nature almost unlimited, waiting to work for or against human purpose. One tiny yeast fungus, scarcely more than microscopic in size, can split ten thousand sugar molecules every second during fermentation. Can you imagine any machine made by humans with that kind of efficiency? We have here a marvelous biological "machine" that is going to become even more important in a future when supplies of oil become limited. Not only can yeasts produce alcohol for use as a clean-burning fuel, but they can "brew" polymer plastics in a process very much like brewing beer. These plastics degrade without pollution, almost totally into water and carbon dioxide.

Growing yeasts and harnessing their energy is the fundamental agriculture. Until Pasteur looked into the matter, the role of yeasts was not understood (although good drinking alcohol and sourdough bread were made for centuries before him—a point not to forget). Most scientists thought the change from sugar to alcohol was a chemical one, and that was true in the sense that everything is chemical in the final analysis. But the role yeasts play in the conversion of sugar into alcohol is fundamentally a biological process. To make alcohol by feeding sugar to yeasts is at least metaphorically like feeding cows hay to produce milk. The yeasts eat until all the sugars are gone or the alcoholic content gets too high, and they multiply like crazy in the process. If oxygen is introduced into the process, other kinds of yeasts take over, the alcohol oxidizes, and the result is acetic, nonalcoholic fermented foods like sauerkraut and vinegar. So managing yeasts is really a kind of farm and garden work, not a test tube maneuver. When you start brewing beer or making wine, or producing sour mash for whiskey, think of yeasts that way: as tiny one-celled plants that you have to provide a fertile soil for. In this case, though, your "soil" consists of the various sugars found in plants. As a brewer or vintner or distiller (or pickler, or baker of yeast breads, or cooker of fermented-grain breakfast foods), you manage a garden of yeasts. Some of these yeasts are "weeds" to your endeavors, while others are your "crop" plants. You must control the former and encourage the latter if you want consistent success.

Fermenting grain for beer is a process very similar to fermenting grain for distillation into whiskey, gin, vodka, or any grain-fermented spirit. Likewise, distilling grain-based spirits from distillers beers is almost exactly the same as distilling brandies from wines. The stills used are practically identical. Granddaddy made both brandy and whiskey in his illegal still. Brandy exudes a taste of fruit and whiskey a taste of cereal; however, the alcohol itself is the same ethyl alcohol. The whole art of spirits-making in fact revolves around giving alcohol, which of itself is colorless and rather odorless and tasteless, unique flavors and coloration so that it is enjoyable to drink, not just something to get plastered on.

The whole chemistry and physics of making spirits rests upon the singular fact that ethyl alcohol boils or vaporizes at a lower temperature than water: alcohol at 173°F and water, of course, at 212°F. That's why anybody can make spirits. All you really need is heat. The reason why it takes skill to make *good* spirits is that there are other ingredients in ethyl alcohol—acetates, aldehydes, and fusel oils—that must either be separated out of the whiskey and brandy entirely, or retained, but in very small amounts, for flavoring. There are in fact a hundred known ingredients that are present in ethyl alcohol in very minute amount and chemists suspect there are some not even known yet. It is interesting to ponder what Tom Stevenson points out in *The New Sotheby's Wine Encyclopedia*, cited earlier: some 99 percent of the ingredients in wine are known, but if these ingredients are mixed with chemical accuracy and the proper amount of alcohol and water is added in, "the result will taste nothing like wine, let alone the specific wine we would be trying to imitate."

Some of these ingredients have a slightly lower boiling point than ethyl alcohol and so vaporize a little sooner. Others have a slightly higher boiling point and so vaporize a little later. The former are called "heads" or "foreshots," and the latter "tails" or "feints." In modern commercial distilling, especially with the use of continuous column stills, separating these substances—and in many cases selling them to by-product markets—is mostly a matter of technology, although the skill of master distillers is always the key ingredient. In pot stills like Granddaddy's, the distiller had only his skills and experience to rely on, not even an alcohol hydrometer, which I would consider a necessity if I were to make spirits myself.

After the family started bragging up Granddaddy's prowess at dodging revenooers as well as in making good whiskey, he opened up a little and began to regale us about his experience as a moonshiner, much to the dismay of Grandmother. I could not blame her for her attitude. She was a good and virtuous woman, but she resolutely, and much against her inclination, carried the moonshine to the house and did the selling, according to my brother-in-law John. Granddaddy's name was on the local FBI docket, as sister-in-law Jean learned when she went to work there. (I can't resist an aside. Because Jean worked for the FBI, the agents had permission occasionally to use the Downs farm as a place for target practice. Another Downs sibling, Jimmy, who was only about sixteen years old at the time, could outshoot them all. Hmmm. Maybe that's why Granddaddy never got caught.) Grandmother must have lived in constant dread of her husband ending up in jail and their farm being confiscated, as the authorities could by law do.

Once on a visit to Bardstown to help another moonshiner solve a distillation problem, Granddaddy saw some suspicious-looking strangers approaching the house. Sure enough, revenooers. He climbed up into the rafters above the attic, where he lay for hours. The moonshiner he was advising, who happened to be a relative, went to jail in Bardstown, where tradition says he was royally wined and dined by the local sheriff's department and, after everyone got a good laugh out of that, sent home.

Granddaddy and his cohorts in "crime" concocted a surefire way of transporting moonshine without getting caught. I've never heard of the method anywhere else. They would haul moonshine with loads of live chickens. Down in a hollow space inside the stacks of crated, squawking, crapping chickens were hidden the jars of moonshine.

Grandmother's mother was evidently morally opposed to liquor. Family tradition says that she so complained about her husband working as a master distiller that he finally quit and went to farming. But his replacement "got everything out of whack," and after much beseeching from Jim Beam, Mr. Kurtz went back until he had the mess straightened out.

None of my generation of the family were born soon enough to have tasted any of Granddaddy's moonshine. His first two sons were just big enough to find the still while playing around the potato house cellar. They went to Granddaddy and asked what it was. "He lined us up against the barn wall and told us we were never *ever* to speak of the still or ever go near it," says Morrison, chuckling at the memory. "But eventually he let us help him a little." I gathered from Granddaddy that he rarely drank any of his moonshine himself. It was in great demand and, at $15 a gallon, too pricey for him to drink. According to the written memento of his moonshining that he left, he ran off only small batches at a time—two 2-gallon batches at a time. Figuring maybe three or four batches a week, that could be as much as $120 a week in spare-time work, mighty fine money during the Depression.

He told me many times that one of the secrets of making good whiskey was not to add sugar to the mash, which of course is what most moonshiners do, yesterday and today. It's far cheaper and quicker to make moonshine with sugar than from grain malt. As one moonshiner once told me, "In fermentation, the sugars have to be broken down out of the grain, so why not just start with sugar?"

"Not at all the same," Granddaddy insisted. "Moonshine from sugar burns the throat." He followed the practice of all quality commercial distilleries and used barley malt, not sugar, as starter food for his yeast. Malted barley is barley grain that has been moistened so that it begins to sprout. Sprouting is then stopped by quick drying, and the grain is ground into a meal. I think Granddaddy made his own malt, but he could have bought it, too. However, buying malt (or sugar in the quantities needed) could draw the attention of revenooers.

Two separate preparations preceded Granddaddy's distillation, and pay attention now, because this is a good recipe for bourbon. In a barrel (55-gallon size) half full of boiling water, he put 50 pounds of cornmeal and let the mash soak for eight to ten hours. His directions mention steam as a source of heat but do not say how he rigged his steamer. Anyway, he could have cooked his corn in the same way one would cook anything, rigging up a firebox of stone or one made from a steel barrel. Using steam instead of a wood fire directly under the evaporator made control of temperature a little easier, I suppose. Steam was safer too, because then the wood fire could be located a little farther away from the still. The alcohol that comes out of the still is as volatile as gasoline, one must never forget, and were it to accidently come in contact with a flaming fire, the moonshiner might find himself scattered all over the hollow.

While the corn mash was cooling to 80°F, Granddaddy prepared the malt and yeast mix. Ten pounds of malt were used per batch.

To this he added 10 pounds of rye mash and ½ pound of yeast. His directions do not say, nor did I know enough to ask when I had the opportunity, what kind of yeast he used. He could have used regular kitchen baking yeast. My theory is that he may have gotten special whiskey yeast from his father-in-law at the distillery, but I have no evidence of that. Distilleries guard their yeast strains jealously, and Granddaddy's father-in-law would have been in deep trouble if he got caught sharing the secret. At any rate, the malt and rye mash were cooked in water rising just to 212°F, then allowed to cool to 80°F. At that point the corn in the barrel and the malt-rye-yeast in the other container were mixed together and allowed to ferment "until the frothy bubbling of fermentation more or less stopped." He figured two weeks for that operation, though it could be more or less. He did not specifically say, but I'm sure the yeast was added only after the malt and rye cooled down somewhat, as boiling temperatures might have killed it.

Then it was time to distill the "beer."

The drawing of his still that he left us is very inexact. His son John, who talked him into writing down his recipe, says that Granddaddy, while answering questions, simply scrawled the still as a sort of word picture to what he was describing orally. His still was a simple traditional copper pot still. It had a cone-shaped top, with a copper tube running out of the top to a "slag box" type of expansion chamber next to it. A typical slag box was an empty chamber, perhaps half the size of the still, in which some of the vapors condensed as they passed through, separating out some of the inferior "heads" while the good alcohol vapors, high in alcohol content, went on through to the condenser. Granddaddy's "slag box" appears from the drawing to have been a small, traditional "thumper" rather than a simple empty slag box. The vapors passed down into hot water in the thumper, which was also heated by steam or direct firebox, then bubbled up through the water, condensing into the "low wines," revaporizing, and leaving behind the undesirable heads. A thumper supposedly did a better job of separation or rectification than a mere slag box. The contrivance was called a thumper because as the vapors bubbled up through the water or sometimes hot mash, they created a thumping noise. The low wines went back to the pot still for revaporization, to wring out the last good alcohol during redistillation.

The tubing from the thumper, or slag box, which was often called the "doubler," because it doubled the alcohol content of the vapors as it redistilled them, carried the "high wines" on into the condenser, where the copper tubing spiraled down to an outlet valve at the bottom of the water jacket. In the spiral coil or condenser, the vapors cooled, condensed, and dripped into a jar or jug below. Cool water had to flow continuously into the condenser during distillation, while the warmed water flowed out. That's why so many moonshine stills were set just downhill of a spring. Granddaddy had a good spring available near the barn (still running merrily), but it is unclear whether he used it or pumped water from the well.

Actually the evaporator and the condenser are the only real necessities in traditional home distillation, but some kind of doubler greatly increases the efficiency of the still. Without it, the whiskey coming out of the condenser must be distilled a second time to achieve a good, high-alcohol spirit. Maybe even distilled a third time. Or fourth. In commercial pot-still distillation, the doubler is much like the first evaporator, only smaller. The second distillation that takes place in the doubler is similar to, but more complete than, that accomplished in a thumper or simple slag box. With a commercial doubler today, redistillation is not usually necessary, though in some cases it is still done.

I will describe a much easier way to distill toward the end of the chapter, but here's how Granddaddy did it. In his evaporator, he heated the fermented mash, which he had stirred into a runny slurry, to 173°F, the boiling point of ethyl alcohol. As far as I know, his still was not equipped with a thermometer, although I would not even contemplate distilling without one. Granddaddy said that some moonshiners dripped candle wax on the copper tubing leading out of the still before cooking off a batch. When that wax started melting, it meant the alcohol vapors were beginning to come and so it was time to cut back on the heat so that the temperature did not rise much above 173°F. But as for himself, he said, "After a while you can just feel how to manage the fire."

Granddaddy probably distilled his whiskey twice, another question I didn't know enough to ask him when I had the chance. With his little thumper/slag box, one distillation would have been about equal to twice without it. The alcohol content of the first run without a thumper or doubler would average about 30 percent. But the alcohol content of the second run, or, with a thumper or doubler, of the first run, should have averaged at least 60 percent or 120 proof. But likely he went through the whole process twice to achieve 140 proof liquor or more. In any event, Granddaddy probably threw away the first few ounces of spirits that came through the still on the second run, if his whiskey was as good as it was said to be. Those first drippings might still be too high in "heads" for safe drinking.

The trick was to stop saving the spirit when the alcohol content dropped below 110 proof, denoting that too much of the fusel oils and other impurities in the tails were now going into the spirit. How did he determine the proof of his moonshine so that he knew when to start and stop saving the good alcohol? Today you would use an alcohol hydrometer that measures alcohol content fairly accurately. Just draw off a little spirit into a glass as it comes out of the condenser and insert the hydrometer. Granddaddy, though, had to resort to old and not so exact methods. He'd use taste, for one thing. Also, by flaming the alcohol, he could estimate its alcohol content. At 190 proof, ethyl alcohol will burn as readily to the lighted match as gasoline. Bend a spoon handle so the spoon body lies level on a metal surface, fill it with alcohol, and light it. If it lights readily and burns for a few minutes, the alcohol content is around 140 proof or higher. When you can hardly light a little puddle of the liquor (about the size of a broken egg in a skillet) poured on a metal table, and when it does not stay burning much beyond a sputter, it is past time to save the liquor, because the proof will be below 100. Another handy measuring device from tradition, Granddaddy pointed out, was to pour some of the new whiskey into a small, narrow bottle or glass, filling it half full of moonshine. Put a top on it tightly, or use your thumb or hand to seal it, and shake vigorously. Then set it on the table. The bigger the bubbles and the longer they last, the higher the proof. A string of bubbles resembling a string of tiny pearls sometimes forms on top, usually in a circle around the side of the glass. That is called the "bead." The larger and more uniform the bead bubbles, and especially the longer they last, the higher the proof. If no bead forms at all, the proof is below 100—definitely time to stop saving the run. If you want to use these methods, try them on a good, high-proof commercial whiskey or vodka first, note how it reacts to these tests, and use that as a comparison with your own spirits.

To give his finished water-clear whiskey the required amber color of aged bourbon and at least a little mellowness, Granddaddy strained his new whiskey through charred oak chips and several layers of cloth mesh to screen out any bits of charcoal from the wood. He did not use caramel for coloring as moonshiners often did. This wood chip filtering removed more impurities and slightly mellowed the whiskey. The longer the soaking, the more the mellowing and the more amber coloring could be achieved. How long he aged the whiskey this way we don't know. Although using oak chips rather than an oak barrel to age whiskey sounds cheap, it is a rather standard practice in the production of some commercial brandies in Europe and not to be criticized. Oak chips are far cheaper than oak barrels, and so are used in cheaper spirits to get some flavoring of the wood. This doesn't of itself mean that the taste of these spirits is inferior. It depends on how long the aging process lasts, whether in chips or in barrels.

But if you go to the trouble of illegally distilling spirits today, you will certainly want to age your hooch at least a year or two, and four would be better. I suppose that is why really good moonshine is seldom available. Takes too long. Aging liquors to mellow them is just as important to the quality of the finished liquor as the distilling process, as we shall see in a later chapter.

But skillful distillers, like skillful cooks, can be frustratingly obtuse about their craft. How do they know *exactly* when a whiskey is right coming out of the still, as well as coming out of the barrel after years of aging? Granddaddy, when questioned about *exactly* when to start saving the alcohol and when to stop saving it in the distillation process, would shrug and say something to the effect that, "It's too complicated to explain," or, "Oh, you just gotta kinda get the know of it."

So when by extreme good fortune (the Downs family must know everyone in Kentucky), I was able to interview Booker Noe, the grandson of Jim Beam and certainly the First Guru of Bourbon in the world, I said to myself, Aha, at last I'll learn the secret. Booker (no one calls him Mr. Noe) had himself been a master distiller. Now retired, he travels around the world doing whiskey tastings to promote Jim Beam bourbons. He is famous for the theory and practice of perfecting the "single-batch" way of selecting the highest-quality whiskeys, which I'll explain in a later chapter. I sat there in his stately home, where his grandfather developed the yeast still used in Jim Beam distilling, my pencil poised, notebook on my lap, ready with my list of questions. Now would come forth the Deep Secrets of good whiskey for the world to read and I would become famous and appear in *The New Yorker* magazine as Booker has, wreathed in bottles of expensive bourbon.

Booker Noe is a big, wonderful bear of a man with a personality to match. People who know him well describe him as "just as common as any of us," which in Kentucky-speak means that he doesn't put on airs even if he is rich and famous. If there is anything a true Kentuckian can't stand, it's a person who puts on airs. I think Booker would rather have talked about his lush garden visible outside the windows, or the wonderful home-cured hams hanging in his garage, but, never mind, these people wanted to talk whiskey. He made us feel right at home. Maybe too much so, because before I could start into my list of studious questions, my wife Carol, brother-in-law Paul, and sister-in-law Joan (who are characters in their own right, believe me) got into one of those family memory competitions about kinship. We were sipping high-priced Booker bourbon, named after our host, which lent itself well to kinship orations.

"Papa was a master distiller at Jim Beam," my wife started it out. "John Wesley Kurtz. Did you know him?"

Booker beamed a great Beam smile. Of *course* he knew old John Wesley. (Even if he didn't, he was a world-traveling diplomat of good bourbon and knew how to handle such matters.) "Yes, yes. Kurtz. Downs. Seems to me we might be related," he offered seductively. "Through the Brinleys maybe."

"Maybe so," said brother-in-law Paul, rising promptly to the occasion. "But I think probably through the Cravens."

"Well, I recollect Uncle Jerry married a Brinley whose mother might have been Kurtz."

And then they were off and running. The room filled with bygone spirits of Beams and Kurtzes and Brinleys and Cravens and fugitive uncles and aunts who on second thought couldn't have been the kinship connection because they had no children or who, on third thought, could have been connected with almost anyone because they had a dozen children. I began to smile. I was reminded of similar kinship recitals that I had been submitted to as a child, when the numerous Ralls and Logsdons and Freys and Thiels and Orians in my home neighborhood in Ohio began toting up scores in their own fertility competition. I would have to stand in the middle of a room surrounded by grandmotherly types staring at me as if I were a calf at a livestock show.

"That chin is all Best, no doubt about it."

"He's got the Logsdon round shoulders." Pause. "Unfortunately."

"But where does that forehead come from?"

"Rall," my mother said, proudly.

"Well, Grady Orians who married that Lucille Frey of the Kirby Freys, as I recollect, *he* had a head like that, and *he* weren't no Rall."

"Ho, ho, don't be too sure. Grady Orians's grandfather was married to a Thiel and they're related to the Ralls by way of the Freys, aren't they?"

And so it continued, but now in Kentucky. Finally exhausted from the intense effort of pedigree debate, or perhaps waiting for another round of bourbon tastings, my in-laws fell silent for a second or two. I managed to ask a few questions about making whiskey. Paul answered them.

When I finally got through to Booker, he waved his hand grandly into the pleasant aroma of good bourbon saturating the air. "Oh, it's too complicated to put into words," he pshawed, just as Granddaddy would have said. "You just gotta kinda know." And that is all I could get out of him on that subject. On other matters of quality alcohol, he had much to say, as I shall relate in a later chapter.

To really understand stills, you need to see one, preferably in action. There are plenty of moonshiners around, but you may have to be patient before you earn their trust enough to be invited to watch or even help with a run. Remember, strictly by the letter of the law, ATF agents can be tough on anyone they catch at an illegal still, even an innocent bystander—the presumption always being that, if you are present at a run, you could not possibly be innocent.

A safe way to see a still in action is to watch for local festivals that are now more often (a good sign) able to get temporary permits to put on distillation demonstrations. The best one I know of takes place in southern Ohio, at New Straitsville, during its annual Moonshine Festival. The town hardly boasts two thousand residents, but on any particular Moonshine Day around the Memorial Day weekend, the population may swell to ten thousand or more. What's that tell you?

Now that Brown-Forman Corporation has restored the ancient pot-still distillery, Labrot & Graham, near Versailles, Kentucky, and is distilling a new bourbon, Woodford Reserve, you can visit there (free) and learn microdistilling in the traditional pot-still manner. To learn more about old backyard stills, you can visit the Whiskey Museum in Bardstown, Kentucky, in the heart of bourbon country. When we were there, the curator also told us about David Beam's ancient pot still, which he keeps in a shed near his Kentucky Home motel in Bardstown. He kindly showed it to us.

Mr. Beam belongs to the famous Beam family, although he no longer works in the company. He found the big old pot still in a long-closed distillery in Pennsylvania, and keeps it as a collector's item. I studied it and wondered greatly if it would not make the perfect still for a microdistillery should the laws ever change to make that a profitable possibility. Mr. Beam wonders too.

Another way to learn about stills is, yep, you guessed it, from the Internet. All the world is on the Internet now. Look under "moonshine and distilling books and supplies." Or tap into http//stillife.com/book.html. If you are not into internetting, or if that website has gone the way of so many websites by the time you read this, the postal address of that stop on the information super-highway is Stillife Publishing, Box 5, Neustadt, Ontario, Canada N0G 2M0. There are probably other websites as well. You can order all kinds of information on distilling, including how to make your own Scandinavian-designed still. One offer includes a fully assembled Liebeg Condenser kit and a copy of a book called *Home Distilling*, for $64.95. Some offers accentuate the fact that it is okay to have a still in your house as long as you don't use it. Others just come right out and say: "Enjoy illicit distilling."

There is a rare *Moonshiner's Manual* floating around used book-stores that is fun to read and gives the most details of home distil-lation of any book I've seen. This softcover manual first appeared in 1975, and the copy I have is the third printing, so it must have been at least fairly well read. The publisher was Oliver Press in Willits, California, and it was distributed by Charles Scribner's Sons, which would be the first place to inquire if you want to track down a copy. The author is one "Michael Barleycorn," which is al-most certainly a pen name.

If you decide to become a spirits outlaw, most certainly the best way to start distilling is on your kitchen stove. Use a pressure cooker or, better yet, a pressure canner for an evaporator; use wa-ter from the tap as a coolant for the condenser; and make your own condenser by bending copper tubing around something that will give the tubing the desired spiral shape without crimping it too much. Granddaddy said the way to bend copper pipe so it won't crimp is to fill the pipe with sand first. (See how smart those old-timers were?) You want to maintain a good open passageway through the tube to preclude all chance of it clogging in that rare occasion when solids in the evaporator might boil up and over into the condenser. The spiral of the condenser must always be slightly downward as it spirals around.

Making a small amount of spirits on your stove is quite simple, and the pressure cooker is a handy container. Its gasket lid ensures no loss of vapor, if it is in good condition. The fact that the pot is a "pressure" cooker is not necessary to its function as a still, because there should be little pressure buildup in vaporizing alcohol. If there were, the little pressure core in the lid of the canner or pot should melt and pop before the canner blows up. That's what it's there for. The valve on top of the canner that sputters and hisses and wobbles when in use can be screwed out and an adapter put in, to which you connect your copper tubing. If you can't do this yourself, any plumber can. You should always use silver solder, not lead, in putting together a still. (The stovetop method is well described in Fred Stetson's *Making Your Own Motor Fuel* [Garden Way Publishing, 1980].)

Some pressure canners have a temperature gauge, and all have a pressure gauge. You don't need the latter, so take it out and insert a temperature gauge if the canner is not so equipped.

Moonshiners today use a more sophisticated version of a slag box or thumper, which they call a "reflux column" (also known as a fractioning column or stripping column), and through which the alcohol vapors rise before passing on to the condenser. A home-made reflux column is nothing but a copper canister full of toy marbles that sits above the pressure canner evaporator, about the same height as, and half the diameter of, the evaporater. (Taller stripping columns to at least 4 feet in length are entirely possible, and are used in homemade ethanol stills where a higher-proof alcohol is desired, as I will describe in Chapter 11.) If you are handy, you can make one from sheet copper, but remember always to use silver solder, not lead. Each marble acts as a tiny, crude condensing plate as found in a commercial fractioning column, and the marbles provide much more surface area for condensation than an empty pipe or slag box would. The canister sits above the evaporator on a short length of copper tubing coming out of the pressure canner. You may have to use some supporting pieces of metal strap iron to anchor it firmly in place, but all parts that come into contact with the alcohol should be copper or stainless steel. As the vapors rise through the canister, the "low wines" tend to condense and drop back into the cooker, while vapors full of good ethyl alcohol rise on through the crude fractioning column and go to the condenser. A little more alcohol can be extracted from the low wines that fall back into the mash, but after a run, what is left in the evaporator is thrown out as waste. The remaining mash makes excellent chicken feed. One run through the still with a reflux column is equal to two runs without it, but with such a short reflux column, it is better to run the alcohol through the still at least twice and best to run it through three times to eliminate the undesirable heads and tails and to raise the alcohol content to the desirable 140 to 160 proof level.

In operation, the pressure canner sets on a stove burner and the temperature is held a little above 173°F. The closer you can keep the temperature steady at 175° to 180°F, the less "tails" will evaporate into your spirit. Of course, you want a wee bit of fusel alcohol tails, because the esters will flavor the whiskey as it ages. (See how fascinatingly fun this art can become?) The copper tube out of the reflux condenser leads over to the spiral copper condenser sitting in a container of cool water on a nearby counter. The container or water jacket for the coil can be fashioned out of a plastic bucket, since only water will be used in it. A bit of hose connected to the cold water faucet in the nearby sink delivers cool water into the top of the water jacket, and warmed water flows out the bottom through another bit of hose back into the sink. If you have good water pressure, you can even run the cold water in the bottom and the warm water off the top of the water jacket for better dispersion of the cool water around the condenser. A jar or jug under the condenser catches the dripping spirits. It is essential to have a good seal where the condenser tube exits the water jacket, because otherwise water will leak out at this juncture and drip into your spirits.

Strain the finished product through charred oak chips placed between a couple of coffee filters. Put the spirits in mason jars along with a handful of seasoned, charred white oak chips in each. Or age the whiskey in a new oak barrel charred on the inside. Let your own taste decide how long to age your whiskey. It will generally grow smoother for many years, but the taste of the wood after ten years of aging may be more noticeable than you might like. More on oak barrels and aging in a later chapter.

Remember, all this innocent and simple, home-centered work, leading to pleasurable and economical drinking after long and interesting experience, is illegal. But it is not illegal to read about it.

CHAPTER 3

From Cider to Applejack

OR PURPOSES of becoming acquainted with all the fermentation processes used in spirits production, let us first consider beverages from the apple, since nearly everyone is familiar with them. Apple juice in the absence of air ferments first to sweet cider, and then either into a "hard," or dry, cider of about 4 to 6 percent alcohol or into an apple wine that contains 9 to 12 percent alcohol or more. Unless you are a master apple vintner using just the right kinds of apples, you will need to add sugar to make an apple wine of that alcohol content. Hard cider or apple wine can then be distilled into brandy or "applejack" in the same way that fermented grain "beers" are distilled into whiskey.

If processed aerobically, that is, in the presence of oxygen (air), the cider will ferment into apple vinegar.

Lately the apple juice business has been hit with a bit of bad news that makes backyard cider an even more worthwhile venture. A few instances of the newly mutated form of *Escherichia coli*—*E. coli* 0157: H7—have made an unwelcome appearance in recent years. Its occurrence in unpasteurized cider and apple juice is rare—a few cases out of zillions of instances of people drinking apple juice, but it can be serious, and even cause death. The good news is that, thus far, in all of the reported *E. coli* outbreaks linked to apple cider, unwashed fruit drops were the culprit, which means that good basic sanitary practices, including not using old drops and not pasturing animals in the orchard during harvest season will eliminate most of the risk. But because we live in a society that has become intensely paranoid about possible toxicity in food, the government has moved swiftly to react (overreact in my opinion), and lots of regulatory red tape is being heaped on orchardists who make and sell apple juice. Most of the new regulations will result in the pasteurization of apple juice, by heat or by ultraviolet light, which small producers will hardly be able to afford, since thermal pasteurization units cost more than twenty thousand dollars and UV units can cost over ten thousand dollars. Government regulators admit that the new rules will drive some small producers out of business. Common-sense sanitation practices around the cider mill and quick refrigeration of the juice will avoid the problem, but as is so often the case in quantity food production, some seemingly easy but expensive "solutions," like heat pasteurization and irradiation, which increase costs, become the regulatory option.

But this is not necessarily bad news for the backyard cider makers, who keep their cider-making utensils immaculately clean, as they must anyway. You can't make real, honest-to-goodness hard cider out of pasteurized juice. It may be good, wholesome apple juice, but it won't ferment naturally. Juice from which cider can be made will thus become harder to buy, and will therefore make your own backyard cider venture a more important activity. And once turned into a stable spirit of 8 percent or more alcohol, the alcohol in the hard cider or apple wine itself protects against bacteria.

If most of us aren't as particular or precise about cider making as the best books advise, we at least can have safe cider that is fairly easy to make and quite enjoyable, even if not of the highest quality. I make the point because I hate to see busy home-centered families get discouraged by the detailed directions of the masters and decide not to try at all. With practice, your cider could become as good as the best imported French hard ciders and not take a lot of time or work to make.

The way we make cider is simplicity itself. We squeeze the apples, strain the juice through several layers of cheesecloth into plastic gallon jugs, let it set in a cool place (55°F is best) for a couple of days, until the solids have settled out to the bottom of the jugs, then very carefully pour the cider into other sanitized jugs, leaving the dregs, or lees, behind. It is better to siphon the juice from one bottle to another, because siphoning doesn't disturb the lees as much, but we don't always bother. In fact, in parts of Spain, where cider is as common in bars as beer, the custom is to keep it cloudy, not clear, by shaking it up regularly, as Frank Browning writes in his new book, *Apples* (North Point Press, 1998).

Then we start drinking it. At first it is just unpasteurized apple juice, mighty fine stuff in its own right. Very soon, in fact almost right away, tiny bubbles begin to rise in the jugs, indicating that fermentation has begun. We keep some jugs in the refrigerator and freeze the rest for later drinking. The important detail is that the fermenting cider must be kept at a cool temperature. If you do a small batch at a time, such as ten gallons, you can generally find room in the refrigerator for five of the gallon jugs and put the other five in the freezer to be thawed and enjoyed later. A cheap, secondhand refrigerator is perfect for storing small amounts of cider, as it is for muskmelons when too many get ripe at one time, or cabbage from the early winter garden. When we make cider in the late fall, as I prefer, we simply store the jugs in the garage.

After siphoning the cider from one jug to another, a procedure called "racking off," fermentation continues, slowly in cool temperatures, faster in warm temperatures. You can see the tiny bubbles rise in the jugs. After about a week, depending on the temperature, the sweet cider develops a snappy bead to it, indicating a slight alcohol content. That's when I love it. I suppose the alcohol content is hardly 2 percent at this point, though I've never tested it. At this stage, it makes a great thirst quencher. I often swig down several glassfuls at a time with little intoxicating effect. (But what that sometimes does to my bowels is horrendous.) We keep loose-fitting plastic or paper lids on the jugs for simple airlocks. The carbon dioxide pushes its way out of the jug around these lids, but the lids settle back down, allowing little air to get in if the jugs are full. You can watch the lids jiggle as the cider works.

The refrigerator works well to control temperature during fermentation. If you allow a higher storage temperature, say 65°F, the cider will ferment faster, but this will not usually result in as high a quality of cider. Even if you do not intend to bottle off high-quality cider, but only drink it as it ferments, as we do, cooler temperatures of about 50° to 55°F and slow fermentation keep the cider sweeter longer. If you don't have refrigerator space, make cider in cooler weather.

My father and grandfather made cider almost that simply, but in larger quantities. They took a truckload of apples from Grandpaw's orchard to the cider mill, and brought home the juice in a couple of 55-gallon barrels. Dad would put his barrelful on its side on a raised platform on the porch of his workshop. The time would be late October. Into the bung, he'd insert an airlock, which consisted of a piece of rubber tubing stuck through a quarter-inch hole in the bung, with the outside end of the tube in a glass of water sitting on the barrel and the other end inside the bung above the level of the cider. (Modern plastic tubing is better to use than rubber.) Carbon dioxide escaped through the tube, bubbled up in the glass of water, and no oxygen could get in the barrel. There was a wooden spigot in the end of the barrel, about four inches above the bottom of the barrel. That allowed enough room under the spigot inside the barrel for the lees to settle, and the cider could be drawn off through the spigot without disturbing the lees. While the 55 gallons of cider fermented away, and the carbon dioxide bubbled out of the airlock, we (my sisters and I when Dad wasn't looking) filled our glasses at the spigot and drank ourselves into a mild case of the trots. At first what we drank was just apple juice, but into November, the juice slowly changed to cider, getting a little harder (drier and more alcoholic) by the day, and Dad getting a little stricter about how much we drank. By Christmas what was left was really hard cider (about 5 percent alcohol) that only Dad appreciated.

When the cider was completely through working and before it turned vinegary (if indeed any remained after the corn-harvesting crews had slaked their thirst through November), Dad would draw off the remainder for drinking or further "experimentation." He would put the saved cider in a smaller barrel with an airlock on it, add some brown sugar and raisins to it, and let it sit till spring. The addition of sugars induced the yeast to work some more, raising the alcohol content hopefully to around 12 percent, or about the level of wine. Sometimes the resulting wine was miraculously dry and champagnelike. But not always. Once he invited Grandpaw over to taste two hard ciders from two different years, one which Dad thought fairly decent and the other not so good. Since he figured that he had made the ciders the same way, he was puzzled. Grandpaw, who loved a good laugh even more than good cider, solemnly sipped one bottle, then the other. He stared into space, as if pondering a heavy and heartrending decision. Finally, winking at me, he looked at Dad and said, "Neither horse will live."

If Mom needed vinegar, some of the year-end cider was put down cellar in a crock covered with cheesecloth, where, over the rest of the winter, it turned slowly to vinegar for table use. A cellar was a good place for the vinegar crock because of the semi-darkness. (A plastic container works better than a crock because crocks get chips in them and the vinegar may, very rarely, react negatively with elements in the burned clay under the glaze.) Acetobacter, a bacteria that turns cider or wine into vinegar, doesn't like sunlight. I don't remember Mom ever doing it, but vinegar that is to be kept for more than a few months can be pasteurized by canning it to keep it from deteriorating. Adding ascorbic acid will also preserve it. Follow the directions that come with the ascorbic acid sold in powder or tablet form, available from canning supply and wine supply businesses.

Vinegar can be made even more easily by using the pomace left over from pressing the apples. Put some pomace in a plastic container, something that will hold a couple gallons at least, and cover it with lukewarm water. Since vinegar requires air, you don't have to worry about airlock arrangements. Just let the stuff sit with a cover on it that will keep out bugs. Soon it will start to foam or cloud. That's the "mother" starting to form. In about two weeks, you should have good vinegar. If it is not strong enough for your tastes, let it sit longer. Maybe add more pomace, or apple peelings and cores from making pies. When you get the strength you want, strain off the vinegar and put it in a container, preferably one that you can draw from the bottom. That way you can keep adding cider to the top to produce more vinegar. A small wooden keg with a spout in the end for drawing off and a bung in the side for adding to, is perfect.

Cider and vinegar can be just that simple. The complexity comes into play either when very high quality cider is desired or when methods that speed up the natural process are introduced. These latter commercial methods need not apply in the home production of comparatively small amounts, and you need to know that, since these more sophisticated methods are often paraded as the "right" way to make cider. Home cider and vinegar makers should not be in a hurry, and, in fact, they usually prefer a process that takes care of itself over a longer period of time rather than a labor-intensive, chemical-intensive shortcut. They have plenty of other things to do in the meantime.

Most of the vinegar offered for sale in the grocery stores today is not real apple vinegar at all, but apple-flavored, distilled grain vinegar, which is faster and cheaper to make. Even the notion that adding "mother of vinegar" is necessary for starting the vinegar process is not really true. This addition just speeds up the process. If you let some cider age where air can get to it readily, it will turn to vinegar in its own sweet time. Then you can save a quart of that with the cloudy "mother" in it, as your starter for the next batch, or do as suggested above. The "mother" becomes a glucky-looking jellied mass. Don't let that bother you. That's your yeast. If you bottle the vinegar instead of keeping it in a barrel and adding to it, you should strain out the mother and use it for the next batch of vinegar. Just remember to keep all vinegar processes removed from cider-making processes.

As with all ciders and wines, you can add an almost unending list of herbs, flowers, or fruits to your vinegar to give it unique flavors. Some people put onions, for example, in with the pomace to make a vinegar with an onion flavor. You can mix in wine left over from parties and let it age awhile. You can add any fruit to a bottle of vinegar to enhance its taste, although this usually works better with wine vinegars or distilled grain vinegars. We put a few raspberries in our vinegar, let them soak for a few months before starting to use the vinegar, and just leave the berries in the bottle until it is empty. Looks pretty on the table, too.

Scrupulous cleanliness is the key to good cider, and that includes the condition of the apples. The apples should be ripe: not overripe, not underripe. They should not have skin breaks, or at least not many. They should not have lain on the orchard floor a long time, where they might have picked up molds, or mud, or even the toxic substance patulin (although I've drunk cider from dirty apples many a time and never heard of patulin). Apples with deteriorating bruises should be discarded (fed to livestock or chickens or used for making vinegar) or have the bad parts cut out of them. Apples slightly wrinkled from a mild attack of scab, or a worm now and then, or healed-over skin breaks, are okay. We use some windfalls in our cider mix, but probably should not. The more particular you are about using only the best apples, the better your cider will be. If fruit is contaminated with *E. coli*, from lying on the ground and rotting, not even washing will remove the bacteria.

It is best to allow apples to cure a bit after picking them and before grinding and pressing them. This "sweating" starts the starch-to-sugar conversion process and also causes the fruit to lose a little water, which you don't need. Aging usually works out automatically on a small scale if your apple trees are like ours. The apples don't ripen all at once, and we try to pick them just before they fall off, which means going over the tree several times. So apples stand in baskets for anywhere from a week to a month before pressing. Some of the high-quality, commercial cider makers, especially in England and France, also let the apples sit for eight hours after they are ground up but before pressing. This is a risky proposition, requiring lots of experience because of the danger of oxidation encouraging vinegar yeasts.

Connoisseurs of apple cider insist that apples should be washed before going into the press. I haven't done that in the past because we don't spray our apples, but my wife, Carol, who is the real boss of this operation, has issued an edict that, from now and hencefor-ward, we *will* wash the apples. I argue (in vain), if the organic ap-ples are handpicked from the tree, why wash them?

At any rate, for best results, wash your apples, especially if you are using windfalls. Mud that gets on apples, debris from the or-chard floor, dust in the air, bird manure, etc., won't do your cider any good. Often it is not the "dirt" that is the problem, but the wild yeasts and bacteria that are floating and growing everywhere. Some of them will be acetobacter, which, to a batch of cider, is worse than an infestation of purslane to your garden.

Obviously, the varieties of apples you use will make a difference in the taste of your final product. So will the weather and soil type and condition, just as in wine production. The search for the per-fect combination of apple varieties, climate, and soil could be just as exacting and complex and never-ending with apple wine as with grape wine, and I think it would be keenly interesting and chal-lenging for those looking for a high-value crop for a small farm. But it would be folly to start naming varieties that make better cider than others, although some obviously do. In general, a more acidy apple like Northern Spy or McIntosh makes tastier cider, and low-acid apples like Red and Yellow Delicious a less flavorful cider: mixing the two kinds might be the best compromise. As far as I'm concerned, a mixture of Virginia Winesap, Liberty, Grimes Golden, Roxbury Russet, and the fruit from a couple of wild apple trees makes a good cider, because those are the apples I have. There is a school of thought that says the old varieties, now mostly gone, that were used exclusively for cider in the eighteenth- and nineteenth-century heyday of cider were better than our modern varieties, but I wouldn't let that discourage you. There are so many varieties out there today, old and new, that high-quality apple ciders and wines are as much a possibility as ever. Some of these old cider apple varieties have been preserved at land grant colleges, particularly Cornell, and are once again available. Wild crab apples often make a good addition to cider because their high acidity and tannin content gives the cider a taste not unlike that of the ancient Yarlington Mill and Kingston Black cider apples of merrie olde England. High acidity and high tannin levels improve the keeping quality of hard cider as well as its taste.

We use a simple hand-cranked home grinder and apple press to relieve the apples of their juice. But we have motorized the grinder, and my clever brother-in-law found a way to use a little hydraulic jack between the press screw and the board on top of the press basket to supply the power to squeeze out the juice. Actually, the real cider gourmets would tsk-tsk a bit at our fast pressing. Old-timers said the apples had to be pressed very slowly so that only pure juice and very little pulp got into the liquid. Hand-turning the screw press ensures slower pressing. Oh well.

For making small amounts of cider, a kitchen grinder can be used, and the apples can be washed and even cored before grinding for extra pure cider. You don't want crushed apple seeds in the mix, as they would release unpleasant tastes. Don't peel the apples, however, because there are good yeasts and flavors in the apple skins. Extra clean conditions can be maintained fairly easily in the kitchen with small amounts if you have visions of making a quality champagnelike wine. You can also pulp the pomace more completely and capture more juice without a tremendous amount of pressure. In this case you may want to mimic wine making. Put the pulp in a cloth bag and press it *gently* in a wine press, or squeeze it *gently* by hand and then let the bag of pomace drip over a pan for a couple of hours to get out all the juice without forcing out the pulp.

Other fruit juices can be added to apple cider with good results, especially pear juice. Perry is pear cider, and it is better to my taste buds when mixed with apple cider than when used alone.

Even elderberry juice blended into apple wine makes an interesting taste, because of the elderberries' high tannin content. But it
will darken the liquid.

The process of making apple wine (sometimes called "applejack," although that term more correctly refers to distilled apple
brandy) is about the same as making any wine. Apple and other
nongrape fruit wines are becoming more popular, as more high-
quality small wineries are turning attention to them. An idyllic,
ideal model in the Ohio territory I roam is Pleasant Valley Winery,
near Mount Vernon, Ohio, operated by Mike Wineberg. (There's a
quaint theory that one's name can influence one's career, but Mike
was a biologist who worked in a laboratory that had nothing to do
with wine in the first half of his working life. Like so many of us,
Mike and his wife, who were working in Florida, wanted to "come
home" and give their two boys the kind of rural boyhood that
Mike had enjoyed.)

Wineberg makes seven (so far) different kinds of apple wines
with the same meticulous sophistication that grape wineries use.
All his wines are blends of various apples. In one of his blends, he
adds grape wine, and in another, cherry wine. He blends apples
that do well in his climate: Rome, Jonathan, Red Delicious, Yellow
Delicious, and two strains of McIntosh. He uses some Winesap,
but the variety is not well acclimated to central Ohio. Empress
wine is mostly made from Empire apples. One wine is aged with
oak chips suspended in a mesh bag in the wine, much as Granddaddy did to flavor his moonshine. "Actually, I believe using oak
chips achieves what I'm after better than aging the wine in barrels," Mike says. "I can control the amount of oak taste more precisely. Apple taste and aroma are more delicate than grape, and you
have to make sure the oak doesn't overpower it. And oak chips are
much less expensive than oak barrels." He has experimented with
American, French, and Hungarian white oak, and found the latter
to be the best for the taste he is after.

As part of the strict sanitation that Wineberg says is the major
factor in making cider or wine, he washes apples a second time (he

buys from local orchards, which have already washed them once). The apples then move automatically into a grinder and then directly into a continuous press where the juice is pressed out as the belt carrying the pulp moves through rollers of varying sizes. "Continuous presses are a vast improvement over the old cloth-and-rack presses," he says. "And they make sanitation much easier too." His continuous press, the smallest model made, costs twelve thousand dollars. The apple juice then is pumped to a settling tank, where he adds potassium metabisulfite powder (easier to work with than the tablets, he says) to kill wild yeasts and to control oxidation, plus pectin enzyme to take out solids and ensure clarity. Sometimes he also adds tannins for flavoring. After twenty-four hours, when the potassium metabisulfite loses its effectiveness, he inoculates the juice with special, laboratory-reared yeast and also adds sugar. His apple juice doesn't have enough natural sugar to raise the alcohol content high enough to achieve the wine stage. The amount of sugar added is determined by what kind of wine he is after: dry, semidry, or sweet. He likes to bring up the apple juice to between 19 and 22 Brix, which is how you refer to sugar content, all determined by careful measurement and sampling at his laboratory table in the wine room. He waves a manual in the air. "It's all here," he says. "The wine industry provides manuals like this, and I'd be lost without one."

Properly sugared and yeasted, the wine is pumped into 275-gallon fermentation tanks. The tanks are plastic encased in metal jackets for extra strength. "Plastic breathes a little, stainless steel doesn't," Mike explains. "More small wineries are opting for plastic tanks because of that, and besides, plastic is much less expensive."

While the wine is fermenting, Wineberg must test it continually for alcohol level, pH, residual sugars, and sulfite. He believes that the optimum alcohol level for apple wine is 9.5 percent, somewhat lower than grape wines, because of the more delicate nature of apple flavor and aroma. "However, I let my wines rise to a 10 percent alcohol level because I want to assure stability." This practice has, incidentally, gained support recently from Robert Kime at Cornell's Agricultural Research Station. Kime's research underscores the practice of keeping most nongrape fruit wines at a lower alcohol content than grape wine, not to exceed 10.5 percent.

Fermentation may last a month to six weeks or longer, with the wine kept as close to 55°F as possible. "A cooler temperature slows fermentation, and that's better for quality," Wineberg says. Over the winter the wine is cold-stabilized, which enhances clarity, then pumped through a filter and bottled. Although the bottles are already clean, he washes them again. Pleasant Valley is producing about 1,600 gallons of wine a year, and Wineberg wants to increase to only 2,500 to 3,000 and no more. "I'm a champion of small operations," he says.

Professional winemakers routinely add some form of sulfite (backyarders use crushed Campden tablets, usually) to their pressed fruit juice then add a commercial yeast, just as Wineberg does. This practice almost always results in a better wine, but ordinary baker's yeast is okay, and wild yeasts, if you're willing to take the chance, might be just as good. Highly acid "musts," the term for juice to be fermented, have built-in natural control over vinegar yeasts.

Sulfites in wine are okay but are not really good for you. Some experts believe that sulfites give some people headaches when they drink wine. For asthmatics and other people allergic to sulfites, they can be, very rarely, deadly. That is why all wines that use sulfur must say so on the label. I think killing off wild yeasts with sulfur is like using herbicides in the garden to kill off unwanted weeds, and as in that situation, there are other methods available for very small operations. For instance, there is a slow movement away from sulfur dioxide to citric acid, which deters unwanted yeasts too in "organic" wines. Home wine making way back into the eighteenth century recommended adding citrus fruits, juice, and rinds to the juice to be fermented. Scalding utensils, and mixing scalding water with fermenting fruits and grains, which many recipes call for, also kills wild yeasts.

Where ultracleanliness is observed, there may be a dearth of natural good yeast (various *Saccharomyces* species), and so even if the "must" has not been sterilized with the usual metabisulfite (Campden) tablets or powders, adding a laboratory-cultured yeast is now almost standard practice, although again, not absolutely necessary. For the backyard cider maker, this is seldom something to worry about. One reason for using old cider, wine, or whiskey barrels for containers is that they are usually teeming with good yeasts. Just stay away from wooden barrels in which cider has turned to vinegar. Or set a fire inside them and char the surface thoroughly. There are no real lab-cultured cider yeasts yet, but ale yeasts (for fermentation temperatures of 60°F or above) and lager yeasts, or white wine or champagne yeasts (for temperatures of 45°F to 55°F) work very well, and are easily available from wine supply stores.

The traditional way of supplying extra yeast power to cider when turning it into wine is to add raisins and sugar. Boil a bit of warm water, and when it cools to a tepid temperature, add the raisins to it. (Be sure to use natural, sun-dried raisins that have not been treated with sulfur dioxide or other preservatives.) A quart of water and a half pound of raisins are enough for 10 gallons of cider, or approximately a handful of raisins to the gallon. The raisins do a lot of things for a fruit wine. They are, after all, dried grapes. The tannin in them can help the taste, and they support good yeast activity. Whether or not you use raisins, you will probably want to add a little sugar. You can be precise like Mike Wineberg if you want to make a good commercial wine, or you can be a bit more casual and experiment on your own. Try a rate of about one part sugar to two parts of cider. For a gallon of finished wine, start with 5 quarts of sweet cider, mix in 2.5 pounds of sugar and a tablespoon of citric acid (or the juice from a couple of lemons or even oranges). This is also the time to add a crushed Campden tablet if you want to. You can add pectin enzyme as Wineberg does, which usually makes the final wine clearer by removing pectin from the must. Let stand for twenty-four hours, then add a commercial wine yeast as Wineberg does if you have inoculated or sterilized the juice previously with some form of sulfur or boiling water. If you can't get a wine yeast, just use a package of regular baker's yeast. Some winemakers also add a tablespoon of yeast nutrient (available at wine supply stores), but this is not necessary either. If you use some of today's quick-acting baker's yeast, it starts working at a fever pitch without special nutrients. Usually the yeast is added by dissolving the powder into a cup and a half of lukewarm apple juice. Orange juice works okay, too.

After the sediment settles, rack off the fermenting wine into glass or plastic or wooden containers that are equipped with some kind of airlock to let out carbon dioxide and not let air in. In about a month, rack again, but do not seal the bottles, as the wine should still be working. Fill the containers nearly to the top so that there is less room for air, and leave the corks in loosely or use airlocks (or loose lids as we do for regular cider). Commercial airlocks are inexpensive and can be purchased at any homebrewing supply store, but you can also make one by drilling a hole in a cork of the right size to fit the bottle and inserting a length of plastic tubing into the hole in the cork. Stick the other end of the tubing in a glass of water. This way, carbon dioxide can escape the bottle, but air can't get back in. When the wine quits bubbling, the bottles can be corked tight.

To make somewhat larger quantities in a traditional way, go back in your mind to my description of my father's barrel of cider. If he had added sugar to his working cider, and maybe honey, raisins, and brown sugar, he would have made the first step toward wine, or what he would have called, incorrectly, applejack. During the "primary fermentation," as it is called, the bung was left off because the tiny yeast plants initially need oxygen to shift into high gear and go crazy with all that sugar. A froth or head builds up on the cider and often boils out of the bung if the barrel is full, as it should be. Karl Kuerner, one of Andrew Wyeth's most famous models, told me when I was writing about him that the only time he was aware that Wyeth was not faithful to the reality he was painting was when he painted one of Karl's barrels of cider. "It foamed up out of the bung like a birthday cake," he said, "but Andy didn't paint all the foam. He said no one would have believed it." Wyeth later wrote in his autobiography that no one could make cider like Karl, and that Karl's secret went to the grave with him. Wyeth then commented in that mischievous way of his, "Maybe Karl pissed in it." I suspect that Karl was adding a good portion of brown sugar, honey, and raisins.

In a few days, with the cider no longer foaming so much, an air-lock was placed in the bung hole, and the cider wine was allowed to ferment until still. It normally was not racked off, as would other-wise be the case, to separate the wine from the sediment, because cider wine to drink could be drawn from the spout positioned in the end of the barrel above the bottom sediment and below the top float-ing sediment, just as my father did. Racking off in the usual way was not necessary. In fact, devotees of this apple wine believed that the settlings in the barrel continued to impart good taste to the wine.

The experts argue about whether cider ought to be fermented in 5-gallon glass carboys or in oak barrels. Glass is certainly easier to keep clean than barrels. Barrels impart more flavor, not only from the wood, as in the case of whiskey, but because during storage there is a better chance for certain "good" yeasts that cause malo-lactic fermentation to come into action, mellowing the cider wine.

The general important rule is not to seal up a container, espe-cially if it is glass, until the fermentation process is over, or very nearly so. Seal too soon and you can have an explosion, and the flying glass might not only turn you into hamburger but detonate other bottles. That's why champagne bottles are recommended for storing all alcoholic beverages where a bit of fermentation is still going on. Champagne bottles are made stronger because cham-pagne (and other sparkling wines, including cider) continues to work a little in the bottle, since a little sugar is added to each bot-tle. Bottles of my father's homemade beer periodically went off like little sticks of dynamite in the cellar, a problem that led my mother to mention the word "Prohibition" occasionally with a certain longing in her voice.

Some people add boiled cider concentrate and a little sugar to the finished apple wine to make it a little sweeter to their taste.

Distilling brandy or applejack from apple wine is done in the same way as described for whiskey in Chapter 2 and for brandy in Chapter 7, using a pressure canner and your stove or a hot plate. It should be aged in oak for at least a year.

Applejack has another designation as well. It is often the name given to the "distillate" you get when you freeze cider, separating out the water as ice, and leaving the alcohol behind as a sort of crude brandy. In old New England, distilling cider by freezing, a common practice, resulted in a potent drink. Some cider makers believe distilling cider in this manner does not fall under the law disallowing home distilling without a permit. They are wrong. It is not only illegal, but it is dangerous. In proper distilling, where the alcohol is driven off the water by heat, most of the fusel oils and higher alcohols and other substances in the ethyl alcohol are separated out, as described earlier, from the drinking alcohol, making it reasonably safe, possibly even healthful, to drink. But distillate made from freezing has the full complement of these "impurities" still in the liquid. That's why applejack from freezing can cause excruciating hangovers and even physical harm, often referred to in earlier times as "apple palsy."

Until government comes to its senses, which is difficult to imagine, real apple brandy will be scarce and well above the affordability of most Americans. Probably the most revered apple brandy in the world is Calvados, imported from France. Like Calvabec from Quebec, it must be made completely of apple juice (no grain neutral spirits), and must be distilled in a pot still and aged in wood under rigid regulation to preserve as much as possible the traditional way of making it. We could all be experimenting with high-quality apple brandy if distillation were legal.

There are several levels of quality in Calvados, with the Calvados du Pays d'Auge from a small area of Normandy being the highest ranked and considered the equal of the best grape brandies. By law the best Calvados must be made from apples crushed in the traditional way, fermented for a month, and distilled to a 75 percent alcohol content, which is cut at bottling to 40 to 50 percent alcohol (80 to 100 proof). Calvados must be aged for at least a year, and Calvados du Pays d'Auge much longer.

American cider brandies are usually not pure apple brandy but a mix of grain neutral spirits with apple brandy. They are cheaper because grain distillation is cheaper than fruit distillation. This is not to say that using grain neutral spirits of itself lowers the quality of a spirit *necessarily*. It just ain't real brandy, and, to real brandy lovers, not nearly as tasteful. As a bartender once told me, "Whiskey slides down your throat, but brandy explodes in your mouth."

There are other apple-based or apple-flavored cordials or liqueurs available. Jim Beam is marketing "Green Apple Pucker," which it calls a cordial. The alcoholic base is Kentucky bourbon with a pert apple flavor, managing to be sweet and tart at the same time, at about 15 percent alcohol. If you want to experiment on your own, there is no limit to the number of new and old drinks you can concoct with apple brandy.

CHAPTER 4

The Fruit Juice:
A Moonshine Story from 1935

*With apologies to the villagers of Harpster,
Ohio, who know which parts of this tale are
true, and which are not.*

"STRAWSTACK in the making is surely one of the most beautiful dramas on the farm," Grandmother Gowler remarked, ascending into her most teacherly tone of voice. She and Emmet, her grandson, were standing in the shade of the great white oak tree next to the ancestral Gowler home, watching the harvest scene on the flatlands below them. Dust and chaff rolled from the threshing machine. Spread out in the wheat fields around it, men labored, loading the wheat bundles on horse-drawn wagons. They looked like industrious ants from the distance, wending their way to and from the strawstack, unloading the wheat bundle by bundle into the hungry maw of the threshing machine, and then returning to the fields for another load. Straw cannonaded in a continuous flow out the blowpipe of the thresher onto the stack, while the threshed and winnowed grain disgorged from another pipe into a waiting grain wagon. "If Thomas Hart Benton lived around here instead of in Iowa, he'd be painting out there in our fields and making us all eternally famous," she concluded.

Emmet stared at her. Twelve years old, he had no idea who she was talking about. His grandmother was "educated," Gramps always reminded him, and had been a teacher. Allowances had to be made for people like that, Gramps said, because they meant well and kept the rest of mankind from returning to savagery. If she

49

thought there was something beautiful about those fly-bitten, farting horses, and those chaff-choked, sweat-stinking men, and that dusty, noisy old separator, well, she could have her whimsy. She didn't have to do the work.

"Look at Avery Bump up there on the stack with his red bandanna over his mouth and that cowboy hat on his head," she continued. "Right out of a picture show."

"He looks like Tom Mix, don't he?" Emmet said.

"*Doesn't* he, Emmet, not *don't* he. I'd say he looked more like Jesse James." She sniffed in disapproval.

Emmet did not answer immediately. He liked the Bumps, even if they were "outlaw trash from Killdeer," as his grandmother sometimes called them. Nate and Nan Bump were far more fun than any of the town pups in Upper Surrey, where he lived with his mother whenever he could not cajole her into letting him stay at the farm on the edge of Gowler Village. Gramps said Killdeer farmers were okay, but their land was so hard to farm that they couldn't afford to be too honest.

"Gramps says nobody can build a strawstack better than Mr. Bump," he said defensively. He paused. "How's come Killdeer farmers are so poor?"

"Houses can't come, Emmet. Quit using that phrase." She paused to consider his question.

"All this flat land around here was a prairie mostly," she said. "A kind of peculiar landscape. Trees weren't growing on it when the settlers came, except on the little knolls and rises such as where Gowler Village, here, sits, or over there on that knoll beyond the thresher where the hickory grove stands. The land looked real good to the settlers. Level, black, no trees to clear. They called the wooded hillocks 'islands' because they stood out like islands of white oak and hickory in the sea of tallgrass prairie. They say the prairies were treeless because the Indians set fire to them every year—huge rings of fire to drive the game into clusters where they could kill a bunch for winter." She pondered her own words and then added, "I wonder if that's true."

"What's that got to do with Killdeer farmers?" Emmet interrupted, not too patiently.

"I'm getting to that. Turned out these prairies were very hard to drain and cultivate. Your great-grandfather had enough sense to run sheep and cattle on them, not try to farm them like we're doing now. South of Gowler Village, down in the heart of Killdeer, you can hardly raise crops at all. Even if you put in drainage tile, that blue jackwax will seal the tile over. And of course the worst of it is pure swamp fit only for hiding moonshine stills."

She paused to see if Emmet was still listening to her, and then continued. "But new farmers coming through here in the dry season couldn't understand why such level black land was selling so cheaply. They made the usual mistake newcomers are prone to make: they figured the locals were ignorant. The strangers plunked down their life savings to buy Killdeer land. Then they were trapped, unable to make enough money to get out and unable to sell for what they'd paid. They had to learn to live on rattlesnake steak and killdeer breast, like those poor Bumps."

Emmet was supposed to be refilling the water jug to take back to the fields, but figured he had time to ride his pony, Pony, on into the village close by to spend the penny Gramps had bribed him with to get the water. He pondered his grandmother's words as he rode along, telling himself that the Bumps weren't really down-and-outers like some of the Killdeer homesteaders. His grandmother just wasn't well acquainted with them like he was. He waved at Sam, dozing away in his barbershop without a customer, passed Doc Halw's house and office, Mrs. Smith's dry goods store, Pickring's smithy, Johnny's Filling Station and Auto Repair, and Herb's Diner. Other than himself, not a soul stirred in the heat. Then he crossed the railroad tracks to the great, gaunt brick building that the oldest inhabitants called "The Hotel." It had served as such fifty years ago. His great-grandfather had built it, and now his uncles used half of it for the Gowler Bank, and Pinky Ghent used the other half for his general store. The store also housed the post office, although there was talk that the government would soon build a new one across the street, next to the fire station. Behind the bank and store sprawled Ramsey's Egg and Poultry Market, and behind that, next to the railroad track, was the grain elevator and flouring mill, which was also owned by the Gowler family. On the other side of the general store stood Closson's Bakery and Confectionery. Emmet often went in there just to smell. At the door, he would exhale every wisp of air in his lungs, and then step inside to inhale a long, slow drag of fresh bread aroma.

With the railroad taking only an hour to bring supplies from Columbus (sixty years later it would take an hour and a half by car or truck), and with shipments from New York and Chicago hardly more than two days away, it was quite possible, Gramps liked to say, to satisfy all of one's bodily needs and comforts except liquor without leaving Gowler Village. Alcoholic beverages were unavailable in Gowler Village legally because great-grandfather Gowler, having turned from unbeliever to Baptist in his old age after getting his start in life tending bar, had put a deed restriction prohibiting the sale of spirits on every parcel of land except his own. So far the Gowlers preferred not to exercise their inherited privilege, preferred in fact not to let it be known that they owned such a privilege. But the lack of alcohol in Gowler was why Gramps took great delight in pointing out that a mile away, Linner (population 72) boasted seven saloons just two years now since Prohibition had been repealed. "Why, the reason's plain as the nose on your face," he said. "All the Methodists and Baptists from Gowler and Upper Surrey sneak into Linner where they think their neighbors won't see them, and drink with the Catholics."

Instead of dismounting, Emmet urged Pony right up the steps onto the platform in front of the general store. The platform was left over from the days when wagons and railroad carts were drawn alongside and unloaded. Then he reached down, still mounted, pulled open the screen door, and held it ajar with his leg as the horse, obviously out of long habit, sidled on into the store. From behind the counter, Pinky Ghent stared at them, pretending to be vexed but unable to stifle a smile. There was no one else in the store anyway. Pony approached the counter, her hooves thumping hollowly on the wood floor, rolled her eyes at the glass canisters of candy on the back shelves, and began nodding her head in a most abjectly pleading way.

"If that horse shits in here, you're gonna scrub the whole floor on your hands and knees, Emmet," the storekeeper said, but with a voice full of good humor.

"Pony won't do that, will ya, girl?" Emmet said. "She says she just wants a piece of candy."

"Gawd, boy, you don't need to speak for her. That horse can talk plainer than a whole trainload of Columbus politicians."

"But she says I've only got one penny," Emmet went on, dropping the coin onto the counter from his perch in the saddle. "And there's two of us."

Pinky glared at the boy. "You're gonna end up richer'n your tightwad old grandfather," he said, but he made the pronouncement sound more like a compliment than a criticism. He reached into a canister and pulled out two Tootsie Rolls, tossing one to Emmet and stuffing the other, paper and all, into the horse's eager mouth.

"Oh Jesus," Pinky said suddenly, looking out the window. "Here comes Gene Autry."

The screen door swung open abruptly. A towering man, revolver sticking out of a holster at a brazen angle, sheriff's badge shining on his chest, and large white felt hat cocked jauntily on his head, infused the room with the overweaning presence of the Law.

"Godalmighty, Pinky, what if that thing poops in here?" he thundered, shaking his head at the horse and rider. "Times must really be hard when you've got to cater to horses to make ends meet."

Although normally the scene would have deserved a more thorough commentary from him, Sheriff Mogan now abruptly dismissed it. He had important things on his mind today.

"Where's Avery?" he demanded. "I got a revenuer in the car and he's got wind of a movement of moonshine outta Killdeer. This could be Avery's butt for sure this time."

Pinky stared at Mogan with a sardonic look on his face. The sheriff, like everyone else, knew damn well where Avery was. Mogan was merely stalling for time, putting out the warning.

"Well, he can't be up to no good," Pinky replied, loud enough for the revenuer lounging against the car outside to hear. "He's right this very minute on top of Floyd Gowler's strawstack."

"Well, he hasn't been up on no damn strawstack all summer long, now has he?" the sheriff roared.

"Aw, Mog, Prohibition's over. Nobody's doin' moonshine anymore." The storekeeper's freckles grew more vividly obvious as his normally pale face turned even paler.

"The hell. Wouldn't surprise me you had some stashed right there behind that counter," the sheriff snorted, but obviously not at all interested in proving or disproving his suspicion. And then in a lower voice: "I'm gonna hafta go out to Avery's place and look around before that agent out there wets his pants."

Then, knowing he had sufficiently warned the community, the sheriff stomped out, muttering something about the government not having enough to do.

The storekeeper and the boy watched him and the revenuer climb back into the patrol car and drive away in a clatter of loose gravel. Pinky went directly to the phone to call Avery's wife, Dorothy.

"She ain't there," Emmet said to him. "She's at the park."

And with that he urged Pony out the door, down the steps, and out into the street, headed west. He knew that Mrs. Bump had taken Nan and Nate and little Karl to the wading pool in the park to wile away the midafternoon heat. She did that often. Emmet kept close tabs. He had his reasons. He was not sure the Bumps were moving moonshine today, but he was not sure they weren't, either. He had heard the talk. Avery Bump's whiskey was said to be as good as anything off the shelves of any bar anywhere. It was aged, not white lightning. And at half the price. Emmet knew his grandmother would be furious if she learned what he was about to do, but he was certain that Dorothy Bump would want to know that the sheriff was heading for her place.

As he approached the school, vacant for the summer, he plunged through the hedge in front, wheeled into the schoolyard, and cut across the playground behind the school building. The scene he now entered seemed like a world far removed from the hot, dusty environment of street and field and the hard reality of scratching a living from the soil and the marketplace. Pony's hooves pounded the manicured grass of a little park, perhaps four acres in size, a horticultural gem full of exotic ornamental shrubs, trees, and flowers, as seemingly out of place in this nondescript Corn Belt village as the Taj Mahal would have been.

The park was a gift to the village from Lieutenant Governor Arnold Clewis, scion of another wealthy local landowning family, a man who continued to live in Gowler and manage the Clewis land when not politicking in Columbus. The centerpiece of the ornamental gardens was an oval, shallow, concrete pond, what late Victorians called a reflection pool, but enlarged by the practical agrarian mind to accommodate a score or more of wading children. Emmet urged Pony at full speed to the pool and the Bumps, who were watching him approach curiously. Mrs. Bump had been reading in the shade while Nate, Nan, and Karl splashed in the water. Emmet reigned Pony in sharply, the way Tom Mix might do, so that the horse reared a bit. He watched Nan out of the corner of his eye for a look of approval and addressed himself to Nate, too embarrassed to speak directly to Mrs. Bump over so delicate a matter. He was not quite sure what he should say, but the uncomfortable ambivalence that sometimes came between the two friends had little to do with the urgent errand at hand. More than anything in the world, Nate wished he had a horse, but there was no money in the Bump world for such an extravagance. On the other hand, Emmet would have gladly forsworn horses forever if he had a mother who would play with him like Mrs. Bump did with her kids, and a father who was still alive, even if he made whiskey.

"Nate, the sheriff . . ." Emmet hesitated, glancing at Mrs. Bump, catching his breath. She had raised her head from the book in her lap to eye him intensely. "The sheriff just stopped at the store," he blurted. "He's headed for your place to look for bootleg."

Nate, age eleven, stared in embarrassment down at his bare legs, dripping water from the pool. He glanced momentarily at Nan, a year younger than himself. She was studying the ground in front of her, too. Only the baby, Karl, played on, unperturbed. Nate did not dare look at his mother. Although only a child, he was adept at playing the tricky pretend game that the Bumps had invented about the whiskey. They pretended it didn't exist. While he and Nan splashed in the pool, they pretended that strange people did not drive into the park, stop next to their old Dodge, transfer the Mason jars of what the family referred to as The Fruit Juice into their own vehicles, leave money under the Dodge's front seat, and drive away, with never a word spoken. It just didn't happen.

Even now, the only sign that his mother had heard news disconcerting to her, Nate noticed, was that she involuntarily closed her book with a crisp slap.

"Well, Emmet, thanks for coming by," she said, smiling. "The heat must have addled the sheriff's brain. It wouldn't take much. But I'd appreciate it if you would ride out to the thresher and tell Mr. Bump what you heard."

"I'll see you tomorrow on the wheat wagon," Nate said. For the first time ever, he wanted Emmet to leave. Nor did Nan roll her eyes admiringly and ask for a ride, as was her habit.

Emmet understood. "Guess I better go," he said awkwardly, hoping Nan noticed how he was holding the reins in his left hand, just like Tom Mix did, his gun hand free for action if need be. He smacked Pony on the rear with it, and headed for the thresher.

Nate, his teeth chattering more from fear than being chilled from an hour in the cold water, wondered what his mother would now do with a car full of The Fruit Juice and the sheriff likely to come by at any moment. She hated The Fruit Juice and hated Killdeer and often told Nate that they were lucky to have such a beautiful little park and pool all to themselves most afternoons, just like rich folks on their estates. When his father had first suggested that her afternoons at the park would be a perfectly safe place and time for Fruit Juice transactions in case the farm was being watched, she had refused, and only finally consented when he promised that she would not have to do or say anything to the people who came by to get their Fruit Juice.

Now the scheme was backfiring. Though a comely woman ordinarily, her face turned ugly with pent-up rage. To no one in particular she began to fume, "This is the last time. I swear to God it's over. I am through with The Fruit Juice forever!" Then she turned anxiously to Nate, who, though only a boy, was Killdeer-trained in the high art of resourcefulness as she never could be.

"What will we do, Nate? What will we do? I can't just ditch a couple hundred dollars of The Fruit Juice. Your father would throttle me. The sheriff will stop us on the road if I try to take the stuff back home and hide it. He's probably found out where we are and is headed here right now. Oh Lord, what'll I do? God help you, Avery Bump, this is the end." She beat her head frantically with both fists until little Karl started to whimper.

"Put the jars in the pool," Nate said. He was not sure himself how the idea had come to him.

Dorothy abruptly stopped her fussing, stared at him for a long moment, and almost smiled. "You could go far in this world, son," she said. "C'mon."

Together she and the two older children quickly transferred fourteen precious Mason jars of The Fruit Juice to the very center and deepest part of the pool, around the outflow pipe. The jars were barely visible, and not at all when the surface of the water rippled from the breeze or from splashing children. The transfer complete, Mrs. Bump pondered her next move: should she drive home and leave the cache till later, in which case someone might steal it, or wait around for the sheriff to find her and search the Dodge?

Sheriff Mogan made the decision for her. While she hesitated, he came driving through the park entrance.

"Nate, Nan, you get in the water," their mother snapped, low and cool now. "Get out there in the center and splash around until he leaves. And don't you stop splashing even if you think your arms are going to drop off."

Then she went back to the shade, opened her book, pulled the baby Karl close to her and assumed an air of serene saintliness.

Sheriff Mogan parked, got out of his car, his pistol handle catching momentarily on the door frame, and gingerly approached her. He would rather have faced Dillinger than have to pussyfoot around this poor woman with some goddamn government agent looking over his shoulder.

"Missus Bump?" he began, clearing his throat.

Carefully marking her page, as if that were the only important concern of the moment, Dorothy looked up at the sheriff with such demure innocence that Nate in the water could not suppress a snicker. Nan threw water in his face to stop him but then began to giggle herself.

"I, ah, do not much beat around the bush, as you well know," the sheriff intoned. "This here is John Jacob of the Bureau of Alcohol, Tobacco, and Firearms."

"Alcohol and firearms?" Dorothy said, wrinkling her face. "Is it a good idea to mix those two, even in government?"

The sheriff either did not see humor in the remark or chose to ignore it. "He has a warrant to search your car for bootleg."

"Are you going daft in your old age, bothering a churchwoman like this?" she flared up indignantly. "Shame on you."

Nate in the water listened carefully, almost forgetting to keep splashing. His mother never outright lied about anything, not even The Fruit Juice, and he was interested in how she would weasel-word her way around the subject this time. Nan's giggling was infectious, like it was in church, and he began to laugh too, pretending it was all part of their vigorous sporting in the water. They both noticed that their swimsuit-clad mother had stretched one bare leg enticingly out in front of her until it appeared to be several inches longer than any normal leg ought to be. And was still growing. And although there were thirty-seven years of hard work in that leg, or maybe because of that, it was quite an enticing thing to look at. Nate and Nan had never seen nor imagined their mother engaging in this kind of tactic before, and it only served to make them laugh and churn the water more frantically. In the frenzy of their splashing, one of the jars, not as full as the rest, started floating towards the surface of the pool. Nate and Nan both moved to block its rise with their bodies and when that didn't work, Nan straddled the bottle and clamped it between her legs. Standing in waist-deep water with the sheriff hardly fifteen feet away and a jar of The Fruit Juice wedged in her crotch while a revenuer was prostrate on his belly in the car trying to see under the seat, was too much for a little girl to bear. This was even funnier than the time her teacher, Theodolina Smarn, had farted during one of those hushed pauses teachers like to make right before they say something grand. She could feel her insane giggles draining the strength from her.

Sheriff Mogan, waiting for the revenue agent to complete his search, was trying very hard not to look at Dorothy's leg.

"Children do enjoy the water now, don't they, Mrs. Bump?" he said, beaming. At that, Nate and Nan wholly collapsed into hyena-like shrieks, whipping water so vigorously that the spray landed on the sheriff's splendidly shiny cowboy boots. Meanwhile, Dorothy's leg defied all laws of physics and biology and grew another inch.

The ATF man returned from the car, muttering under his breath.

"Somebody must be putting you on," the sheriff said to him. "What the hell would a mother and her kids be doing with a load of moonshine in Clewis Park anyhow?"

The agent was also pretending not to see Dorothy's bare leg. "Goddamn, I wish I could get that much fun outta life," he said, watching Nate and Nan, and then turning abruptly back to the patrol car.

"Our apologies, Mrs. Bump," the sheriff said, obviously pleased with the outcome of the search. Occasionally he liked a drink of really good whiskey himself.

"And I suppose you've been on our property, sniffing around again," Dorothy retorted, going on the offensive now, but internally still full of dread. "Didn't find anything, did you?"

"No, we didn't. Not this time." It was a warning.

She had pretended to go back to her reading, so the sheriff could not see the enormous relief that she was sure showed on her face. The sheriff drove away. Nate and Nan crawled weakly out of the water, collapsed in the grass, and gave themselves up to uncontrollable fits of laughter. This time their mother joined in.

Nate knew there was going to be another Fruit Juice Fight when his father got home from threshing. Twice his mother started to pour the contents of the Mason jars down the sink, and twice she was not able to bring herself to do it. Her need for the money was stronger than her fear of the Law.

Now she sat on the porch, watching the road, waiting for her husband, letting the anger build. Ordinarily, Nate went to the woods during a Fruit Juice Fight, but sensing that this one would be the all-time most memorable one, he only retreated to the repair shop in the barnyard, where he could watch and listen unobserved. Nan joined him.

They could tell by the way their father's shoulders hunched up around his ears as he drove the team into the barnyard that he knew he was in for it. He must have heard most of the story already, no doubt by way of Emmet. He did not hurry the unharnessing; perhaps she would simmer down before he came to the house. He should have known better.

"Avery Bump, I've a mind to pour your damn whiskey down the drain and leave you."

Since she never used the word, "whiskey," for The Fruit Juice, Nate knew she meant business this time, and so did his father.

"Mogan didn't find anything, did he?" he asked softly.

"See, that's all you care about. I could be in jail now and the kids in some foster home for all you know. All you care about is the money."

Although he had come to America from Switzerland nearly twenty years ago, Avery still spoke with a lingering touch of the old country, especially when he thought it suited his purpose. "Now, my luffly, you know that's nicht so."

"Don't you try to pull that luffly crap on me, Avery Bump. You quit making whiskey and start living like a law-abiding citizen under God or I will luffly myself and the kids right off this godforsaken farm."

Nate and Nan cringed at the shop window. Bringing in the law-abiding argument, especially in the same breath with God, was not a good way to talk to their father.

"We break no law of God," he said coldly, "but only rich men's dummkopf finagling with the law. Seagram makes whiskey. Does your God say that's wrong? My grandfodder made the best wine in Switzerland. Does God say that was wrong? Where does your Bible say we are supposed to pay revenue tax?"

"Render to Caesar the things that are Caeser's," Dorothy answered righteously.

"This is not Caesar's whiskey. It's my whiskey," he thundered, suddenly distraught out of his accent. "The rich put on the taxes because they can afford to pay 'em. It's just a way to keep me down, keep me from competing with 'em. Whiskey allows a little farmer to make a little money on corn if he wants to work hard. But the sonsabitches don't want little farmers and they don't want little whiskey makers either."

"Avery Bump, you will think what you will think, but I can't live this way any longer." A note of pleading had come into her voice. "You've got to stop The Fruit Juice or you will ruin me."

Nate watched his father turn away in silence and go back to the barn to feed and water the horses now that they had cooled down from the day's work. Nate followed him. In the barn, his father seemed preoccupied, staring off into space, evidently coming to some hard decision. Finally he turned to Nate. "Have you got the chores all done?"

Nate nodded. When there was a Fruit Juice Fight in the offing, it was wise to have every lick of work done up spick and span.

"Go back there to the far end of the horse stable. In the corner there, up on the last beam, you will find a tin box. Bring it here."

Nate did as he was told, a little fearful at his father's solemnity.

Nate thought he knew every hiding place in the barn, but, sure enough, there among the cobwebs was a box, so well hidden between beam and ceiling that it had escaped even his eyes.

His father carried the box to the house, sat down heavily on the back stoop, sat the box on his lap, and tenderly opened it. To Nate's astonishment, it was stuffed with paper money. He even saw a couple of bills with the figure 100 on them. His father pulled a pencil stub from the bib of his overalls and handed it to him. "I'm going to count out this money, and every time I say a hundred, you put a mark there on the side of the house."

Nate's eyes bugged out. His father must have robbed a bank.

"*Ten, twenty, twenty-five, forty-five, a hundred. Make a mark,*" Avery intoned. "My mistake was not whiskey, it was pride. When I came here, I thought this land was undervalued. I bought this farm against good advice because I thought I could make any farm pay at that price." He seemed to talk to no one or to everyone. "That's the way Bumps are. We think we can do anything. But by God you can't make Killdeer jackwax pay with ordinary farmin'. *Twenty, forty, fifty, a hundred. Make a mark.* Maybe if you had a thousand acres and grazed sheep on it, like old Gowler did, but I bet they'd get foot rot running on such wet ground. *Fifty, seventy, eighty, a hundred, make a mark.* So I did the onliest thing I could see to do. I learned to make whiskey. *Ten, sixty, eighty, a hundred, make a mark.* Not rotgut, but good whiskey. *Ten, twenty, fifty, seventy, seventy-five, a hundred. Make a mark.* I'm sorry for the shame you have had to bear, but I bore it too, you know. I didn't even drink any, not for ten years, to save the money. *Twenty, forty, ninety, a hundred, make a mark.* We are peasants and have no power. *We* knew Prohibition was stupid. *We* know the taxes always benefit the rich, doesn't make any difference if kings or Democrats run the government. *Five, twenty-five, thirty, fifty, a hundred, make a mark.*" The counted pile of bills grew on the doorstep as the uncounted ones in the box diminished.

Dorothy had come to the screen door behind Avery. She stood there in silence, stupefied, looking down over his shoulder at the money, the pot she was drying with a dish towel forgotten in her hands. If Avery knew she was behind him, he gave no notice. He kept on counting and talking and Nate kept jabbing marks on the wall.

"Your ancestors made some of the best wine and beer in Europe and they were honored for it. Making good whiskey ought also to be a respectable profession, not something that forces you to hide in the swamp or go to work for rich people in distilleries just because you can't afford the tax. *Fifty, seventy, eighty, a hundred, make a mark.* There would be no poverty in Killdeer if small farmers were allowed to make good whiskey and sell it without paying the profit to the government. Some days I swear there's a plot to keep small farmers poor. *Fifty, a hundred, make a mark.*"

Nate was trying to keep a running count of his marks. He was up to thirty and his father was still counting.

"So I did what I had to do and it's worked out because the price of good land goes down about as fast as the price of good whiskey goes up. Now we are going to buy ourselves a real farm and you kids won't have to wear patches anymore and your mother can strut right up there with the Upper Surrey snobs, by God, and no one will ever call us trash again. *Hundred, hundred, hundred, make three marks!*"

Nate leaned over to take a closer look. He had never seen a hundred-dollar bill before this day. Or a fifty, for that matter. His mother's mouth moved, opening and closing soundlessly. Karl in his highchair was banging his spoon on his dish, but no one heard.

Eventually all the money was counted and Nate added up the marks one more time. Seventy-seven. Seven thousand and seven hundred dollars.

"My God," Dorothy gasped. "Avery Bump, did you make all that on The Fruit Juice?"

"Nearly. Made and sold a few stills too."

Words failing her, Dorothy went back into the kitchen and banged away at her pots and pans to try to hide her shame at her earlier outburst.

"How many farms can you buy with that much money?" Nate asked in awe.

His father chuckled. "Well, I think there's enough for one anyway. I've got one in mind, too, the 140-acre Weiling place over above the river on the other side of Linner, out of this damnable Killdeer jackwax. I hear the bank's got it now and is desperate enough to sell for fifty dollars an acre. Remember, Nate, all things come to him who waits."

Then Avery stood up. There was still business to attend to. He went to the cellar and took the remaining jars of The Fruit Juice from behind the false wall and carried them into the yard.

"Dorothy, come here. And bring Nan and Karl along."

He then proceeded to unscrew each lid and pour the contents of each jar on the ground, doing so with slow and purposeful ceremony.

Then, staring solemnly at each family member in turn, he said, "I never again want to hear The Fruit Juice mentioned."

And it never was, at least within his hearing.

CHAPTER 5

Homemade Beer

S TRIVING to find ways to make his barley crop more profitable, North Dakota farmer Philip Omdahl began to think "crazy" in 1988. Microbreweries were booming, thanks to more lenient regulations on making beer. People loved the high-quality beer that many small, local breweries were making, probably because the beer actually tasted like something and was usually ultrafresh. If small breweries could make money on beer, reasoned Omdahl, why couldn't farmers cash in on the new market too, making malt from their own barley and selling it to microbreweries at a higher price than they were receiving for barley on the open market—the old value-added concept of farm marketing. Or, what the heck, he mused, why not become a partner with microbreweries, or become a farmer-brewer of high-quality beer himself?

He decided on a light-bodied pilsner beer that would have a unique local flavor, featuring Dakota-grown Azure barley, Cluster and Cascade hops grown in the state of Washington, a special isolated yeast strain to ferment the beer, and pure deep well water to go with it. He called the beer Roughrider Premium. His plan was to establish the beer first, then act as a malt-marketing facility for what he likes to call the craft beer industry. Without the wherewithal to do everything himself, he found an established brewery to brew his Roughrider.

Roughrider sold well, strangely enough, under contract to over-seas markets. But the brewery making his beer closed, and his overseas contracts expired. Retrenching, Omdahl decided to concentrate on the local market in the Dakotas and Minnesota, and turned to the Minnesota Brewing Company to brew Roughrider Premium. He took on a partner, Judd McKinnon, who was in the beer distribution business, to market the beer in his region. "Sales are not sensational yet, but okay," says Omdahl. "If the beer gets established locally, we will branch out. My dream is a hundred-million-dollar brewery and malting cooperative built locally and run by farmers, modeled on the way white wheat growers have organized the Dakota Growers Pasta Company."

I don't know how to explain my motivation for writing this book any better than that. The farmers who produce the raw materials of the food business must hook into the consumer market a little more firmly and a little more directly if they are to survive in an economy that aims to keep food as cheap as it can. Toward this end, producers can learn a lot from homebrewers, people who make beer for their own consumption and who often tell me that, once you learn how to make good beer, it is hard to go back to drinking the popular commercial brands. Microbreweries are the natural outgrowth of backyard breweries.

The decentralization of the beer industry has had another salutary effect. You can now buy organic beer (and of course you could make your own). I'm relatively certain there is more than one brand, but the organic beer currently making the media is Wolover's Pale Ale, Brown Ale, and India Pale Ale from Panorama Brewing Company, Santa Cruz, California. Currently they are available on the West Coast and in Florida.

I used to watch my father brew beer. It must not have been entirely legal, because he warned me, the child, to keep my mouth shut about what went on in our cellar. Now that the last restrictions have been removed from homebrew, as long as you don't homebrew in commercial quantities, I watch and listen to friends who make beer openly and drink the fruit of their labors. I'm not

much of a beer drinker myself, except after a hot day playing soft-
ball, in which case almost any beer tastes fine to me. But that has
more to do with camaraderie than savoring the taste of beer. A bottle of good homebrew (I've tasted some pretty terrible stuff, too)
has rich tastes and aromas and needs to be sipped and sniffed
leisurely, as with good wine or whiskey. My test of good beer is to
see if I like it just barely cool, straight from the cellar. The poorer
the beer, the colder it needs to be for me.

Making beer is not difficult, though you'd never arrive at that
conclusion from reading the better books on how to do it. These
books are written by experienced homebrewers who want you to
know everything they know in one pass through a book. I think
these books, as excellent as they are, discourage the beginner. For
one thing, they smother the neophyte with a new vocabulary, the
same way woodworking books do with that craft, leaving the poor
beginner dizzy before he's even tasted his own beer. No wonder
people want teachers, want to watch someone else do it, rather
than try to read instructions.

When I was trying to learn how to brew beer from books, I was
fortunate enough to find an article in Taunton's *Fine Cooking*
magazine (of all places); the premier (February/March 1994) issue
included a simple, easily understandable article on making beer at
home. In five pages, taken up mostly by intelligent and helpful
drawings, David Ruggiero, who is described as a nationally
certified beer judge and teacher of brewing arts, gives the reader all
the information needed to make that first batch of beer. I highly
recommend it. After that you can go on to more complicated
methods if you want to.

Ruggiero's instructions are pretty much the standard way to
brew beer when you buy all the ingredients, which is what you
should do, at least at first. You can buy a "beer kit" that has all the
ingredients in the right measured quantities for a small batch.
Most longtime homebrewers turn their noses up at beer kits, but
that is the best way to start. Learn by doing. You can get fancy and
discriminating after you have the mechanics down pat.

The first thing you should do to make beer if you don't have another brewer to observe, is to find a store that carries beer-making equipment. If you can't find a store under Brewer's Supplies in your phone book's yellow pages, you can contact Home Wine and Beer Trade Association, 604 North Miller Road, Valrico, Florida 33594, and ask them for the address of the store nearest to you, or The American Homebrewers Association, P.O. Box 1679, Boulder, Colorado 80306-1679. The Internet is full of sources. Or better yet, go to a newsstand or library and read some copies of beer- and wine-making magazines. While reading them, you will get a load of information, and when you go to a brewer's supply store you will get an overload. But that's okay. That's part of the fun. About a million and a half Americans are making beer, so statisticians say, and it appears every one of them has something to say on the subject.

For your first brew, equip yourself with a 5-gallon stockpot or similar container that you can boil your brew in, a thermometer, a funnel, some plastic tubing, a glass carboy with an airlock to put in its neck, fifty-two beer bottles, and a bottle capper. It may be possible to rent or borrow the capper. You'll probably spend about a hundred dollars getting set up, and every 5-gallon batch will cost about twenty dollars worth of ingredients. If you are going to make lager, you might think about buying a used refrigerator. The reason is that lager beer needs to ferment at a 35° to 55°F temperature (like good cider). For ale you can do okay with a room temperature of 55° to 70°F. Obviously, without a very cool place or a refrigerator, you'll want to make ale. If you do decide on the used-refrigerator route, be sure it is one that has removable shelves, to provide enough space for a container that holds 6.5 gallons.

So you go to the supply store and, with your beer recipe in hand (and there are as many recipes for making beer as there are for making fruitcakes), you buy malt extract, malted barley, some bittering hops and some aromatic hops, some Irish moss (a clarifying or "fining" agent), a package of yeast, and some corn sugar (you can use regular sugar as well, though some people say it gives the beer a "cidery" taste). If you buy a kit, all you need will be included. You will find that there are many kinds of malt, many kinds of hops, and many kinds of yeasts. Homebrewers can spend hours over a mug talking about the fine points of one versus another, but whichever choice you make, especially among various strains of yeast, brewers say you should stick with it until you know how that particular kind works for you. There are so many variables in brewing that you don't want to make it any more complicated than you have to.

As with any fermented drink, cleanliness is absolutely essential. Get in the habit of washing all utensils right after every use, and then, right before using, wash again in a weak chlorine solution (2 tablespoons bleach per gallon of water) and rinse thoroughly. Or sterilize them in the dry cycle of your dishwasher.

The first step is to adjust your water to the proper pH. Most household water is a little soft and needs a tablespoon of gypsum for every 2 gallons of water. But if your water is fairly hard, as from a well, with a mineral content exceeding 300 parts per million, no gypsum is necessary. Really hard water, below a pH of 5.0, might need the addition of a little limestone or calcium chloride. Directions that came with your beer recipe will keep you informed.

To begin brewing, crush your malt coarsely with a rolling pin and steep it in about 2 gallons of brew water in a muslin bag, as if you were making a huge cup of tea. Slowly heat the water, but don't let it reach boiling temperature until you have removed the malt, or your beer will probably taste harsh. When the water boils, add the malt extract as directed by your recipe, stirring vigorously until the extract dissolves. That will lower the temperature a bit. When the water boils again, set your timer for an hour. About 10 minutes into the boil add the bittering hops, and after 30 minutes the Irish moss, if the recipe calls for it, to help clarify the eventual brew. At 50 minutes, add half the aromatic hops, and the other half 9 minutes later. Your liquid is now called the "wort."

The trick now is to bring the temperature of the wort down as quickly as possible. The best way is to put your brew kettle of wort in the sink and pack ice cubes around it. When the temperature drops to about 120°F, add enough cold water to the wort to make 5 gallons. The temperature should drop to about 70°F when it is ready to ferment if it is ale. For lager, the temperature must be reduced to about 50°F. Then siphon the wort into a carboy.

In the meantime you will have your powdered yeast dissolving in a cup of lukewarm water. To begin fermentation, pour the yeast into the wort and seal the carboy with the airlock, keeping the brew at the proper temperature: 35° to 50°F for lager, 50° to 70° for ale, or whatever your recipe prescribes. In about ten hours or sooner, the beer will start to bubble, the carbon dioxide escaping through the airlock. A rather thick brown foam, called the *kraeusen* (literally, "crown," in German) will form on the surface of the wort, just as foam forms on top of cider. In a few days the kraeusen will disappear. Fermentation is complete. The yeast will settle to the bottom of the carboy.

In about ten days after fermentation began, the beer can be bottled. First siphon it out of the carboy into a bucket that has a spigot on the bottom of it. Pour into the bucket the amount of sugar or corn syrup that your recipe calls for, which will cause a bit of secondary fermentation and carbonation to take place in the bottles. Fill your beer bottles from the spigot, again using a length of plastic tubing from the spigot to the bottle so as to keep oxidation from splashing at a bare minimum. Cap the bottles. Store in a cool cellar. Start drinking in about two weeks.

Having mastered beer made with malt and malt extracts, you can go on to brewing all-grain beer, that is, beer made entirely from malted barley and other unmalted grains rather than malt extracts. Most serious homebrewers believe all-grain beers taste better, but that's something to argue about. In any case, all-grain beers bring the homestead brewer one step closer to entirely homemade brew. Grow your own grains, and after you make beer out of them, feed them to your chickens.

All-grain beers take more time and perhaps a little more expense. The steps are slightly more complicated. You are going to be crushing more barley malt than in the example above, so trying to do it with a rolling pin will not be practical. You'll need a grain mill. One of the little, hand-cranked table mills will do, but slightly larger, motorized table mills make the job a lot easier. Yes, you can buy precrushed malt, but most homebrewers advise against it if you buy it in large quantities, such as a hundred-pound sackful, which you should because of cost savings. But then you have to store the precrushed malt between batches, and it picks up moisture and gets musty easily.

Now we have to start defining terms. Malted grain is grain that has begun to sprout, then has been artificially dried to stop the sprouting process. Generally speaking, even the most intrepid homesteader will want to buy the malted grain for homebrew, but it is possible to make it yourself following the instructions below. But in all-grain beers, that is, beers that are not made with malt extract, malted barley is only part of the recipe. Fermented with the malt are unmalted grains, usually corn but in some cases wheat or even rice. I'll talk only about corn and wheat, partly because these are the most popular "adjunct" grains used with malted barley in American beer making, and partly because nearly everyone in the United States can grow corn and wheat, but not rice.

To prepare the unmalted corn (or any other grain) for fermentation, it should be cooked. It could be ground and soaked, but the usual practice is to boil it to soften the outer coating, so that the yeasts and enzymes can get into it to unlock the sugars. The easy way to use unmalted grain is to buy it already boiled, flaked, and dried. That's what most homebrewers do. But understand that you can boil your own corn quite easily. It doesn't need to be flaked. (Also understand that this process is similar to making the "beer" from which whiskey is distilled.)

The malted barley and boiled corn (or flaked corn) is then mixed together in warm water in a big kettle. One and one-third quarts of water per pound of grist is about right, but follow your recipe. I am using, as an example, a 5-gallon batch of beer, which means you will need a container that holds 6.5 gallons. (I'll explain why later.)

Adjust the pH of your water as described above, if necessary. Allow the mash, as it is now called, to sit for half an hour, which is called the "protein rest." Keep the temperature between 120°F and 130°F. At the end of the half hour, raise the temperature by slow increments to about 150° to 155°F, stirring frequently all the while. If you hold a mash temperature of 150°F, it will take about two hours to complete the mash period. At 155°F, figure an hour and a half. The warmer the water, the shorter the time, but do not go beyond 159°F. If you let the mash get hotter, you might destroy some of the important enzymes.

You'll be able to tell when the mash time has ended because a surprising change will take place in your pot of porridgelike material. The liquid will clear, with the bits of grain, husks, etc., either floating to the surface or settling to the bottom. The wort (the clear liquid) is now sweet. The starches in the grains have been converted to sugars.

At this point, heat up the wort to about 168°F for 5 minutes. This effectively stops enzyme activity.

Now you are ready to strain the wort from the grain and rinse all the wort from the grain particles and husks. To do that, you will have prepared another kettle of water, heated to 168°F, enough water to make up the total 6.5 gallons that you will later boil down to 4.5 gallons. This extra water, called the "sparge water," should be adjusted for pH like the original mash water.

The mash is now dumped into what brewers call a "lauter tun." It's just a container with some kind of screen a couple inches above the bottom and a spigot that comes out the side below the screen. There needs to be some space below the spigot for the dregs, or "draff," as it is called, to settle into. Some homebrewers use two plastic buckets for a lauter tun, one fitting snugly inside the other, the inner one with lots of ⅜-inch holes drilled in the bottom for a screen and resting just above the spigot. Some brewers also put the mash in a loose-meshed cloth bag before putting it in the lauter tun. You can either buy lauter tuns in a brewing supply shop or examine them closely and make your own.

Set the lauter tun on a table so that the spigot sticks out over the table edge and set a large boiler under it, with a smaller stockpot inside the boiler. The warm mash is then dumped into the lauter tun. Wait about five minutes, open the spigot, and, with a handy pitcher, catch about a quart of the first runoff, which will be full of pieces of grain and husks. Pour that back over the mash in the lauter tun and keep doing this until the liquid coming out the spigot clears somewhat. In the meantime, most of the dregs or draff will have settled below the spigot, and the grain above the screen will form into a kind of filter bed. Keep pouring the runoff back over the filter bed until the liquid runs completely clear. You can quit using the pitcher fairly soon and let the wort and draff flow into the stockpot, continually pouring it back into the lauter tun until the wort clears. Then let the clear liquid flow directly into the boiler pan. (The reason for the stockpot is that, if the wort cools below 165°F, you will want to reheat it before pouring it back into the lauter tun. Your thermometer should be handy at all times.)

At this point, it is wise to attach a length of plastic tubing to the spigot to prevent splashing. Splashing churns oxygen into the wort, and oxidation can cause an off flavor in your beer, just as it will in your cider.

Then you start adding sparge water from your other kettle, having kept the temperature of that water as close to 165°F as you can. Pour the sparge water over the filter bed slowly, so that the level of the liquid stays just above the level of the filter bed and no higher. The sparge water cleanses all the wort out of the grain and thins the wort. By the time the kettle is full, you will have washed all the wort possible out of the grain. Feed the grain to your chickens. Or make cookies out of it.

You are now ready to boil the wort, which proceeds in a manner similar to that described in the first example. All-grain wort is boiled for at least ninety minutes, but it may take longer in your situation to reduce the 6.5 gallons of wort to 4.5 gallons. Add hops as your recipe directs you.

Chilling the wort is also about the same as described earlier. The faster the temperature drops to a fermentation level of about 50°F for lagers and about 60°F for ales, the better. Packing ice around the container is a good way to do this, but you can also run cold water through a coil immersed in the hot wort. (For more about how to make or find suitable coils, see Chapter 2.) Add cold water to bring the 4.5 gallons to 5 gallons, which also cools the wort rapidly.

Fermentation and bottling proceed in the same manner as described earlier. Follow directions that come with your yeast. There are other practices of lagering, kraeusening, and maturing your brew about which you can find tons of information, so I'll not scare you with their seeming complexity here.

Let us instead go back to the beginning of making homemade beer and start really from scratch, that is, by sprouting and malting your own barley. My reason is twofold. Sprouting and drying barley malt represents not only the beginning of good beer, but of good whiskey, too, should our government ever concede that citizens who are responsible and intelligent enough to make their own beer and wine can also make their own whiskey, vodka, and gin.

I'm not sure why we take it for granted that malting barley on a small scale is too difficult for the ordinary American to manage. Philip Omdahl would strenuously disagree, I'm sure. The Scots have been doing it on a rather small scale for at least ten centuries. Are they smarter than we are? Their weather may be more conducive to growing and malting barley, but—again, especially on a small scale—those differences aren't that crucial.

Americans in general don't know how to grow barley, let alone malt it, because they've never been given the chance and mostly don't have the space or time to do it. Too busy growing computer programs.

If you can plant a lawn, you can plant a patch of barley. The latter is a lot easier, in fact. Broadcast the seed on freshly worked soil in the fall and go over it very lightly with a rake to bury most of the seeds just beneath the surface. The crop will grow just like lawn grass will, become dormant over winter, then put on a burst of growth in spring. Barley ripens in early summer. The whole process is very similar to growing winter wheat. For 10 bushels of barley, more than you'll need for a year's supply of homebrewed beer, you need about one-sixth of an acre of growing space (or about one-third the area of a reasonably large backyard).

The harvesting of any of the small grains—barley, wheat, rye, or oats—is best done with a modern grain harvester, but, alas, today's harvesters are so big you can hardly turn one around in a typical homesteader field much less a large backyard. I've described in other books how to cut the ripe grain stalks with a scythe or sickle bar mower, rake them into sheaves or bundles, then tie the bundles and stack into shocks or indoors in ranks until you have time to thresh. You can beat the grains out of the seedheads with a child's plastic ball bat, or run the stalks and seedheads through a leaf shredder, or even lay the stalks and seedheads out on a sheet of plywood or clean barn or garage floor and run over them with your garden tractor tires. Then sift and winnow out the grain from the chaff, spread your barley out someplace out of the weather, and let in dry thoroughly. (See my *Small-Scale Grain Raising* (Rodale Press, 1977.) Sounds like tons of work, I know, but remember that a mere 5 to 10 bushels of barley will yield all the malt you'll need for a typical year's supply of homebrew. Also keep in mind that if you have chickens or livestock, every calorie of energy you expend has a double purpose: first for beer making, second for livestock feed.

Making your own malt may not be "practical" in modern economic terms, but someone has to do it, and if the huge malting facilities in Minnesota can do it, so can you. If you've ever sprouted grains for salads or just soaked seeds before planting to get a fast start in the garden, then you are familiar with the first step in making malt, whether you know it or not. The barley (other grains might be used for specialty beers) is moistened and spread out on a clean surface about 4 to 6 inches deep at room temperature or a little cooler. The grain needs to be turned frequently, as it generates heat as it sprouts. A sprouting temperature of about 65°F is right for barley. For a small batch of beer, you can use a large pan or sink or a small tub and stir the barley with your hands.

You must watch closely the development of the grain as it starts to sprout. First the grain swells. Just when the first little white tip of rootlet shows itself, before it gets more than an eighth of an inch long, put the grain into a large shallow pan and pop it in the oven (or other kiln-drying device), where it will dry quickly at a fairly low temperature. Keep the oven door slightly ajar. A clothes dryer might work if you put the sprouted grain in a mesh bag. Better yet, you could do small amounts in electric food dryers or in solar food dryers. Dry until the grain is hard and crunchy.

Your dried, slightly sprouted barley is now malt. Crush or grind it only as you use it since it stores better uncrushed. The tiny white rootlets are usually screened out; they make good chicken feed.

Now you know everything you need to know about making beer except for the most important part. Experience. Do it. Then, like Philip Omdahl, you can start thinking about beer on a grander scale. If you are a farmer with a strong streak of entrepreneurship running through your veins, you might dream, like Omdahl, of establishing a regional brewery and malting cooperative. If you are a backyard brewer, you might dream of founding a neighborhood microbrewery. Most of the economic analyses concerning profit in the brewery business emphasize large size and large quantities of product, because such analyses assume a large company and a large payroll, with executive types making large salaries. However, the microbrewery business is most often successful when it is tied directly into a restaurant that sells the beer retail to customers. Once you suppose a very small operation—one that would aim to make no more than, say, five thousand dollars a year from backyard and cellar labor—then you open the gate to all sorts of interesting possibilities. Maybe you could become a hop gardener and supply all the local homebrewers. Who says imported hops are better? Who says Washington hops are better? Hops for beer used to be grown all over northern Ohio. Was beer made with Ohio hops any less tasteful? Maybe it was better. How many beer drinkers could tell the difference?

Most microbreweries make a point of saying that their beers are unpasteurized and so, presumably, more flavorful. Great Lakes, a popular microbrewery in the Cleveland, Ohio, area, states in its advertisements in large bold lettering: "Louis Pasteur be damned."

CHAPTER 6

The Backyard Winery

HE MODELS for home wine making that I keep in my mind as I write are not the commercial vineyards that produce high-quality wines in Europe and California, as much as I admire them, but the backyards of German and Italian immigrants to America in the late nineteenth and early twentieth centuries, which I admire even more. Making "the best" commercial wines just isn't possible for most of us who don't live in the most favored climates. Nor can most of us afford to buy "the best" except on special occasions. But anyone anywhere can enjoy their own decent wines, and at a fraction of the cost of buying "the best" wines.

My German models are those of my ancestors on their small farms and in their village backyards in central Ohio up until scarcely thirty years ago (and often to this day). They made wine out of everything from rhubarb to dandelions, but especially Concord and Delaware grapes. I observed the Italian models in Philadelphia, where I worked in the late 1960s and early 1970s, and later in Cleveland, where my son-in-law was born and raised. His parents as children remember their backyards as amazing cornucopias of food. On less than a quarter-acre lot with house in place, their parents raised a full complement of vegetables and fruits, sometimes a goat for milk and occasionally a kid for meat, chickens for eggs and meat, and rabbits for meat. And, casting a nice shade over walks and fences and house walls, there were always grapevines for wine, the food of the spirit. As Kathleen O'Neil, an Extension worker who promotes gardening and urban farming in Cleveland, says, "These gorgeous backyards and their grapes are still to be found here, especially in Little Italy." It seems to me that this is the kind of ageless agriculture that must continue, or be returned to, in city, suburb, and countryside alike for social stability and economic health as well as bodily health. That we have seemingly been able to get away from it for half a century is an aberration soon to come to an end.

Deciding which are "the best" wines is a most difficult undertaking to begin with. Wine quality and human taste preference are two extremely complex subjects. Not in all the centuries of civilization has anyone come to any conclusion about either that everyone agrees with. After a long discussion of what constitutes quality in wine, Tom Stevenson concludes in *The New Sotheby's Wine Encyclopedia* (which you know by now I am fond of quoting) that "it is always personal preference that is the final arbiter when you are judging wine." Yet more than one expert wine taster's book contains this seemingly preposterous statement: "Liking a wine has nothing to do with whether it's good." That makes sense only after you learn what expert wine tasters define "objectively" as "good." As Mike Wineberg, who operates Pleasant Valley Winery near Mount Vernon, Ohio, said to me recently, the correct statement should be: "Liking a wine has nothing to do with whether it's good to *someone else*."

It seems to me that trying to solve the wine-tasting mystery of where "objective" leaves off and "subjective" begins is not very productive of anything. Much of the talk and writing about wine is little more than people trying to impress other people with their knowledge, or trying to keep the enjoyment of wine an elite pastime of Very Special Snobs. I suppose it is much like posturing about music or art or poetry. Beethoven may be better than Buffett, but be careful saying that around Buffett fans.

There are great wines and great winemakers, of course. How

many of us backyarders would be so intent on producing a great wine that we would pull the leaves from the grapevines two or three times a season to let more sunlight into the ripening grapes? In some European vineyards, special kinds of rock are laid beneath the vines (or are there naturally) to reflect daytime heat back up into the grapes. Great vintners know that the intensity of sunlight, the amount of rainfall, and the level of humidity are crucial to a great wine, not only on an annual basis, but month by month. Some European wineries do not just differentiate and bottle wines by grape variety, but by the soil type in which any particular variety is grown. They know that small differences in the amount of major and minor nutrients in the soil can mean big differences in the taste of the wine. There is no other agriculture that so clearly demonstrates the connection between food quality and soil quality. The culture of growing grapes in France is to the culture of growing field corn in Illinois what a sculpture by Michelangelo is to a salt block licked by a flock of sheep. But the bourbon whiskey industry, which prides itself in staging whiskey tastings similar to the vintner's wine-tasting rituals, simply buys distillery-grade, No. 2 yellow corn on the market with no concern over whether or not it comes from humus-deficient soils pounded by heavy machinery and heavy doses of chemical fertilizers. But this attitude is, like all things, in flux. Some restaurants, like McFosters in Omaha, now offer not only organic wines and beers, but organic spirits as well.

Judging the "best" wine does not end with soil culture and climatic influence. Wine is alive in the bottle. A "best" wine from a "vintage" year may prove after another year of storage not to be so superior after all. Some wines taste best when sipped with certain foods, and taste only so-so when sipped with other foods. A particular wine of a particular year will taste different if aged in glass or cask, and taste different if the barrel is old oak or new oak. Kermit Lynch in his wonderful book *Adventures on the Wine Route* Farrar, Straus and Giroux, 1988), tells how he learned that the very best wines of France lose quality during shipment if not refrigerated.

Very often, a wine is deemed "best" for no inherent perfection, but simply because the wine or the vineyard has become faddish or fashionable, like styles in clothing.

Nor is it easy to judge which wines are *not* good enough to merit serious consideration by backyard vintners. It is fashionable to show sophistication about wine by tilting one's nose in the general direction of the North Star when mentioning grape wines from areas other than California and Europe. Some high-tongues do not even recognize wines made from fruits other than the grape. And since the "objective" definition of what is good and bad in wine is controlled for all practical purposes by California and Europe, in the same way that judgments on art are controlled by New York and Paris, this attitude is not going to change; never mind that there are many decent wines coming from small and large wineries all over the world. Indeed, the number of AVAs (Approved Viniculture Areas) increases every year, as vintners learn how to adapt grapes and wine to new areas and new climates. Argentina is coming on strong. Eiswine, or Icewine, made from grapes frozen on the vine by winter's wrath, is now not only a treasured German product, but American and Canadian, too. Valley Vineyards, near Cincinnati, is noted for its Icewine. Some treasured wines are made from grapes that are covered with botrytis mold, which winemakers call the "noble rot." Considering how grapes love to rot in the humid Midwest, all we might need in central Ohio is a skilled vintner willing to give the noble rot a try. Our rot is more noble than anybody else's rot. We might even become an ARA—an Approved Rot Area.

There are interesting wines from just about everywhere. The Huguenots, French Protestant pioneers in Florida, made do with what was at hand and produced a creditable wine, so I read, from our native southern scuppernong grape—the first wine made in America. On Middle Bass Island in Lake Erie in the first half of this century, George Lonz and his father made a fortune (and eventually lost it, but not because of poor wine quality) from wines made out of such hardy, old-fashioned grapes as Concord, Catawba, and

Delaware varieties that descended (or perhaps more accurately, ascended) from the lowly native fox grape, *Vitis labrusca*. Lonz was totally American, as was his wine, but he could trace his wine ancestry back to Europe. His father, who started the Lonz grape enterprises, worked first for Andrew Wherle, also of Middle Bass, who had learned wine making in Germany. Wherle was so convinced that the Lake Erie islands were perfect for wineries that he carved a huge wine cellar out of the limestone rock under Middle Bass. A couple of wineries have burned and been rebuilt at the location over the past century, but the wine cellar is still there. Some Lonz wines have even won silver medals at wine competitions in France. Lonz maintained, and many Great Lakers would agree, that carefully made Delaware grape wine was as good as any other, though he admitted that, even in his heyday from the 1930s to the 1960s, California wines outsold him in his own marketing area.

While it is de rigueur now to ridicule Concord grape wine, let us for the sake of argument consider this ubiquitous labrusca variety and its supposedly improved strains. Concord makes a much too heavy, much too sweetish, cloying wine by the standards of winetasting juries. Once you have tasted great wines, Concord is never as enjoyable as it was before you got educated. But hundreds of thousands of backyarders have made and still make Concord grape wine. Why? First of all, they like it. Second, Concord-type grapes may be the only grapes they can reliably grow in their climate without having to use fungicides and put in extra time they don't have in order to maintain the vines. Third, the Concord grape is a curious fellow. It has been so reliable and so popular (for jellies and pies and grape juice if not wine) that it has become a standard part of the traditional Northeastern and Midwest garden. Because of that, there is a wide variation in the quality of Concord grapes found in gardens, and a correspondingly wide variation in the Concord-type grapes that clutter the garden catalogs. I think that many garden Concords are in fact seedlings that resemble a good Concord grape only remotely. Seedlings are easily started and spread accidentally from grapes left to fall and rot under carelessly maintained arbors, or from birds eating and spreading the seeds in their droppings. I have observed very inferior "Concords" in some gardens, although their owners were unaware of that fact, having nothing to compare their Concords to. My own "Concords," from different sources, all vary among themselves, and even the best are not as good as some I've encountered in other gardens. Therefore, backyard wine made from Concord grapes is going to vary in quality also.

A better garden grape for wine in my opinion is the Delaware, and to some extent also Niagara and Catawba, all of which are white grape soulmates of the blue-black Concord in Northeastern and Midwestern backyards. Delaware, unlike other labrusca varieties, is usually named in lists of wine grapes in botanical encyclopedias because it has French wine grape heritage. It makes a white wine, but the grape itself is more pinkish red than white. It was originally grown in New Jersey, but brought to Delaware, Ohio, from where it gets its name. Then it was taken to the Lake Erie region, where it became more or less famous as a wine grape before all the new *Vitis vinifera* hybrid varieties were developed. The Winery at Wolf Creek, at Norton, Ohio, just west of Akron, makes what I think is a delightful wine from Delaware grapes, and owner Andrew Wineberg has been so pleased with the result that he is planting more Delaware vines. He doesn't think last year's vintage (1997) is up to top quality, but I, the wild wanderer in the wine fields, love its fruity taste.

The Winery at Wolf Creek is a good example of the new small-farm wine business. Mr. Wineberg "came home again" from other pursuits to start the winery so that he could keep the home farm alive. (Mike Wineberg, mentioned in Chapter 3, is his brother.) The family farm is pressed all around by suburban development. What the Winebergs developed is a great example of how farm and city can benefit from each other instead of facing off in a battle over urban sprawl. A rather small operation, Wolf Creek sells only the wines it makes. Some 80 percent of them are sold right at the winery, and the rest in the local area. Sometimes Mr. Wineberg runs out of wine before the next vintage is ready. He caters to the walk-in public, and his spacious tasting room overlooking Barberton Reservoir is a heavenly place to sit and relax and drink wines and gaze out at woodland, grassy hillsides, and rows of grapevines, or into your lover's eyes. The winery sells baskets of fruit, crackers, and cheese to snack on while enjoying the various wines. Visitors are encouraged in summer to bring picnic dinners and blankets and eat and sip Wolf Creek wines on the lawn outside the tasting room. Because Mr. Wineberg operates a bona fide farm, growing grapes and producing his own wine, he qualifies for special, lower-cost permit fees in Ohio, evidence that the state is finally understanding that by encouraging spirits production, not taxing it to death, it can generate a better all-around economy. Visitors can sign up to help pick grapes, and, for every bin of grapes picked, a little money is set aside for charity. Andrew says he gets more help than he can use.

Wolf Creek is noted most of all for its Seyval wine, which it now calls Rhapsody. One of the secrets of Rhapsody, says Mr. Wineberg, is that he harvests the grapes before they are completely ripe, something I was taught should never be done. "The higher acid content gives the wine very good aroma of peach and apricot and even grapefruit," says Mr. Wineberg. "I handle the grapes very gently, barely breaking the skins, and then pressing them only softly so as to get out only the good first juice. Then we use cold fermentation processes, fermenting at 53° to 54°F. That means a longer fermentation time, but a better quality wine with Seyval." I climbed up the top of a big tank of fermenting Rhapsody and stuck my nose in under the lid. The aroma of peach was so forceful it nearly knocked me off the ladder and cleared out my nasal passages in an instant. Who needs sinus medicine in a winery? Rhapsody took a gold medal in 1995 in, believe it or not, Los Angeles. "Oh, we Ohio wineries are making world-class wines now," says Mr. Wineberg, "but Ohio just doesn't have an identity as a wine-producing area the way California does. . . . Yet."

Another thing you can do with lowly garden grapes is to blend them. River Rouge, a top-selling wine in the Great Lakes region, is a blend of Concord and Niagara. At our county fair, you will find plenty of homemade wines that are combinations of Concord and Niagara, as well as Concord and Delaware and Concord and Catawba.

I don't wish to leave the impression that labrusca varieties are to be preferred over viniferas, the latter considered the "true" wine-making grapes if they will grow for you. If you are serious about starting a small winery, the right way to get educated is to journey to wineries in your area and find out what grapes grow well there. Nearly every state now has at least one area favorable for commercial wine making. To use Ohio for an example, the climate along Lake Erie and the climate in the southern part of the state along the Ohio River are both designated AVAs and home to successful wineries. Chalet Debonné along Lake Erie at Madison is an excellent one to visit for Great Lakers. Although it is expanding, it is still small enough to be a practical model for other small-scale commercial wineries. During June, July, and August, it holds Country Gourmet Dinners every Wednesday, Friday, and Saturday. You can sip good wines and eat good steaks and learn what might be practical for you if you live in more or less the same climate. Even the master wine tasters give a nod of approval to Chalet Debonné's Vidal Blanc, a wine from a French/American hybrid grape, but you can try some River Rouge, too, just to show yourself what might be possible in your own backyard. And perhaps Vidal might work for you even outside the approved AVAs. Surely, Seyval, which is favored at Wolf Creek, just barely within the Lake Erie AVA, would be a good possibility. In New Hampshire, which has a forbidding climate for grapes, good, simple wines are made from European/American hybrids such as Chancellor, Marechal Foch, and De Chaunac, all hardy to −10°F.

So while the first consideration in wine making might be which varieties make the "best" wines, the first practical move is to provide yourself with reliable grape varieties for your backyard. If you are outside an AVA, keep your eyes peeled constantly for good strains of the old reliable labruscas when you visit other gardens. It is easy to transport them to your garden. When the vines are dormant, in late fall or early winter, cut lengths about a foot long that have two or three buds on them. Bundle the cuttings and bury them until spring. Then stick them in the ground (use an iron rod to make a hole) so that one or two buds are below ground and one above. At least half of the cuttings will root, in my experience.

Second, and also very important: grow your grapes (of any variety) in full sun. Lots of Concord wine is not very good because the grapes were grown in partial shade.

I first learned about wine making from my father. The way Dad made wine, with knowledge from his traditional roots, is still an acceptable way to do it and is a million times simpler than the worrisome directions given in how-to books on wine. He picked the grapes when they were ripe and stripped them carefully from the stems so that no stem parts remained in the grapes. He then put the grapes into a crock and squished and mashed and pressed them with his hands, getting the fruit as juicy as he could. Hand mashing—or barefoot mashing, as tradition enshrines for larger amounts—avoids the possibility of crushing seeds, which would give a bitter taste to the wine. (However, many old-time winemakers, like my son-in-law's Italian family in Cleveland, used a traditional hand-cranked grape grinder to mash the fruit.) Then Dad left the purple slurry to stand for several days with a cloth covering over the crock, occasionally stirring the "must," as the juicy mass is called. This seemingly insignificant detail also gives the grape skins a chance to impart flavors throughout the must and an initial exposure to oxygen to get the fermentation process started. Then, after about three days, he poured the must into a big fold of cheesecloth inside another crock, gathered the ends of the cheesecloth together, and tied them together to make a bag. He then raised the bag above the crock and hung it there on a hook. Only the weight of the bag pressed the liquid out through the cloth. He said that the best wine came from the juice that flowed of its own accord through the cloth, which I would only much later learn, from people like Andrew Wineberg, was exactly the case even in commercial wine making. The bag full of grape pomace was allowed to drip all night. He then poured the juice into a wooden cask laid on its side with a wooden spigot in its head. He put an airlock in the bunghole, and let the wine work. That was all there was to his process. That's the way my in-laws remember their fathers making wine, only they charred the barrel with a little, brief fire before putting the wine into it, to burn out any residues from what had been in the barrel previously. To my memory, Dad hardly ever racked the wine off into bottles, but simply drew a glassful from the spout, as I described for cider, when the wine finished working, if not sooner. That is also the correct way according to my in-laws. The sediment would collect on the bottom of the barrel, where it could not get sucked into the spigot, so the wine came out of the spout clear. Unlike most professional and backyard winemakers, Dad did not add any yeast; he said the powdery white coating (or "bloom") on the blue grape skins contained yeast enough. He also did not add sugar. There was enough sugar in grapes for wine, unlike most apples. Letting the wine ferment in the barrel may be the reason his Concord tasted better than some. I didn't know it then, nor do I think he did, but oak imparts distinct malolactic and vanillin flavors to wine. Most important of all, perhaps, he kept his barrel of wine in the cool cellar so as to benefit from slow, cold fermentation.

Today winemakers, even the backyard variety, want more control over the process, and go to way too much trouble to get it in my opinion. Many will add Campden tablets (sodium or potassium metabisulfite) to the must to suppress wild yeasts right after the must is strained, wait twenty-four hours, and then mix in a laboratory-cultured wine yeast. They then rack off the wine from bottle to bottle several times, to separate the clear wine from the sediment. Many also add a pectin enzyme to the must at the start of fermentation to help clarify the wine, even though wine will usually clarify of its own accord in time; the pectin enzyme merely hurries up the process. None of these practices are obligatory for small-batch producers in my experience, although they might increase one's chances of producing a superior wine. But there is never a guarantee that the wine will be good, and that is half the fun of it.

A farmer I once worked for in Minnesota loved wild grape wine, which has even more foxiness (meaning a kind of muskiness to the flavor) than domesticated Concord. He taught me that there was some variability in the foxiness of these little grapes and to gather only the fruit that tasted lightest, sweetest, and least cloying. He added sugar to the fermenting juice and a little water, too.

Nor is the grape the only fruit that makes good wine, despite what wine connoisseurs say. Robert Kime, food science pilot plant manager at Cornell University, points out that excellent wines can be made from other fruits and even vegetables like rhubarb. The secret, he believes, is to keep the alcohol level no higher than 10.5 percent. Backyard winemakers make the mistake of trying to get their nongrape wines up to the alcohol content of grape wine at 12 percent or a little more, he says. But alcohol at that high a content will actually dissolve flavor compounds in nongrape fruit or vegetable wines. The alcohol vaporizes the flavors and they escape with the carbon dioxide through the airlock. Kline halts fermentation leading to higher alcohol content by controlling the amount of sugar he uses and by refrigerating the wine quickly at 28°F when the alcohol content measured by the hydrometer reaches 10.5 percent.

Just as you can buy vinifera grape juice to make "the best" wine, so some juice suppliers also offer nongrape fruit juices to winemakers, including specialties like cherry, peach, and even rhubarb juice. The supplier of specialty juices I know about, thanks to a press release from Cornell, is Walker's Juice Company, based in Forestville, New York.

Steve Semken, one of my favorite writers (*Moving with the Elements* and *River Tips and Tree Trunks*, from his Ice Cube Press, North Liberty, Iowa), makes a hobby out of fermenting wines from wild and backyard fruits. He tried wild black cherries last year. He says the cherries vary in taste from tree to tree, and it pays to be selective. He describes his latest black cherry wine as "horrible—it tastes like highly toxic cough syrup. However, my wife thinks it tastes okay, so I guess it's not all bad. She's got her own wine reserve now." I didn't think to ask him, but it is important not to crush the seeds when pressing out the juice. The seeds of wild cherries (and the fresh wilted leaves) are somewhat toxic. Semken says the best wines he has achieved so far are wild blackberry and rhubarb. "I'm often confused with some sort of addict or crazed alcoholic as I roam through forest and field with friends, because of my constant observation and questions regarding the potential of items I pass for wine: pears, apples, cherries, crab apples, raspberries, strawberries, whatever. What seems to be lost in the modern and conservative mind is the appreciation of homemaking and the charm of creating your own from possibilities in nature. Sure, it would be easier to purchase wine, but it wouldn't taste the same, be as exciting or as fulfilling."

Semken believes that part of the charm and benefit of wine making at home is turning it into a social event involving friends and family. Harvesting the fruit is easier with a group than alone; there is much good conversation, and, if others in the group are winemakers, one can learn a lot about the craft just by keeping one's ears open. "People have strong opinions about making wine," he tells me, and I nod with vigorous agreement. "A person who goes to the trouble almost always cherishes the methods of making wine at least as much as drinking it. It is fun to invite a bunch of friends in for the first tasting. The goal isn't some sort of drunken hysteria, but the pleasure of creation and sharing that creation."

Semken says rhubarb wine is extremely simple to make. For a batch, he dices 3 pounds of rhubarb stalks, places the stalks in a crock, and adds about 2.5 pounds of sugar. In about twenty-four hours the diced rhubarb and sugar reduce to a mushy consistency. Then he adds a gallon of water and a crushed Campden tablet and waits a couple of days before adding a wine yeast. He lets the brew bubble for about six more days, stirring occasionally at first and then letting it alone. At the end of this time, he strains the must into a glass jug or jar, puts an airlock on the jug, and lets the wine work until it is finished. This takes a couple of months. Then he racks off the liquid into bottles, being careful to leave the sediment behind. In about six months if not sooner, depending on one's curiosity, the wine is ready to drink. "Last time I used all whitish stalks and got a real clear wine," he says. "This year I used more red stalks to give the wine a nice red color."

I once made a wild plum wine that came out tasting more like bad beer than good wine, but, like Semken and his wild cherry wine, the plums started me thinking about the wine-making possibilities in wild fruit free for the picking. Some of that fascination produced better stories than it did wine. I, or rather "we," since the following wine-making story was a very social event, turned to elderberries, mostly because there's something about the taste of elderberry pie that I hunger for, once a year. Old herbals say that elderberries are good for warding off colds. (They say that about nearly every wild fruit.) I was supposed to be studying theology in a seminary at the time, not herbal remedies (although there may be a similarity there), and of course activities like making wine would have been strictly forbidden had the priestly authorities known what we were doing. It so happened that the more notorious (by seminary standards) students had been assigned in their spare time to barn work on the farm from which the seminary derived much of its food. This may not have been entirely coincidental. The rector, in portioning out the workload, might have consciously or unconsciously appointed the more ornery students to the barn because he knew we would survive kicking, shitting cows, and forking hay away in the loft, where summertime temperatures sometimes reached 105 degrees. Anyway, in the barn, away from the constant surveillance of seminary life, we almost always found some deviltry to get into. We justified our wine making by insisting to ourselves that we needed fortification for the sometimes brutal work.

We had to proceed with our nefarious wine making like moonshiners evading the law, and that part was more fun than actually drinking the vile stuff we made. We knew nothing about wine making other than that fruit juice would ferment, and with sugar added would ferment fiercely. We procured sugar by secretly emptying all the containers on the dining room tables into a paper sack. The disappearance of sugar should have been a tipoff to the priestly authorities, but, fortunately for us, none of them had training with the Bureau of Alcohol, Tobacco and Firearms.

If you want to do elderberry wine right, you scrupulously keep out of the fruit to be pressed all the stemmy material to which the tiny individual berries are attached. Or keep out as much of it as you possibly can. But since we were always just a step or two ahead of our priestly revenooers, we were in too big a hurry for such niceties. We just threw the fruit clusters into a crock, stems and all. We first tried pressing the berries by wrapping fistfuls of them in pieces of muslin cloth and then squeezing out the juice with our hands. This is a good and time-honored method if you don't squeeze too hard and press out too much pulp. But much too slow. I borrowed a mechanical mop squeezer and bucket from the cleaning closet. I don't remember, but I hope we cleaned the mop bucket first. Then we added sugar (no one knew what constituted the correct amount, but now I would advise a cup or two per gallon of juice) and we let the furtive brew bubble in a crock with a cloth over it to keep out flies, hopefully. Since all the work had to be done on moonshine time, we worked fast. Too fast. We bottled and corked the stuff up before it had finished working, and hid it in the haymow. I don't remember if the corks blew out or the bottles blew up, but two mornings later, when we went to the barn, there were the most beautiful streaks of purple coursing down the wall where we milked the cows below the mow. The decor was especially noticeable because we had, just the week previous, newly whitewashed the walls. We worked feverishly to obliterate our purple wallcovering and re-whitewash, but the aroma, which was far more delectable than the taste, was not so easy to obscure. We decided on an original solution to mask the smell. We did not clean out the manure gutter behind the stanchioned cows for two days.

Today, when I hear wine connoisseurs waxing eloquent about the "husky vitality" of such and such a red wine, I laugh. I have survived the King Kong of husky vitality.

But do not on my account write elderberry off your list. Had we let it work a little longer in a cooler place with an airlock to exclude oxygen, let it settle out better, carefully racked it off several times, and then let it age for three months, our elderberry juice should have made a tolerable wine. If we had poured boiling water in an amount equal to the amount of elderberries into the mix at the very start, then skimmed the thicker stuff that floated to the top of the pot while the juice was still hot, as all good eighteenth-century housewives knew how to do, then added a wine yeast, the final product would possibly have been quite wonderful.

So I repeat: the practical course for the backyard winemaker is to make wine out of what you have available. If the priority is on cheap availability, dandelion wine would be a logical first choice. Not a whole army of alcoholics with nothing else to drink could even make a dent in the dandelion population of our farm.

I have not made dandelion wine myself, but have observed and tasted the work of others, and our neighbor used to win a blue ribbon for her dandelion wine nearly every year at the fair. Dandelion wine is surprisingly light and delightful. I suspect that it is really sugar/lemon wine, with the dandelion blossoms adding a bit of color and a delicately sweet breath of honey to it. At any rate, it is easy to make. For six bottlefuls, pick a gallon of dandelion blossoms (you are welcome to pick in my yard). You would want to pick blossoms where no chemicals have been sprayed, of course, and you might want to rinse the petals in cool water to allay our modern paranoia about dirt or bugs harbored therein. Old-timers say to pick the blossoms early in the morning, a standard bit of advice that applies to most herb collecting. Remove all the green plant parts around the blossoms and all stem parts. Put thblossoms in a crock and pour over them an equal amount (in this case, a gallon) of boiling water. Let that stand overnight. In the morning, strain the liquid through cheesecloth into another crock or enameled pan and squeeze all the juice out of the blossoms with your hands. Add 4 to 6 cups of sugar (the more sugar, the faster and more feverishly the liquid will ferment) and the juice of six squeezed lemons. Bring the liquid just to a boil, lower the temperature, and let the potion simmer for about half an hour. Then pour your brew back into your crock, which you have meanwhile scalded clean, and add, for this amount, two cakes of yeast or two packets of powdered yeast and stir until the yeast dissolves. A common old winemaking practice if you are using cake yeast is to spread it on a piece of bread and let the bread soak in the must. Let your wine ferment for a couple of days and then rack off into jugs or jars that you can seal with an airlock, so that carbon dioxide can escape but little or no air can get in. On no account seal the container while the juice is still fermenting energetically, unless you are a Fourth of July freak and enjoy spontaneous explosions. When the wine quits bubbling, in about two weeks, more or less, you can rack it off again into other jars if there is sediment present (with dandelion wine there may not be enough to worry about), but in any case do not stopper the bottles tight, as some light fermentation will still take place. Set the corks in tight only after all signs of tiny rising bubbles disappear and the wine becomes still. Store in a cool place for six months to mature, but drink some of it right away, too, just to satisfy your curiosity.

The yeast in the above recipe is regular store-bought baker's yeast. If you go to a wine supply store, you might find a special wine yeast better suited to your purposes. But I imagine if you asked the shopkeeper about what yeast goes best with dandelion wine, you might not get a firm answer. What you are really "yeasting" in this case is mostly the sugar, anyway.

Some dandelion wine makers add strawberries or red raspberries to the mix to give the wine a nice pinkish color and a bit of fruity taste. For the above amounts of ingredients, a pound of berries will do fine, but don't be afraid to experiment. Pulp them a little and mix into the must when you add the sugar.

Other dandelion wine makers add a half pound to a pound of

raisins to a batch of dandelion wine, which I think is a good practice for succeeding with any exotic flower wine. I don't think you can go wrong adding raisins to any backyard wine, in fact, and when you get into herbal and nut wines, the raisins are invaluable because, like all grapes, they almost always contain lots of *Saccharomyces* yeast strains. In fact, I will go way out on a limb (vine?) and declare that a handful or two of raisins added to every batch of wine substitutes well enough for special wine yeasts and some of the sugar.

A close study of the myriad recipes for various herbal and flower wines indicates that what you are really making is raisin-sugar-citrus wine, flavored by the various herbs, spices, or nuts after which the wine is named. Understanding this, you will find it easy and fun to make wine out of almost anything vegetative. To make fermentation and taste even better, add a half pint of concentrated white grape juice to any or all of these wine musts. To make your own concentrate, boil down white grape juice to a syrupy liquid. You could use black or purple grapes, too, but the wine would then be dark and everyone would assume (partly correctly) that they were drinking grape wine. Add a few ounces of a spice like cloves, or of a nut, like almond, and call your creation clove or almond wine. Be careful if you make and serve hazelnut wine. A rare few people are very allergic to hazelnuts.

A friend of mine makes a very praiseworthy wine from red raspberries and gives me a bottle every year. Considering his simple methods, his wine is amazingly clear and tasty. He doesn't use pectin enzyme for clarification. He doesn't use Campden tablets to kill off wild yeasts, either. He does use a purchased wine yeast he gets through a mail-order wine supply catalog. First, he squishes the red raspberries into a juicy pulp in a crock with his hands, adds dissolved sugar syrup and yeast, and lets it sit for ten days, stirring occasionally. Then he strains the must into a big glass carboy and puts an airlock in the carboy mouth. When the bubbles subside and the wine clears, which he says last year took five months, although it usually takes less than three, he racks the liquid off into bottles.

Encouraged by him, and with a tame blackberry patch over-flowing with surplus fruit, I decided to make blackberry wine last year. What I really had in mind was blackberry brandy to make blackberry brandy Alexanders, my favorite after-dinner drink, but I'm getting ahead of my story. Our blackberries are huge, luscious fruit of the Thornfree variety, but they are seedier than wild black-berries, and when they are really ripe enough to eat, they fall off. So I picked very carefully, mindful of the old advice to use only completely ripe fruit. Berries that fell into my hand when I pulled gently were the ones I kept. I decided to make only a gallon of wine to start with. For that I weighed out 2.5 pounds of berries, put them in a 2-gallon crock, and smashed and squished them to a juicy pulp with my hands. Since the juicy slurry was superthick, I added 2 quarts of boiling water and let it stand overnight. Why so many wine recipes call for adding *boiling* water I do not really know, but it is true going way back to the eighteenth century at least. That direction is always accompanied by another calling for adding yeast to the must *after* the must has cooled a little, so I presume the boiling water is for sanitary reasons, both to kill wild yeasts and to keep bacteria at bay.

Next day I strained the stuff through a couple of layers of cheese-cloth, and when no more juice would soak through, I made a little sack of the cheesecloth and squeezed out a little more juice, but did not squeeze hard because, as in most wine making, what comes through the filter easily makes the best wine. Second pressings make lower-quality wines. (The same goes for olive oil—hence all of the "extra virgin" and "first cold pressing" designations on the la-bels of the most expensive brands.)

I let the strained liquid sit only a day in the crock, to expose it to a little initial oxidation. This period of time is supposed to be for a few days, but I'm always afraid that I'll get too much exposure to air and encourage acetobacter, which can turn a potential wine into vinegar. Then I added 2.5 cups of sugar. I stirred the juice very gently to dissolve the sugar without stirring in air. Then I added two packets of baker's yeast, which I had dissolved in a cup and a half of pure orange juice. The yeast began working immediately in the orange juice and was bubbling over the glass when I added it to the must. Then I poured the whole business into a gallon jug, added water to fill it to an inch from the top (it needed only a little), and closed the jug with a cork and airlock. For an airlock, I drilled a hole in the center of the cork just the right size to accept the end of a plastic tube. The end of the tube through the cork had to be positioned above the wine, not in it. The other end I inserted into a glass of water. That allowed the carbon dioxide a way out of the jug, but air no way in.

The wine worked for three weeks before the bubbles began to subside. I let it sit another two months so that sediment settled in the bottom. Then I siphoned off the wine into another jug, being sure that the tube I used did not stick down into the sediment on the bottom of the first jug. The wine was clear and purple-red in color, very pretty. I did not sock the cork in tight right away, just in case the wine might still be working a little.

My blackberry wine may not win the applause of wine tasters, but my wife, who is very particular, thinks it is pretty good for homemade. It has no unpleasant aftertaste at all. It is a bit too sweet for my taste, though, and next time I make it I will halve the amount of sugar. All I can add is that it was extremely simple and easy to make, and I wonder exceedingly why wine books make it all sound so complicated. I did not use Campden tablets or any form of sulfur. I did not use pectin enzyme.

How I eventually made my blackberry brandy Alexanders without violating the law will have to wait until the next chapter, on brandy and liqueurs.

You can age your wine in wood barrels following the simple method I've described or you can cork it in glass bottles after it finishes working. As to which is better, the argument goes on. I think the main reason glass carboys are used is because wooden barrels are hard and expensive to come by. If I had a good used whiskey barrel, I'd surely keep my wine in it.

It seemed almost a bit magical, but just as I was finishing

research on this chapter, the government seemed to have finally heard my (and many others') complaints about the unfair health cautions it required on wine labels. Now a winemaker can advertise the health benefits of wine drunk in moderation. With the increase in popularity of organic wines, this governmental show of enlightenment proves once more that progress is possible. Onward and upward.

CHAPTER 7

The Adventures of a
Brandy & Liqueur Illiterate

NTIL two years ago, I knew nothing about one of life's little pleasures, good brandy. In the realm of spirits, I was a macho corn-likker man, mostly because my Kentucky wife led me into bourbon sin. In Ohio restaurants, when this lovely lady of refined and feminine appearance hauls off and orders "Old Fitzgerald on the rocks," the waiters invariably step back, a bit shocked (or at least pretending to be) and greatly amused that a *woman* would be ordering what is evidently considered a man's drink every place but in Kentucky. Their eyebrows arch higher if I, with my newly gained knowledge, affect a slightly feminine voice and try to say through my nose, "Cooovahseeaye, please."

I am a brandy illiterate mostly because good brandy is too expensive for me to indulge in except on very special occasions. Courvoisier costs over forty dollars a fifth. I'm sure that most Americans consider good brandy too expensive, which is why you, like me, are also brandy know-nothings. Wisconsin is the only exception. For reasons nobody has figured out yet, Wisconsin, often thought of as a beer and cheese enclave, loves its brandy. America's general brandy illiteracy is a direct result of our government not allowing home distillation. If it did, by now those of us so inclined would be drinking our own brandy regularly at not much more than the cost of our labor. And the brandy industry, far from being hurt by this

98

competition, would have a much larger market, because brandy would be at least as much a part of our culture as bourbon. We would understand the worth of good brandy, would have cultivated a taste for it, and would be buying more of it as well as making it, just as we do with beer and wine.

The story only gets worse. True grape brandy and, occasionally, true apple brandy are the only real fruit brandies generally available in America as far as I can find out. Brandies made *entirely* from real, honest-to-goodness peaches, apricots, blackberries, and all other fruits are very hard to find in the United States. (St. George Spirits, in Emeryville, California, and Clear Creek Distillery, in Portland, Oregon, make highly touted real fruit brandies, but such domestic products are rare.) What you can buy is mostly neutral spirits from grain alcohol or from grape brandy, with various fruit flavorings and a little generic grape brandy mixed in. These drinks taste okay if they are aged in wood to mellow them, but are not true brandies or *eaux-de-vie*, as they are designated in the trade. To get the most famous *eau-de-vie*, you have to journey to the nooks and crannies of Europe and pay handsomely. The good news is that this situation is changing. Keep your eyes peeled for real *eau-de-vie* when you visit large liquor stores. Some European *eaux-de-vie* are being exported to the United States now, especially to the West Coast. But it is not always easy to tell from labels. Labels are often masked in wording that is strong on the word "flavor." Beware. As everyone knows by now, "genuine fruit flavor" does not necessarily mean "fruit flavor derived 100 percent from genuine fruit." Here's a label from a generic brandy product, and I'll not name the distributor because I'm sure the same pretentious wording appears on other distributors' bottles: "An elegant brandy that combines true brandy *flavor* with the traditional aroma *characteristics* [emphasis mine] of the world's finest brandies." I may be brandy-illiterate, but I'm not language-illiterate. That label, to me, could describe a brandy made from sugar beets and infused with genuine artificial flavoring. A brandy made from sugar beets and artificial flavoring might be good, don't get me wrong, but it is not real brandy. The only nongrape fruit brandy label that I would believe to represent the real thing would be one with words to this effect: "This is a true *eau-de-vie* distilled from 100 percent real peaches"—or blackberries, or whatever fruit the brandy is being represented as. So far I haven't found such a label, but remember, I am still a brandy illiterate who has not traveled in big American cities, much less Europe.

Distilling brandies is just like distilling whiskeys, as pointed out earlier. If I were to distill my blackberry wine into brandy for making blackberry brandy Alexanders, I'd use the stovetop method described in Chapter 2. I would, however, leave some pomace and sediment in the wine, not strain it all out, to help build flavor in the brandy. I would not treat the wine with Campden tablets or other forms of sulfur (I don't anyway), because in the brandy any taste or characteristic of the wine is amplified, and the taste of sulfur could be noticeable. Commercial brandy makers usually use wine that has not been sulfured.

A simple stovetop still is not as simple as the traditional French models for distilling cognac, the best of all brandies (according to the French). The traditional cognac still did not have a slag box, or thumper, or any kind of doubler at all. The vapors traveled from the evaporator directly to the condenser, and the first run was redistilled at least once.

The early distillers kept getting cleverer, and eventually they learned how to use the wine itself instead of water as a coolant for the condenser coil. The wine to be distilled was warmed by letting it pass first around the condenser on its way to the evaporator. The condenser was at the same time cooling the vapors from the evaporator into brandy. Prewarming the wine increased the efficiency of the still because less fuel was required to heat the evaporator and no water was used at all. Also, the vapors rose in the evaporator through a series of plates, the forerunner of the rectifying column in a column still. This column of plates worked like a reflux column in a moonshine still or homemade ethanol still. As the vapors passed through the plates, only those of higher alcohol content passed on through to the condenser; some of the low wines condensed on the plates and fell back into the still. This still is sometimes called the Armagnac still, Armagnac being considered (except possibly in California, which also makes good brandy) as the second-best brandy in the world. Redistillation in an Armagnac still was not as necessary (but on a small backyard scale I would surely do it) as in the older cognac still.

Early Armagnac stills were often mobile. Since a source of water was not needed, they could be operated anywhere a vintner chose to distill. The still could be moved from one vineyard to another, enabling the small distillers to share costs. This is the kind of efficiency that takes place when government keeps its taxing nose out of things. Eventually, however, the French government descended into the same kind of totalitarian stupidity that America did. In the 1970s the "cradle of liberty and reason" decided to issue no more permits for home distillation—in an effort to curb alcoholism, officialdom piously announced. Has anyone noticed any curbing of alcoholism in France lately? Nonissuance of permits merely gave the commercial French brandy interests a lock on the market and made alcoholism cost more, to the detriment of the families of the alcoholics.

Eaux-de-vie, that is, brandies made from fruits other than grapes, are traditionally distilled in cognac stills in Europe, although an Armagnac-type still would work too. Stone fruits such as cherries, plums, and peaches are squished into a runny must for fermentation, taking care not to crack the seeds, which would give a bitter taste to the brandy. Fermentation takes longer than for grapes because there is less natural sugar in these fruits, and it is illegal in most parts of Europe to add sugar to true *eau-de-vie*. The juice is not strained from the fruit pulp during fermentation, and both are distilled together to saturate the spirit as much as possible with the aroma and flavor of the fruit. Heat is applied very carefully, usually by way of a double boiler arrangement so as not to scorch the pomace, but if you are doing this by stovetop methods, where temperature is easily controlled, this should not be a problem. Distillation proceeds just as described for cognac, but the final brandy after the second distillation has a little less alcohol content than grape brandy, usually around 60 percent (120 proof) instead of 70 percent. But if you decided to add a bit of sugar to the fermentation, not being regulated by European laws, the alcohol content might be about the same. The Alsatians would say that your *eau-de-vie* with its added sugar was not as good as theirs, just as Granddaddy insisted whiskey made with sugar was not as good as whiskey made from grain malt alone.

Although a far cry from today's continuous column still, the original Armagnac still was its forerunner, in the sense that distillation was more or less continuous. Also, its little rectifying column over the evaporator was a primitive model of the stripping column in the modern continuous column still. But continuous column stills today loom five stories high and can distill 1,000 gallons of brandy an hour. From a distance, a brandy distillery looks a little like a petroleum refinery. Scary. But actually, this method of manufacturing spirits has some advantages over pot stills other than quantity production. Distillers of pot-still spirits, and many drinkers of spirits, insist that pot-still products taste better than continuous column products, but continuous column distillers claim that they have more control over the impurities in spirits. The aldehyde "heads" in the spirit are more easily volatilized out of the ethyl alcohol, and the fusel oils in the "tails" are more easily separated, too, although, like everything else in spirits making, that latter claim is disputed. In distilling brandy in a continuous column still, the preheated wine is pumped into the top of the first, or stripping, column, where rising steam evaporates the alcohol. The water and some of the tails drop to the bottom and are drained away, while the alcohol ascends to the top of the column and is piped to a rectifying column next to it. The alcohol vapors condense on a series of plates one above the other, according to alcohol content, and in this manner the "heads" and remaining "tails" are separated from the middle fraction of ethyl alcohol to varying degrees on the different plates. The most volatile "heads" ascend to the top as almost pure neutral spirits and are shunted off to their own condenser, where the aldehydes and acetates are separated and sold as by-products.

In a continuous column still, it is easier than with pot stills to produce nearly pure (95 percent or 190 proof) alcohol off the highest plate. The middle plates on the column yield the best drinking alcohol. Fusel oils collect more on the lower plates, but even then they are not easily separated or rectified to give the proper content for full flavor to the drinking alcohol. Some of these lower, fusel alcohols are desirable in the spirit for flavor, but most Americans don't like the taste of a brandy if its fusel oil content is on the heavy side. Think of the difference between red and white wine. Although the differences being discussed are very slight as to volume in any case, red wine has more fusel oils in it than white. While lots of Americans love red wine, not so many have acquired a taste for fusel-charged brandy. Brandy lovers believe that achieving just the right touch of fusel oils for flavorful spirits can be accomplished better by the artful master distiller in a pot still. A column still tends to produce a purer, but somewhat less flavorsome alcohol, they argue. That doesn't really mean that brandy (or whiskey) from a column still is second-rate, but that is why, at the chemical heart of it, most brandy and whiskey gourmets believe pot-still distillation produces a higher taste quality than column stills do.

It is really a matter of preference and sometimes of historical necessity. French peasants learned to like a highly fusel-charged brandy, known as marc, that is made from grape pomace. The feudal lords gave them the pomace and kept the good wine for themselves. So, over the centuries, the peasants turned the pomace into a pot-still brandy that costs as much as the good stuff today, and to some palates tastes just as good.

The commercial pot stills used to make brandy in Europe today are bigger and more sophisticated than the simple pot stills of the French backyard distiller. But, in every practical respect, these new pot stills by law must imitate the centuries-old way of making brandy. In making true cognac, no kind of doubler or rectifying

column is permitted, but only the oldest-fashioned way of distilling twice. Distillers usually don't bother to take out any heads or
tails on the first run, but on the second run, which delivers a
brandy of around 70 percent alcohol, the first bit of brandy out of
the condenser is used for by-products and only the strictly middle
fraction is kept, leaving nearly as much tails to be redistilled as the
amount of brandy saved. For *eau-de-vie* made from other fruits,
the standard run is bottled at 80 proof, the grand reserve at 86
proof, and the most select heart of the run *(coeur de chaufe)* at 90
proof. The *coeur* may amount to only 12 or 13 gallons out of a typical 320-gallon run, says R.W. Apple Jr. in an interesting article,
"*Eau-de-vie*: Fruit's Essence Captured in a Bottle" in the *New York
Times*, April 1, 1998.

This keeping to tradition is the reason, I think, that these cognac
stills are so pleasing to the eye. Art follows function, perhaps. They
strike me as works of sculpture. The evaporator looks more like a
large, glistening stove with an artfully shaped, ovoid copper top.
The copper "tube" coming out of the top is gracefully swan-necked
in a most pleasing form, and leads on through a big onion-shaped,
copper *chauffe-le-vin*, or wine preheater (not all cognac distillers
use one), where the vapors on their way to the condenser heat the
wine that is headed for the evaporator. The condenser is a round
tank, also of glistening copper, where the brandy condenses and
drops into a receiving barrel. The barrel is also beautiful, made of
Limousin oak. A room-size version of this whole affair would make
a wonderfully decorous piece of furniture. Hey, don't laugh. The
still might be used as an attractive woodstove and fireplace, the
chauffe-le-vin could be turned into a refrigerator, and the condenser
pressed into service as a liquor cabinet.

But none of this knowledge solved my problem of how to make
blackberry brandy for my blackberry brandy Alexanders without
breaking the law. (Actually, all the information was helping indi-
rectly, but I didn't know that yet.) Good grape brandy makes a fine
brandy Alexander along with equal parts of crème de cacao and
heavy cream, but I have this quirk: when I mix brandy with dairy

cream and crème de cacao, I want it to have a blackberry flavor. I can't explain this strange desire other than that the first brandy Alexander I ever tasted was made with blackberry brandy at the William Penn Inn, north of Philadelphia, which was a tremendous restaurant in those days and probably still is. We lived close to it. So close, in fact, that we could saunter from our property through a bit of woodland and meadow to get there. Elegance personified. Brandy Alexanders are not all created equal, and I've tasted some truly vile ones over the years, but the one at the William Penn turned out to be the most heavenly after-dinner drink of my lifetime up until then. I didn't have to worry about putting on weight in those days, so I had two.

Trying to find other options out of my dilemma of brandy illiteracy and the law, I learned that an already distilled spirit could be mixed into a macerated fruit, and then the whole redistilled to permeate the spirit with the flavor of the fruit. In fact, this is the way many of the best liqueurs around the world are made. A "liqueur" is best defined as an alcoholic spirit with lots of sugar in it, along with almost any kind of fruit or herbal flavoring under the moon. "Maceration" means squishing and squashing the fruit as you would do to make wine. Making cordials (the terms "liqueur" and "cordial" are synonymous today) this way is far easier than regular distillation: you only have to distill once and don't have to worry about heads and tails, because you are dealing with a finished spirit. Commercially, neutral spirits are redistilled with fruit to make liqueurs and then cut, if necessary, with water. You may have a difficult time finding a source of neutral spirits, but a high-proof vodka or brandy works fine—even better, in fact, than using neutral spirits.

Since this method did not actually call for making a new spirit, but simply evaporating and condensing one already made to infuse it with a stronger taste of the fruit involved, was this against the law, too? Of course, no one in authority wanted to give me a firm answer. Did that mean I could go ahead with making my cordial this way? Don't be silly.

So now I was down to my last option and becoming less illiterate as time went by. Many liqueurs can be made entirely by infusing a spirit with the fruit or herb of your choice, no distillation involved. The process is the same as infusing vinegar with fruits or herbs. To my delight I learned that the number of liqueurs one can make in this manner is limited only by one's imagination. The result is only partly homemade and can get expensive, of course, but it's perfectly legal. Actually, it may not be so expensive, now that I think about it, because when you mix the macerated fruit with the brandy, you make more liquid than the original brandy volume, albeit a little less in alcohol content.

Once headed in this direction, it seemed as if whole new worlds of spirit delights had opened before me. (A most helpful book for the brandy illiterate is *Brandies and Liqueurs of the World* by Hurst Hannum and Robert S. Blumberg [Doubleday, 1976].) In fact, liqueurs are probably the reason drinking alcoholic spirits became popular. Early attempts at distillation produced something that was akin to the harshest moonshine, which was okay since they were made to be taken as medicine, and everyone knows medicines should taste awful. Infusions with sugar, spices, and fruit flavorings were a way to make the stuff endurable to the tongue. The medieval alchemists who made some of the first liqueurs believed that there were elixirs to be discovered in nature that would lead to eternal life, literally (which is no more far-fetched than their dream of turning base metals into gold). So they started infusing alcohol with every herb or fruit available to them. If spirits made you feel good, then, as bitters makers much later learned, you could ascribe the good feeling to any damn-fool thing you put in the spirit. Those looking for an excuse to drink alcohol would believe or pretend to believe that they were merely drinking medicine, not enjoying liquor. When people still died despite these elixirs of eternal life (or maybe because of them) the alchemists decided that the secret was in finding the right *combination* of herbs and seeds and fruits to blend. That meant almost an eternal life of trying all the possibilities. Some liqueurs were blends of at least a hundred herbs and flavorings!

The medieval monks, perhaps not so much enamored with the idea of eternal life in heaven as they pretended to be, embraced the possibility of eternal life on Earth. Monasteries became the first important distilleries, and from them came liqueurs that exist to this day, like Benedictine. Those Benedictine monks were evidently interested not only in *ora et labora*, but a little *libatio*, too.

Most liqueurs made by infusion use neutral spirits as the alcohol base. Neutral spirit of itself has no taste and so is easy to infuse, and it also has a high enough alcohol content so that the infusion of fruit and herb juices and sugar does not lower the alcohol content too much. (By law a liqueur must be 15 percent alcohol, but most are much more than that.) Almost all infused liqueurs as well as distilled liqueurs are quite heavily sweetened with sugar.

Making infused liqueurs is simplicity itself, but the infusion, which means soaking flavorings in the liquor, should last at least two to three months to get a good transfer of flavor. Sometimes, in the case of commercial liqueurs of great price, the aging time is much longer. One hundred proof brandy and 100 proof vodka both make good infusers—vodka because it has little taste of itself and brandy because it hits the mouth like fire and benefits from being toned down a bit.

For an example, here's how a small batch of lemon liqueur is commonly made. You need a fifth of 100 proof vodka, eight lemons, 2 cups of sugar, and 2 cups of water, though you can vary the proportions of each to suit your taste. (If you like the resulting drink, you will probably want to make a larger batch the second time.) You are going to use the skin or rind of the lemons, so they have to be peeled carefully so as not to include the bitter white pulp under the skin. Wash the lemons beforehand, of course. Let the lemon peelings sit in half the vodka in a glass jar at room temperature for a month and a half. After that time, dissolve the sugar and water in a pan of boiling water and, when it cools a little, add it to your peelings/vodka mix along with the other half of the bottle of vodka. Let the whole stand for another month and a half (if you get real curious, you can shorten the time a bit). At the end of the aging period, strain out the lemon peelings. To enjoy the liqueur best, put a bottle of it in the freezer to get icy cold and then drink it from a frosted martini glass on a hot summer afternoon.

Don't let the skinned lemons go to waste. Make lemonade out of them and spike it with a little gin. That makes a great hot-weather drink, and might be served, for instance, during haymaking time, but watch out. Once in my theologically wild oats days in the seminary, a friend and I surreptitiously slipped a fifth of gin into a milkcan full of lemonade that had been prepared for our haymaking gang. The general consensus among the innocent seminarians was that this was the best lemonade anyone had ever tasted. One of the guys was a big bear of a young man, and, after downing several large glasses of "lemonade," he felt himself to be the equal of a bear in strength. A hay bale lay in the path of the tractor and baler coming across the field, and he decided to run out from under the tree where we were drinking and kick it out of the way. He bore down on the bale with a whoop and, imitating a football place kicker perfectly, drove his foot into the side of the bale with great gusto. The bale may have quivered, and then again it may not have, but the kicker went sailing through the air toward some unseen goalpost on the horizon. We would have burst into hysterical laughter even had we been cold sober, so you can imagine the effect this scene had on us, aided and abetted by our "lemonade."

*   *   *

You may have guessed by now how I made my own "blackberry brandy" legally. Using as a guide a recipe for infusing red raspberries in grappa, I filled a quart jar half full of blackberries, mashed only a little, added a cinnamon stick, then filled the jar with grape brandy (not grappa—much too expensive), put a lid on the jar, and let it sit in the cupboard for a month. The recipe I was using as a guide called for 4 tablespoons of sugar, but I left that out, hoping to end up with more of a brandy than a sweeter cordial. I used half of a fifth of Hennessy VS brandy, which, at twenty-six dollars a fifth, was not the most expensive brandy, but still a lot of money to experiment with. (I tried to get my publisher to underwrite my strange experiments of the drinking kind, but no luck.) Then I strained out the blackberry pomace, poured in the rest of the bottle of Hennessy, and let it age for another month. Not bad stuff, but a little weaker than the Hennessy would have been alone. It did impart a blackberry taste to my brandy Alexanders. Even the dollop of whipped cream on top tasted like blackberry. I enjoyed my almost-homemade after-dinner drink for about four dinners and gained two pounds. When I make more blackberry bounce, I'll probably gain weight faster because I'll leave the sugar in—and probably add more than 4 tablespoons. Also, in the second half of the aging period I'll use either more brandy or less blackberry juice.

Cherry bounce, popular in Michigan backyards, is made in the same way I made my blackberry bounce. In fact, you can use almost anything edible with sugar and a high-powered spirit to make a liqueur: any fruit; angelica (this herb is almost standard in all great liqueurs, and to think I have tons of it growing along the creek); artemisia (avoid this one, though, because the herb is related to wormwood and that's what the dangerous and mostly illegal green liqueur, absinthe, is primarily made of); dill; ginger; maidenhair fern; licorice; fennel; cocoa; coffee; sage; thyme; vanilla; and rose blossoms. Chartreuse, say Hannum and Blumberg, dates from 1605 and is a blend of some 130 plants! It is now owned by a secular corporation, which says that the formula is a secret known only to three Carthusian brothers. (Oh sure. If you believe that, you need to live in a seminary awhile.)

Those three Carthusians may not know it, but they are spawning a value-added idea for an American backyard gardener and spirits maker. Since liqueurs are not difficult to make, at least not basically difficult, start experimenting and come up with your own blends. Use lots of sugar and a good bonded spirit, which will cover a multitude of sins, and call in your friends to taste your homemade liqueur. Tell a gripping story about a secret recipe handed down through your family and just recently rediscovered in a chest in Aunt Matildebee's attic. Or tell them you use a secret blend of herbs all native to your backyard known only to three skeletons in your closet. Call it Homebody.

The recipe for Benedictine contains a secret blend of "only" twenty-seven herbs and dried plants. Make one with twenty-eight. When Benedictine is mixed with brandy, you get a spirit well-regarded in America called B and B. It's about 40 percent six-year-old brandy and 60 percent Benedictine. Why not try making your own version of it for your own table?

Everybody knows Drambuie and half of everybody likes it as an after-dinner drink. But most of us liqueur-illiterate everybodies do not know that it is made with scotch and sugar plus a ritualistic secret blend of herbal oils. Drambuie was made from a family recipe for a century and a half before it went commercial. There's no reason to think that all the great secret herbal essences were discovered in past centuries. It's just that monks had plenty of time on their hands. Make up some new blends—a perfect hobby for the retired or people determined to stay home and care for their babies. Some water is involved in the final Drambuie mix, too, which means that if you whip up your own blend of Scotch whisky (when in Scotland one must drop the "e" out of "whiskey") and sugar and herbal secrets, you can, by adding water, probably double your money on the scotch you buy to make it with. You, too, can say it's from an old family recipe, if you define "old" loosely.

I've a notion an interesting homemade drink might come from American whiskeys, sugar, and a secret blend of herbal oils, too. Rock and Rye is an original American cordial—whiskey flavored with citrus. The "rock" in this case stands for, or at least once stood for, rock sugar. The original recipe had oranges, lemons, and cherries in it. Southern Comfort is a standard bourbon liqueur much loved in America. It is more often used in cocktails, but can stand alone as an after-dinner drink as well. Maybe even after-breakfast, at least on special occasions.

The Carthusian monks would probably start praying for my eternal salvation for saying so, but I liken the liqueur maker to the jam and jelly maker. If you use proper amounts of sugar and patience, you can make jam or jelly out of just about anything, including corncobs. Don't laugh. My aunt's corncob jelly was pretty good. In a parallel sense, you can make liqueurs out of almost anything alcoholic, along with sugar and patience, and all those bottles of different-colored spirits glistening from your shelves will look even better than all those jars of jellies.

CHAPTER 8

The Midnight Fox:
A Bootlegging Folktale

An elaboration of a folktale, "Max and Magi,"
told on the shores of Lake Erie.

OW THAT she was full grown, Jake did not know what he was going to do with Mosey. He had in fact never known what to do with her. He had found her one morning, in, let's see, it would had to have been 1898, a baby snuggled among dirty rags in a washtub along the bank of the Portage River. Peering through the early misty light from his rowboat, he had spotted the tub on the shore, the rags in it heaving up and down, two tiny arms flailing and thrashing among them. He had rubbed his eyes, shook his head, cried out in wonder, but the apparition, which reminded him immediately of the story of Moses, did not go away. Had the poor tyke's mother brought the baby to the river with the intent of drowning it and then not been able to do so? Had he interrupted the grisly deed? Had someone deliberately abandoned the baby where he would surely find it as he ran his daily trapline along the river? "Oh God, sonuvabitch, hellfire," he mumbled over and over again as he rowed with the squalling baby back to his cabin. "What the goddamn hell am I supposed to do now?"

Still muttering an unending monologue of foul language, he had taken the baby inside, put a big fire in his stove, heated some milk, and fed the child just as he had fed orphaned fawns many times, with a lamb nipple on a bitters bottle. The child took the milk ravenously, choking, but coming back for more immediately, grabbing at the bottle with both fists in the fierce tenacity for life that would always be characteristic of her.

Jake had a mind to call her Moses, but since she was a girl, he settled on Mosiana. Every night he made up his mind that the next day he would deliver her up to the proper authorities. But he could not bring himself to do so. A runaway from an orphanage himself, he had lived a solitary life, fishing and trapping the more remote shores and backwaters of Lake Erie and its tributaries from Port Clinton to Vermillion, shunning human society as much as possible. Remembering his own unhappy foundling years, and finding the baby somehow fulfilling after years of solitary living, he finally decided on another course of action. He enlisted the help of Suzanna, the old woman upriver, who lived as hermitlike an existence as he did. She took to the baby, too, and together they raised the child.

By the time Mosey was five, she was accompanying Jake on his fishing expeditions almost daily. When anyone on the docks asked him, which happened rarely, for Jake was not one to invite inquiry about anything, he said that her parents had died of smallpox and that he was the only known relative. And so the girl grew up, happy to wander with Jake along the lakeshore or sailing the open water: trapping in winter, fishing in summer, delivering their catch to the fish markets of Port Clinton and Marblehead and Sandusky and Lakeside, and, at the height of the tourist season, to the islands that were strung out like iridescent green pearls between Catawba and Canada—Kelley's, North, South, and Middle Bass. By the time Mosey was ten, she could have found her way alone across the lake had Jake allowed her.

When she was fourteen, he told her the truth. She stared out across the water for a few minutes, picked at her bare toes absentmindedly for a few more, then turned to look at him with a malevolent eye. "Jake," she said, "if you ever tell anyone and they try to take me away, I'll sink your goddamn boat." They both grinned. No two people so different in sex and age could be so much alike in character.

Mosey loved the wild, solitary life on the lake with an almost savage intensity and, as she grew aware of the outside world, lived in fear that someone might take her away from her beloved life with Jake and Suzanna and make her go to school or live with some more reputable family. Jake wondered if she was altogether human; perhaps, he thought, she was the offspring of the mermaid that Erie fishermen swore they saw regularly off uninhabited Mouse Island. Her instinctive knowledge of the lake's waters and its fish seemed too keen to be wholly human. As he grew older, Jake more and more depended on her skill with both boat and fish to make a living for them. Like him, Mosey learned to sense accurately their position out on the lake when they were miles from shore by a sort of eye-gauging triangulation, using the islands and the mainland as points of reference. She could estimate distances to the islands or various points on the mainland by the height of the landmass on the horizon and its degree of visibility. Eventually, she could sense where the water was no more than three to four feet deep far out in the shallow lake by the color of the light in the water, or the way the waves broke, or how hard the wind stirred the surface, or by some instinct she could not articulate. She distinguished a dozen different kinds of waves where most fishermen saw only swells and whitecaps and holy rollers. "Dragon tails" whipped up from the east and warned of storms; "chicken wings" were the white, frothy-tipped waves that came only from the south wind on a calmish day, and meant good fishing. "Wind from the south, blow the bait in the mouth," Jake would say. She marked in her mind in some uncanny way the position where boulders lurked off the shores of the islands when the wind churned deep troughs between the waves. Every year she made a new mind-map of where the sunken, waterlogged tree trunks lay barely submerged in the mouths of the Portage, the Touissant, the Huron, and the Vermillion Rivers. She could even snake up between deadfalls and mudflats in the lesser creeks of Turtle, Crane, Lacarpe, Cranberry, and Chappel. With any moon at all, she could navigate at night both East and West Harbor next to Catawba Island, and the whole of Sandusky Bay.

Her knack of locating schools of fish became uncanny. By the time she was seventeen she had gotten into the habit of shucking her clothes and diving into the water to check out her hunches about the whereabouts of shoals and rocks and schools of fish. She would surface as much as a hundred yards away after what seemed to Jake like much too long a time to be underwater, and yell at him to bring the boat around to where she bobbed casually on the surface. She had found the fish. It was a rare day that she and Jake did not chug back home in their troller, *Old Hookeye,* with a full load of walleye, bass, and yellow perch. Other fisherman learned to watch where the old man and girl trolled or put down nets, and cluster around them hoping to share their finds. Mosey would snarl openly and curse them under her breath, but Jake only laughed. "There's enough for all," he would remind her, and in those days that was true.

She feared no storm, boasting that she could swim to shore from any point within the Catawba–Kelley's–Bass Islands–Pelee archipelago with no more aid than a short length of two-by-eight pine board for a little extra flotation. The secret, she said, was to ride with the waves, not go against them, even if the waves were carrying you away from the nearest island. To Mosey, Lake Erie was as familiar and reassuring as a pasture field to a farmer.

For more than twenty years, she and Jake worked the waters of Erie. He taught her everything he knew, which was considerable, and as she bloomed into her mid-twenties and Jake's energy began to wane in his sixties, she more and more took charge of the fishing business, her name becoming legendary among the North Coast and Island dwellers. Fishermen who viewed her beauty, unspoiled by the fashions of so-called civilization, or who claimed that they had seen her swimming naked, diving deep to check on the schools of fish, thought of her as a sea nymph, something to dream about at night, not to approach or to touch lest she disappear or lest Jake wrap an oar around their necks. They called her Mosiana of the Islands.

But now, in her late twenties, Mosey was showing signs of a

vague restlessness and irritation, and that was why Jake pondered so worriedly about what to do with her. He noticed how she stared intently at the shirtless young men around the wharves when they weren't looking, and he decided that it must be sex that ailed her, a subject that forever remained a mystery to him. With heavy heart, he knew he should encourage her to get out "into the real world" (no world could have been more real than theirs, and he knew it) and see what she could see, as he put it in a tone that clearly implied that what was out there was not worth seeing. How he might encourage her he did not know, because he was convinced she was better off with him, and felt sure that her loyalty to him would never let her leave him far behind, wherever she went.

Unloading iced fish at Put-in-Bay on South Bass Island one summer evening in 1925—Mosey would never forget the day—a sleek thirty-foot Belle Isle Bearcat slid up to the dock across from where she had moored *Old Hookeye*, and off of it hopped a young man whose swarthy complexion, piercing eyes, and almost furtive agility—like a deer's—caused her, in spite of herself, to pause and stare at him. Their eyes met momentarily as he flashed past her. Then he stopped and turned his head back, as if he did not believe what he had just seen. She was fair-skinned with straw yellow hair, in contrast to his dark visage, but the real reason he stood still, momentarily stunned by her appearance, was that he had mistaken her for a man under the slicker and rubber hat, hoisting the boxes of iced fish onto the pier with effortless strength. He smiled casually, without any of the sexual cunning that Mosey often saw in the wolfish grins of the fishermen she encountered. His glittering eyes almost caused her to drop the box of fish she was holding, but, gaining composure, she went back to work as if she had not noticed him. Out of the corner of her eye she studied the Bearcat. She would have given five years' catch of fish for a boat like that.

Who *is* that?" she asked Jake when the man had gone ashore. "Never seen him before. Nor the boat."

"Canadian. Max Fox. Fisherman and winemaker over on Pelee.

Or used to be," Jake replied. Something in his manner struck Mosey as evasive. "I never seen him before either, but I know that name on his boat. *Midnight Fox*. Fastest boat on the lake, they say. Faster even than the gray ghosts."

"What do you mean, he *used* to be a winemaker?" Mosey asked.

Jake shrugged. "They say he's a bootlegger now. Dangerous way to get rich. The Coasties will catch up with him someday and blast him out of the water."

Mosey's eyes widened. She knew all about the rumrunners. Since Prohibition had gone into effect in 1920, a lively illicit trade in liquor had flourished between Canada and the United States. Hundreds of thousands of cases of beer, wine, and whiskey were being bootlegged across the water, usually between Long Point in Canada and Erie, Pennsylvania, in the low-lying "gray ghosts," boats designed to outrun the Coast Guard and often clad in armor to thwart the Coast Guard's bullets. But increasingly, as the Coasties focused on that more eastern route, or the equally lucrative trade to Detroit in the western part of the lake, the rumrunners had shifted operations to the North Coast. It was a short run from Pelee Island in Canadian waters to the Bass Islands in American waters and then on to Catawba or Port Clinton or Sandusky, where the mainland would swallow up the haul and smuggle it on to Cleveland or Toledo and all points beyond.

As was their habit after selling a good catch at the South Bass tourist market, Jake and Mosey dined royally at the Commodore Hotel, where they planned to stay the night. Mosey had her own room now that she was grown, lolling in luxury in a huge double-mattressed bed instead of the cramped hard cots of the boat, and bathing in a large porcelain tub with gold-plated spigots instead of in the waters of the lake.

Brought up practically outside the bounds of conventional civilization, Mosey had a sense of morality and refinement that was totally honest and unaffected, but that often appeared to the confining and hypocritical conventions of the time neither virtuous nor refined. For proper Victorians, virtue was no more than a synonym for exterior politeness, which Mosey lacked entirely. In her lake-faring dungarees and rubber hat and coat, she had learned little of the artificial culture of wealth that drew people to the lakeshore and islands to "vacation" while never leaving the luxurious quarters of their hotels or yachts. Floating into the hotel dining room for dinner, wearing a dress, Mosey could be a shock to people who had seen her only in fishermen's clothing. As comely and feminine in appearance as any of them, she was nonetheless hard muscled and hard talking like the grizzled fishermen on the lake. Jake did not mind her seeming roughness. In fact he liked her that way. He knew that underneath the crude mannerisms was a gentle soul who would react tenderly to a need for help or reciprocate a kindness with a soft femininity, as she had nursed Suzanna in her dying days. He thought that his training and upbringing had been proper enough. He had never given her any rules to follow except that she dared not swim or fish naked when boats were close enough to observe, a rule that mystified her. On a warm day on the water, clothes were a botheration, she said. In the water, clothes were a positive danger.

So she sat now at the table in the Commodore, in her yellow dress (her only dress), her hair carelessly brushed, the effect somehow only increasing her beauty, and smoked a cigar with Jake. Around the room, the trimmed brows of the rich rose, and long fake eyelashes fluttered till they nearly fell off. This amused Jake greatly.

"I tell you, if you let me go it nekkid, I can swim from Catawba to Pelee without hardly gettin' tired," Mosey was arguing expansively between puffs on her Havana. Jake shook his head but smiled, humoring her. "I'd just paddle over to Mouse Island," she continued, "then backstroke on to Starve, and float on into South Bass. Then I'd swim over to Middle Bass and then from Ballast Island on to Middle Island in Canada and ease on in to Pelee. No big deal. Hell, the longest stretch is hardly six miles."

"Come on, Mosey, it ain't like you'd be ice skatin', you know. If a wind came up, you know how damn rough the waves can get. You might not make any headway atall."

"You have to go with the waves o' course, not fight 'em," she replied. "Easier to go three miles with the waves than a mile fightin' them." She paused, then added with a little grin. "And if I got halfway there and didn't think I could make it, I could always turn around and come the hell back." She laughed loudly at her joke, but suddenly her voice caught, causing her to wheeze on cigar smoke. Across the room stood the stranger with the piercing eyes, Max Fox, the first man who had ever caused her breath to catch, if only for an instant. He was laughing at her joke.

Apparently Fox decided on something he had not even considered a second or two earlier. Across the restaurant he walked, straight up to Mosey, and with a nod toward Jake and still smiling, he said, "I hope you will forgive my curiosity, but it is not often that I see a beautiful young lady smoking a cigar. Down on the docks, I was told you were the famous Mosiana of the Islands, but I must say that the person referred to then, throwing fish off that old troller, did not quite, ah, do you justice."

There was neither ridicule nor slick compliment in his voice. Just a friendly, challenging banter. Mosey thought she might swoon, but steadied herself. "Yep, and I noticed that old troller had a helluva lot more fish on it than your Bearcat did," she snapped back. A smile wreathed Jake's face. There was no one anywhere like his Mosey.

Fox laughed heartily again and sat down between Jake and Mosey, although neither had invited him. Neither protested either. It was evident that no one told Max Fox what to do or not do. An aura of suspense, maybe even danger, seemed to linger around him that drew wildlings like Jake and Mosey as a magnet draws steel filings. Jake offered him a cigar, which he took and lit while he studied Mosey.

"And might I offer you a glass of Lonz's best grape juice," he proffered, pulling a flask from his inside coat pocket. Jake and Mosey both smiled. George Lonz was the only winemaker on the Islands who had not gone broke because of Prohibition. He had switched to marketing his grapes as juice instead of wine with instructions on how to handle the stuff if, heaven forbid, it began to ferment. It was not against the Volstead Act to sell grape juice nor to pass out instructions on how to make wine or at least vinegar. The fact that on its way to vinegar the juice first became wine did not escape the notice of the law, but what could the alcohol police do? Vinegar, like juice, was perfectly legal. But when people referred to "Lonz's best grape juice," what they really meant was grape juice on its way to vinegar but not nearly there yet.

Mosey sipped the amber liquid. "Delaware," she said. "The best." Fox nodded. Like all Erie shore people, she knew her grapes. "Too bad you had to ruin it by letting it ferment," she added wickedly. Fox laughed again. What had he found here so different from any woman he knew? Before long, they were deep in conversation about fish and grapes, a conversation that Jake found himself more an observer to, rather than involved in. But that was all right with him. The light in Mosey's eyes was livelier than he had seen it for a year, and that was good.

As it turned out, Fox was a great admirer of Lonz, being himself a grape grower and winemaker on Pelee Island when he was not fishing, he informed them. Fox liked the way Lonz had found a way to beat Prohibition. By the time the flask was empty, the wine had worked its charm: the three spoke to each other as if they were longtime friends. Fox made another of his lightning decisions and abruptly excused himself but was soon back. This time what issued from his flask was a clearer and more potent liquid.

"Ugh," said Mosey, wrinkling her nose. "Tastes like boat varnish." Again Fox laughed with delight. Leaning over the table, he whispered, "This is some of the finest scotch in the world, I'll have you know, and I have literally risked my life in bringing you a taste of it."

Mosey and Jake, already knowing of course, asked questions in a way that pulled his dark "secret" from him. He had indeed thought of starting a brisk grape juice trade as Lonz had done, but then a much more compelling temptation had overwhelmed him. When he learned that 900,000 cases of liquor had been bootlegged into the States just during the first year of Prohibition, he did a little calculating. He could make a profit of about fifty dollars for a case of scotch this way, could carry maybe twenty cases in his Bearcat at a time without slowing the boat down much. Better income than fishing by far. With a souped-up airplane motor for power, he could make several trips a day, no sweat, if the Coasties did not interfere. What's more, the *Midnight Fox* could go fifty-five miles per hour with an airplane motor for power, he said, faster than any Coast Guard cutter even equipped with the new Liberty engines, faster even than the gray ghosts that the Coast Guard had captured from rumrunners and were now using against them. When Jake asked him why his Bearcat could outrun everything, Max only smiled mysteriously. "Someday I will tell you. Someday the whole world will know."

"Well, they're buildin' new boats that will give you some competition," Jake said.

Fox was immediately attentive. Where had Jake heard this?

"At the Mathews Boat Works over in Port Clinton," said Jake.

"Hmmm. I will have to see them," Fox said. Then again, that quick decision. "Tomorrow is a good day. Would you like to come along?" He directed the question at Jake, but almost instantly turned his eyes to Mosey so that she'd know she was also being invited.

Jake started to decline, but Mosey cut in with a firmness of voice that surprised even her. "I'd like that very much," she said.

The same natural instincts that had served Mosey well in remaining aloof and distant from the sexual advances of men she did not like or was suspicious of, now worked in the opposite way. Sensing in Max Fox a similar spirit, she fell immediately and unreservedly in love with him. As they sped in the Bearcat toward Port Clinton, she stared at him like a rapt teenager. Jake had stayed behind, to do a little walleye fishing east of the Islands, he said. Alone with Max, Mosey waited only for the least hint of invitation to embrace him. But Max seemed preoccupied with the future. Prohibition would not last forever, he said, just hopefully long enough for him to save the money he needed to expand his farming and fishing. She did not even pay much attention to the watercraft at the Mathews Boat Works, although she was surprised how keenly her idol inspected the carburetors of the new motors and asked seemingly stupid questions about fuel. Boat gas was boat gas, wasn't it?

Headed back to the Islands, Max seemed in an unusually jolly mood, which he should not have felt, Mosey thought, having just viewed the technology that could bring his bootlegging to an abrupt halt. When she said as much, he laughed. "Oh, they aren't quite as technologically advanced as they think."

"Why were you interested so much in boat gas?" she asked him as he allowed her to take over the Bearcat, a move that they both knew would bring their hands together on the controls.

"You seem to have a knack of asking the right questions," he answered, pressing against her.

She wrinkled her nose, not understanding, not caring about anything but feeling their bodies melting into one.

"You must not repeat what I'm about to tell you, at least not until the insanity of Prohibition has passed," he said, somehow knowing that she would not if he so desired. "Whiskey is a great motor fuel, better than gasoline. Burns hotter and cleaner." He watched her disbelief with amusement. "Really. Whiskey is alcohol. Distill it to 140 proof, and it makes mighty fine drinking. Distill it to 190 proof and you've got race car fuel. Whiskey is nothing more than expensive ethanol. Henry Ford is talking about ethanol as the fuel of the future. I listen to Henry Ford. I persuaded a guy on Pelee who is a mechanical genius to tinker with carburetors until we got one that could handle nearly pure ethanol—I run some of that whiskey I'm hauling through a still we made to beef up the proof. Too expensive a fuel to use all the time, but when the Coasties are after me, I switch tanks and carburetor and zoom right away from 'em." He laughed. "Kind of poetic, don't you think? The very stuff they are trying to stop me from selling is what I use to outrun 'em. I've got the still set up in one of my wine cellars. Could make fuel out of wine too, you know."

Mosey hardly knew what he was talking about and did not care. His voice and his resoluteness hypnotized her. She understood that she not only loved him, but loved the thrill of being part of his activities. Soon she was leading two lives. Publicly she was still Jake's partner. Privately she became the official navigator for the *Midnight Fox*. Within a year she was bringing home enough money so that Jake could retire, except for an occasional fishing run with Mosey to "keep up appearances," as she said.

Local officials usually looked the other way or even helped the bootleggers, but the federal government had decided to stop the illegal trade in liquor no matter how much money and lives were lost, no matter how obvious was the fact that they could not stop even half of the bootlegging. It became a matter of pride. The most powerful country in the world would not be confounded and ridiculed over a bottle of good scotch. Open warfare prevailed. Machine gun sputters filled the air occasionally; men died, boats sank. Even then there was a certain "understanding" between the Coast Guard and rumrunners because of heavy bribery in place. The Coast Guard would attack, kill, capture any bootlegger caught on the water, but if the outlaws evaded them and made it to port, the Coast Guard would leave them alone. As the patrols increased, some bootleggers started flying liquor across the lake. A favorite trick was to set up a temporary airstrip in a farm field, lighted by flashlights pointing straight up. From the roads, revenue agents could not see the flashlights, but from the air they were easy enough to spot.

Another ruse, which involved the complicity of Canadian officials, was to load ocean-going vessels with liquor bound for some port in Europe or South America, according to the ship's log. The boat would be back in a few hours for another load.

But with Mosey on board and his ethanol fuel system in place, Max Fox learned he could bootleg over the water with impunity. On the open lake, he could always beat the Coast Guard cutters back into safe Canadian waters if other alternatives failed. He often ran at night when few other sailors would have dared, because

Mosey needed only a touch of moonlight to find her way. Daytime hauls were more dangerous. Once two Coast Guard cutters seemingly had the *Midnight Fox* bottled up off Ballast Island. Max raced the Bearcat through a stretch of shallow offshore water studded with boulders, with Mosey in the prow of the boat pointing the way. As she directed Max through them, Mosey turned and watched with a smirk as the closest Coast Guard cutter bearing down on them scraped one of the rocks, gouging the hull and panicking Captain Lokker, in command of the cutter, nearly out of his wits. Before the cutters could rally to the chase again, the *Midnight Fox* was in Canadian waters, only a few miles away.

Jake loved to tell stories of Max and Mosey's daring escapades, even as he worried that sooner or later they would be captured or killed. No doubt he even enlarged a bit on the narrow escapes. "Mosey can make a pretty good-size boat disappear," he liked to tell anyone who would listen. "She knows of nooks between rocks around the Island shores just big enough to hide a Bearcat in, and swampy inlets and creek mouths on the mainland shore where she can vanish as if by magic." Then he'd draw himself up grandly and add, "I taught her most of those hideouts.

"The best hiding, howsomever," he would go on, "was what they did in the mouths of some little cricks flowing into the Portage and the Touissant. They had whiskey dropoffs up both rivers. She and Max would rig a dead tree with a block and tackle so it could be swung out across the mouth of the creek. Sort of was my idea. Caught in the river by the Coasties, Mosey could ease the *Midnight Fox* into one of these creek mouths, swing the old tree trunk across the creek hiding them from view, and wait. The Coasties, believing that they had the *Fox* trapped ahead of them up the river, would roar past, their hands on their machine guns sweaty with eagerness. Hee hee. After they went past, headed upstream, the *Fox* and Mosey would swing the tree trunk out of the way, back into the river, and tear off out into the open lake again.

"They got other tricks. They know where the submerged logs lay in the channel of the Portage. We *own* the Portage, you see. Our landing is on the Portage not so far from where Mosey showed up in that washtub, and we know every eddy in that channel. Once when Max and Mosey was comin' in with a load of bootleg, suddenly there's old Uncle Sam behind them. He's been hiding till they got into the river and now he thinks he has 'em trapped finally. Max hits the throttle and roars straight up the river, Mosey again in the prow, her eyes sparkling like fireflies, watchin' the water like a hawk watchin' for mice, motioning Max so close to a big ole sunken log she coulda kissed it. Uncle is right behind, limbering up his guns when he hits that log. You could hear the bottom of that boat shredding into toothpicks half a mile away. Whewwweeee, it was somethin' else.

"They never brought contraband to our landing again, however. That was close enough. Max got to thinking where would be the safest place to unload on the mainland." And now Jake would pause and smile to let listeners know he was about to tell his favorite story. "It hit him one day that Lakeside was the place. Lakeside is a Methodist encampment, you see, and as dry as a desert breeze. So he finds a resident who likes a little nip now and then and likes a little extra money even more, and pretty soon the *Midnight Fox* is making midnight stops at the Lakeside dock when all good Methodists are asleep, and no one else the wiser. Neither the Methodists nor the Coast Guard ever dreamed what was goin' on. Oh my, ain't it great.

"But there were other close calls. Once two cutters were closing in on the *Midnight Fox* from two directions and it looked like the end for sure. So Max dumped the liquor stealthily off the side of the boat and then gave the appearance of trying to outrun Uncle but not so fast that the Coasties were not soon on top of him, bristling with machine guns. Max hove to and pretended great astonishment that the law thought he was runnin' whiskey. Nothing was found, o' course, and the law says you can't arrest a guy if there's no liquor aboard. That son of a bitch Captain Lokker, who had sworn he would kill or jail Max if it was the last official act of his career, acted like he'd swallowed a handful of marbles. After the Coast Guard had gone on its way, Mosey took charge, swung the boat around, and knowin' her way around like the lake was her kitchen, brought it back to where they had dumped the liquor. The water warn't but ten feet deep there, and she just dove in and swam around like she always did to locate a school of fish, and soon found the cache. She and Max got all the cases back on board, and a couple of hours later they cruised right past the Coast Guard cutters standing off Port Clinton. They waved at Lokker as they went by. Whewwweeee."

But Max knew it was only a matter of time before he would be caught if he persisted. He had just about met his goal: enough money laid by to build a nice house for Mosey somewhere in Canada and then work easy-like at farming and fishing until the rest of it was all gone. "One more big run to do before the July fourth holiday," he told Mosey, "and then we're outta here."

"You've said that before," she replied.

"This time I mean it. And remember, if something goes wrong, we'll put our emergency plan into action. If you can swim to Pelee, by God I can too." She smiled and nodded.

Captain Lokker sat back in his office chair, looking as if someone had just given him a sack of gold. He had received a tip of a big movement of liquor before the Fourth, and the principal man involved was none other than Max Fox, so the informer hinted. After dark, the *Midnight Fox* would be delivering a shipment at Oak Point, on Middle Bass Island in the vicinity of Ballast Island. By God, Lokker would be ready and waiting this time.

There was a low waning moon the night of July 2, just enough light for Mosey to guide the *Midnight Fox* through the shoals off Ballast to the dropoff dock. Max and Mosey worked with feverish intensity unloading the cases of whiskey. In a few minutes all this danger would be behind them forever and they could go on to the happy, peaceful life they had planned. The transaction had barely been completed and the cash had barely found its way to Max's pocket when suddenly spotlights pierced the night from two cutters lying in ambush. The voice of Captain Lokker boomed over a bullhorn, "Max Fox, you goddamn sneaking rumrunner, hove to or suffer the consequences."

Max and Mosey dove onto the *Midnight Fox* and Max hit the throttle. The boat, now running on pure ethanol, leaped forward with such a surge of power that it came partway out of the water. Machine gun bullets screamed through the dark and their staccato thuddings could clearly be heard, ripping holes into the hull of the *Midnight Fox*. For a few seconds it seemed as if the *Fox* would even then make its escape, as it surged beyond the fingers of light and disappeared into darkness before the cutters could get up speed. But then, far out in the darkling water, *Midnight Fox*'s motor began to sputter, roar, and sputter again. Suddenly, an eye-blinding explosion, then, in the silence, only Lokker's chuckle.

The searchlights picked out numerous bits of flotsam. In the morning, more wreckage that could have been pieces of the *Midnight Fox* floated in the vicinity. "Whole damn thing musta gone down," Lokker said, as if God had been avenged.

No bodies were ever discovered. Max, Mosiana, and the *Midnight Fox* were never heard of again, and the Coast Guard, without much other evidence, marked their mission successful. Soon thereafter Jake disappeared from his usual haunts.

That might be the end of the story except for a mostly unnoticed little news item that appeared in a back-country Ontario newspaper in 1974, forty-six years later.

"Mr. and Mrs. Maxwell Fox are retiring, their sons and daughters taking over the successful dairy and vineyard operation, which Mr. Fox is fond of describing as 'milk for the body, wine for the soul.' Mr. Fox is well known locally for demonstrating that he can run his tractor on brandy, a project he plans to pursue more seriously in his retirement."

CHAPTER 9

Wandering Wide-Eyed
through the World of Whiskey

HISKEY is ethyl alcohol from the distillation of fermented grains, almost always a combination of malted barley and unmalted corn, wheat, or rye. Other grains could be used for malt but rarely are. In commercial production, whiskey is distilled at least twice, first into so-called low wines at about 20 percent (or 40 proof) alcohol, and then again into finished raw whiskey at around 100 to 140 proof, more or less, which is then cut with water to reduce the final strength to between 80 and 120 proof. Care is taken in malted whiskeys not to distill the finished product into too much of a "neutral" or flavorless spirit. Single-malt Scotch whiskies may be distilled three times. Bourbon whiskey by law can't be distilled beyond 160 proof. This limitation ensures a proper content of congeners, or flavor agents, for the taste that whiskey lovers love.

Blended whiskeys, as opposed to straight whiskeys described above, are mixtures of straight whiskeys or a mixture of straights with grain alcohol distilled to a near neutral spirit. In addition to their own straight whiskeys, most distilleries sell liquor in bulk to "rectifiers," or blenders, who mix them with or without neutral spirits from grain alcohol to achieve myriad blends that have a sort of overall milder uniformity than straight whiskeys. Because there is usually less aging involved, and because a near neutral grain alcohol is cheaper to make since the advent of continuous column stills, blends are generally cheaper than straight whiskeys, though not always. The higher the proportion of straight whiskey in the mix, the higher the price.

Comparing blended whiskeys to straight whiskeys is like the old apples/oranges cliché. More expensive blends always surprise me with their smooth, if somewhat characterless taste, since I prefer straight whiskey. Cheaper blends I am suspicious of. In itself, adding neutral spirit is not bad—some of the most expensive liqueurs in the world use neutral spirits to raise their alcohol content, as we have seen. Champions of blended whiskeys argue that the blends in fact are more healthful, because a more neutral spirit, that is, an alcohol distilled to a purer state, contains less of the impurities or congeners found in straight whiskey, some of which, in anything but very minute amounts, might be unhealthful. But my personal thinking is that if neutral spirit is added to whiskey to bring up the proof in the blend, it could mean that a rather cheap, lower-grade whiskey is involved that has *more* congeners in it than would be desirable from a health point of view. Drinking the cheapest blends simply because they are cheap does not make sense to me, unless the aim is just to get drunk cheaply, which is a shame, not only for the sake of one's dignity, but for enjoyment and health reasons as well. As for cost, I would argue that drinking an expensive whiskey is more economical because you know for sure that a higher-grade whiskey is involved. Also, because of the higher proof, you can add a wee bit of water or ice to suit your taste and make your sipping time or your bottle last longer. With cars, most of us can't afford the higher-priced models, but drinking higher-priced spirits doesn't cost that much more than drinking rotgut if you are drinking moderately, as you should be.

Canadian whiskeys are blends in which rye usually plays an important role in the mix of nearly neutral grain alcohol and straight whiskeys. Seagram's is the brand name that most often comes to mind when the term "Canadian whiskey" is mentioned.

I will limit my discussion to straight whiskeys because there are so many blends that I must draw the line somewhere or this chapter would never end. Kentucky bourbon and Tennessee whiskey are the principal straight whiskeys in the United States. They both are American originals and are so similar that, for all practical purposes, they are both considered bourbon. The difference is that Tennessee "bourbon" is filtered through charcoal before aging. Twelve legal distilleries in Kentucky and Tennessee make almost all the bourbon in the world. (There's also one in Virginia known for its Virginia Gentleman brand.) Most bourbon distillers make straight rye whiskey too, which is similar to bourbon, but of course contains more rye and less corn than bourbon does.

In the 1960s, humans, being rule-making animals as well as alcohol-loving animals *(Homo bossiens* as well as *Homo sippiens)* gave bourbon its official, legal definition, believing it was not safe to allow us to rely on our individual taste and intelligence to buy what we like and not buy what we don't. To be called bourbon, the whiskey must be at least 51 percent corn and must be aged at least two years. Many bourbons are aged longer, up to twenty years, and all of them I know about contain more than 51 percent corn. Bonded bourbons must be aged four years by law. Bourbons must be at least 80 proof in the bottle and must be aged in new oak barrels that have been charred on the inside. No artificial coloring or flavor other than what the barrel imparts may be added. The whiskey must finish its second distillation at no more than 160 proof. Tennessee whiskeys like Jack Daniel's must conform to these regulations, too, but in addition they must be filtered through sugar maple charcoal before they are barreled. The charcoal filtering is done in big vats where the charcoal must measure 10 feet deep. It takes a week to ten days for the whiskey to filter through. That filtering gives Tennessee whiskeys their slightly sooty sweet taste that many people love and some do not.

The term "bonding" has a long and curious history, originating with the government's inane taxing practices, but ending up being something good for sippers of good straight whiskey. When taxes were again imposed on drinking alcohol in the 1860s after a long hiatus from the time of Jefferson's presidency—"to pay for the Civil War," as the excuse went—distillers had to ante up taxes as soon as their whiskey came from the still. But they were not allowed to sell it until it was two years old. By 1865 the tax had risen to a ridiculous two dollars per gallon, pushing the cost of whiskey out of reach of the typical pocketbook. Moonshining exploded on the scene. The ponderous bureaucratic mind finally realized that, if legal distillers were being forced out of business by moonshining and heavy taxes that had to be paid before the whiskey was sold, government was getting less in taxes, not more. So to protect the whiskey industry (actually to protect its cash flow), the government allowed distillers a grace period, or, as it was called, a "bonding period," of one year, before they had to pay taxes on whiskey in storage. That bonding period was soon increased to four years, and eventually to twenty years. The whiskey had to placed in "bonded" warehouses, so the government could keep an eye on it. Eventually bonded whiskey had to be aged at least four years under supervision by the government. It had to be bottled at 100 proof, and only straight whiskey could be bonded, not blends. This led to more battles because the blend industry claimed the law was unfair to them, and that their whiskey, blended with near neutral spirits, was actually "purer" than straight whiskey because it had less of the taste-defining congeners that make straight whiskey what it is, as mentioned above. The upshot of these battles was that a whiskey bottle today must say if it contains "straight" or "blended" liquor and let the buyers make their own decision—as good a solution as one could wish. But, if the whiskey is bonded, you know for sure (as long as Uncle Sam can be trusted) that it is at least four years old and is a straight whiskey.

Fortunately, the laying down of minimum standards for bourbon has not resulted in a bourbon world where the minimum became the rule, as so often happens in the wacky world of regulation. Bourbon distillers, in spite of being bought up by large corporations today, continue a tradition of making bourbon as they always have, each distillery with its slightly different methods, mashbills, and yeasts. (A "mashbill" is simply the grain recipe for a particular whiskey.) As a result, within the bounds of true bourbon, there is a wide selection of whiskeys. Once, in a liquor store in Kentucky, I started writing down the names of all the straight bourbons on the shelves (not counting all the blends and other kinds of straight whiskey) and got to number sixty before my fingers grew numb.

Because of all this wonderful variety (yes, it is possible that two bourbons under different brand names could be nearly identical), you must read the labels carefully when shopping. Even within a single brand there may be several offerings, differing in proof, in age, and as to whether the whiskey came from mixing liquor from many barrels together, from a few select barrels mixed together, or from a single barrel. The exact location of the barrel in the warehouse also may influence price. That's why you get so much confusing argument among neophyte sippers.

"I paid twenty-six fugging bucks for this Rip Van Winkle, watcha think a that?"

"They musta seen you comin'. Old Rip is only fifteen ninety-nine in my liquor store."

"You both better quit drinkin'. Rip Van Winkle costs twenty-four dollars, and my old lady chews me out good for spending money like that."

"You were lyin' to her even then. That stuff costs thirty-nine ninety-five."

All four observations are correct, in a way. A fifth of Rip Van Winkle Special Reserve, twelve years old and 90.4 proof, was selling for $24.95 at the store where my fingers cramped up from writing down brands and prices. (And you thought I was making that name up.) There was also Old Rip Van Winkle at twenty years of age, a real rarity, for $39.95. Regular Old Rip Van Winkle, at 90 proof and four years' aging, was $15.99; Old Rip Van Winkle at 107 proof and ten years old was $16.79 (a good buy); and Old Rip Van Winkle at 107 proof and fifteen years old was $26.79. To confuse matters even more, these Kentucky prices were considerably less than the same bottles cost in Ohio because of a bigger tax ripoff in the latter state. (You can't even get Old Rip in our Ohio village liquor store.) Also, when you start arguing brand prices, make sure everyone is talking about the same size bottle. Most whiskies are sold by the pint and by the fifth, with "fifth" standing for a fifth of a gallon, or not quite a quart.

The least expensive bourbon I could find on the shelves in Kentucky was Old Crow at $5.99 a fifth. The most expensive was Henry Clay Rare Bourbon at $82.50 a fifth. Needless to say, I've never tasted the latter. Wild Turkey, a brand we often buy, was priced at $11.99, but Wild Turkey Kentucky Spirit Single Barrel, twelve years old, 101 proof, limited edition, was $47.99, and Wild Turkey Rare Breed was $25.95.

The appellation "single barrel" means the whiskey in the bottle comes from a particular barrel, not from many barrels mixed together, as is usually the case. A master brewer or taster samples all the barrels in the warehouse and, encountering a really great taste in a particular barrel, reserves that whiskey for single-barrel status. A single-barrel label will carry the number of the barrel it came from and the position where the barrel stood in the warehouse, which, as I will explain, is important to a bourbon gourmet. The bottle will be a fancy one, a collector's item. We bought a pint of Blanton's Single Barrel at some outrageous price (I didn't write it down because I didn't want to remember) and found it very good, but, quite frankly, not appreciably better to our palates than seven-year-old Jim Beam 80 proof or seven-year-old Jim Beam 90 proof, at half the price. This is the lesson we have learned: the higher the price, the more interesting and unique is the taste, but some medium-priced bourbons taste just as good as the high-priced ones or have their own unique flavor that we actually prefer.

We now have an organic vodka (from Kentucky! See Chapter 10), so organic bourbon is surely in the offing. All that is necessary is a dependable supply of organic grain, which the organic beer industry is pioneering. (As I write, Brown-Forman Corporation has organic whiskey in the barrel, not yet ready for bottling.)

*   *   *

Whiskey comes out of the barrel at around 120 to 140 proof, a little higher proof than when it went in because of a slight loss of water through evaporation during storage. Most palates consider this alcohol content too strong, and prefer a lower proof than that, from 80 to 100 proof, or a little less than half alcohol. That's fine with distilleries, which cut the whiskey, often with pure limestone spring water that is believed to enhance the flavor, but in some cases with ordinary tap water that has been thoroughly filtered and purified. (Says something about drinking water when it is unfit for whiskey until filtered.) Adding spring water to bring proof down from 130 to 80 or 90 proof makes a barrel go further. Since most people make mixed drinks from whiskey, or add water, or at least pour their whiskey over ice, I have often wondered why anyone would want to pay for 110 to 130 proof liquor and then water it down to 80 proof. Why not just buy 80 proof in the first place, add no water to it, and save money? The answer to that question came when Booker Noe, grandson of Jim Beam and a master distiller before he retired (see Chapter 2) treated a group of us to a whiskey tasting at his home.

Booker (I will presume on his good graces to use his first name, as most everyone does, because he is a delightfully informal person), whose likeness appears on all Jim Beam bottles along with the five previous patriarchs of the Beam family whiskey business, poured us tastings of four special Jim Beam brands into little sherry glasses: Booker's, Basil Hayden's, Knob Creek, and Baker's. We were first instructed to smell only. "Good bourbon, properly aged, should suggest the aroma of vanilla at least," Booker explained. "A strong woody smell indicates a longer time in the barrel, maybe too long for some tastes."

While we sniffed the whiskies, he directed us to study the liquid. "If the glass is clean and the whiskey seems to hang on the side surface, or even 'climbs the glass,' as we say, that's indicative of a high-proof, quality whiskey," he pointed out. Sure enough.

Then we were supposed to wet our lips and tongue with the whiskeys, each in turn, while munching crackers in between, then swirl a small sip in our mouths. Actually drinking the whiskey was against the rules of the first part of the tasting. It did not take Booker long to realize he was dealing with amateurs. We swallowed too soon, for one thing. And none of us could articulate the characteristics of the tastes that slid across our tongues—at least not the way he could. Once past "hint of vanilla and just a touch of oak," I was lost. In fact, in other circumstances I would have suspected I was being scammed.

Booker mercifully did not press the taster's vocabulary on us. But here are some examples of how professional tasters describe the varying tastes of whiskey, taken from the very informative *Book of Bourbon* by Gary Regan and Mardee Haidin Regan (Chapters Publishing, 1995). And I'm not making any of this up.

"The palate is wonderfully old-fashioned, bearing tobacco, leather, wildflowers, oak, and the 'feel' of an old bar steeped in tradition." (Maybe switching to vodka is not a bad idea after all.)

"A big, soft, thick, round body—honey, vanilla, cigars, caramel, overripe oranges. The finish is very long." (I dare not write what these words conjure up in my mind.)

"Sweet sandalwood, leather, pine, mint, eucalyptus." (And maybe a hint of composting sawdust?)

One thing's for sure. The bourbon crowd has learned how to one-up the wine crowd.

What I *could* taste was excellent smoothness in all the whiskeys and a difference among them that I learned derived from their different mashbills. I've always appreciated the husky lingering taste of grain in whiskey (and beer) because I like the taste of cereal grains. I like good breads and good pasta, and I'm sure I eat more corn on the cob than anyone in the world. Basil Hayden's had a higher rye content than the others. I could not tell the difference was rye, but I could taste a distinct difference. Knob Creek had a higher barley content than the others, and again I could taste something different without knowing what it was. Baker's and Booker's were higher in corn compared to the other two, and, true to form, I liked them the best of the four. Lighter and more corny.

Booker Noe is known particularly for introducing these four "small-batch" whiskeys to the world. "Small batch" means something different than "single barrel" or scotch's "single-malt" appellations. It does not mean distilling whiskey in small batches, as so many people think. "'Small batch' is a selection of the best barrels of whiskey in a warehouse, based on taste. They come from the middle racks of the warehouse, not the top barrels close to the ceiling nor the bottom ones close to the floor," Booker explained. "Proof can vary from 140 on the top rack to 110 on the bottom." He uses the term "center cut" to refer to the barrels he selects for his small-batch brands.

The whiskey from the center-cut barrels is mixed and bottled. Booker's, unlike the other small-batch bourbons, and unlike whiskey generally, is not cut with water, but is bottled at the alcohol content at which it comes out of the barrels, around 126 proof—"the way whiskey is meant to be," said Booker. Also unlike the others, Booker's is not filtered before bottling. The main reason for filtering is to remove possible lingering specks of charcoal, but unfiltered whiskey has a good chance of being better flavored.

All four brands are high-proof and rather expensive, with Booker's the priciest, at about forty-four dollars a fifth. "Real bourbon lovers buy a high-proof whiskey because then they can mix it with water to *exactly* the strength they like," Booker explained. "Or drink it just as it is." He himself, much to our surprise, added room-temperature water to his glass of Booker's. He called his mix "Kentucky tea." Why not ice? "You can't really taste the quality of a good whiskey if it's cold," he said. "And of course, if you're sipping slowly, the ice begins to melt, and that changes the content of alcohol in your glass. With ice in the glass, what you start out sipping is not what you end up sipping." This is the same reason Booker uses sherry glasses at a bourbon tasting session: they are small and rounded and fit nicely into the cup of a hand, to warm the whiskey to body temperature, more or less.

"What about using small-batch or other expensive liquors in a mixed drink?" I asked. Booker fixed me with a withering stare, as if I had asked for ketchup on my steak at a high-priced French restaurant, as a friend of mine once did.

Most distilleries have developed their own "jug" yeasts, and make a great show of guarding their particular strain carefully. But yeasts are also available from commercial laboratories. Since whiskey yeasts all seem to be strains of *Saccharomyces cerevisiae* yeast, I've always wondered whether the secrecy was a sales gimmick. Booker shook his head. "There really are different strains of this yeast. What you look for under the microscope is a nice plump individual to propagate. The cigar-shaped ones are weak, won't work as hard. When you find the best one you can, you culture it. A vigorous strain will have its own particular properties slightly different from others. Once a distillery gets what it believes is the almost perfect strain, it cultures that strain forever. If you lose your yeast, you could lose the distinctive taste of your whiskey."

It is important in this regard to remember that it is not the yeast itself that turns grain starch into sugar, but the enzymes that the yeast excretes as it "eats" the starch. The same yeast strain may act or react differently in different mashbills, depending on enzyme behavior. The process is first biological—agricultural to my way of thinking, like feeding a cow to get milk—and chemical only second. The addition of hops, which some distillers use in the mashes, as do all beer brewers, affects the yeast activity. Lactic bacteria added to mashes, another frequent practice, also affects enzymatic action and therefore taste in the finished product.

"The worst thing you can do to good whiskey," Booker said, "is to mix it with chlorinated water or ice from chlorinated water." Soft water, well filtered, is good for mixing, or clean limestone spring water. Distilled water is okay, too. "The perfect pH for spring water to mix with whiskey is 7.2," he said. Most well waters used in mixed drinks will darken the whiskey, as country people know, because of the sulfur or iron in them. Sulfur and iron both affect spirits taste negatively. Waters noticeably high in either mineral should not be used when distilling or drinking whiskey.

The biggest surprise for me was the freshly distilled whiskey that Booker offered me: raw whiskey, clear as water—moonshine by any other name. It was unaged Jim Beam whiskey destined for his center-cut barrels, hopefully to come out as Booker's. I sipped cautiously. I had long ago tasted some excellent moonshine given to me by workers who were laying drainage tile behind the ditcher I was operating, but I had tasted other offerings that could peel paint off a barn door.

Booker's unaged whiskey was too strong to be called smooth, but it had a very discernible, fresh grain taste. For a fleeting second it made me think of chewing cornmeal. I looked at Booker in surprise. "I think this is pretty good," I exclaimed.

He smiled, pleased. "Me too."

Asked what less expensive whiskey he would prefer if he couldn't get his small-batch brands, he answered without hesitation: "Seven-year-old Jim Beam at 90 proof."

*   *   *

I can't resist the story of the smooth white lightning referred to above, that my hillbilly friends (don't accuse me of political incorrectness—"hillbilly" is what they called themselves, adding "and damn proud of it") on the ditching crew gave me on that winter day long ago. It was a brutal cold Monday, the kind of day when ditching in an open field in half-frozen ground makes hell seem almost inviting. My workers were fresh back from a weekend at their ancestral home in the Kentucky mountains, which is why they could offer me the moonshine. Up to that time, I had rarely tasted any whiskey at all, and then only in mixed drinks. I had only the vaguest notion of what moonshine was or how it was made. The liquid they offered me was crystal clear, of course, which further assured me, falsely, that it must be mild and harmless. I drank a half glassful down as if it were water. It reminded me of plum juice for some reason. I climbed back on the ditcher and throttled back into action. As we chugged along across the field, I fastened my gaze as usual over the sighting bar on the ditcher and lined it up with the parallel bars on the grade stakes across the field ahead of me. Suddenly the stakes began to dance around like crazed rock stars in concert. I stopped the ditcher and walked out from behind it to get a better look. Grade stakes don't ordinarily move around like that. A warm fuzzy fogginess overwhelmed me, and I knew I had to sit down before I fell down. The crew howled in laughter. Somehow the awful day suddenly became a little easier to endure, and we all sat in the half-frozen mud and giggled awhile. My workers told me I had just tasted some of the best whiskey made in the hills.

*   *   *

The most effective way to gain an understanding of the whiskey-making process is to take tours of distilleries "in the hills," that is, in Kentucky or Tennessee. Maker's Mark in Loretto, Kentucky, goes out of its way to welcome visitors. You should by all means also take in, not far away, the newly restored Labrot & Graham Distillery (owned by Brown-Forman Corporation, which also owns Early Times distillery). Labrot & Graham's distillery stood empty and in decay for many years. Recently restored, it has begun the distillation of a new whiskey, Woodford Reserve, by the old pot-still method originally used at the distillery.

Other distilleries that give public tours at this time are Ancient Age, at Frankfort, Kentucky; Heaven Hill, Bardstown, Kentucky; Wild Turkey, Lawrenceburg, Kentucky; Jack Daniels, Lynchburg, Tennessee; and George A. Dickel's Cascade, Tullahoma, Tennessee. Call for details. Or contact the Chambers of Commerce in Louisville, Bardstown, or Lexington for the latest updates.

The first reason for visiting these distilleries is because they are located in a rural paradise of bluegrass horse and cattle farms: acres and acres and *acres* of manicured and fenced meadows, great comely barns, sedate old houses, and quiet countryside. On the final lap of our journey to Labrot & Graham, I thought I'd died and gone to heaven. I have an unshakable conviction that the whole world could look like Woodford County, Kentucky, if humans ever evolved into truly rational beings. It wouldn't really take a lot of money, just intelligence.

Maker's Mark and Labrot & Graham are a contrasting study in

whiskey making. Maker's uses what has become the conventional column-still method, but in a comparatively small-scale operation. It produces less than 50 barrels a day. By contrast, Jim Beam Distilleries can produce 600 barrels a day. The Samuels family has operated Maker's Mark from its beginnings, and though it is now owned by Hiram Walker & Sons, the Samuels family still runs it.

The Brown-Forman people behind the reincarnation of Labrot & Graham dream the almost impossible: a quality bourbon from the old pot-still method, which means, by necessity, a small-scale operation—an enterprise that in today's economy would be difficult to make profitable. Distillation in a pot still is more or less by batch, not continuous as in a column still. You can study the big copper pot stills and get a good grasp of what Granddaddy did on a much smaller, moonshine level, or what the single-malt scotch distilleries do in Scotland, and generally the way most of the cognacs and Armagnacs are distilled in France. Although I can get no one in the whiskey business to agree, at least not publicly, when I look at Maker's Mark and at Labrot & Graham, I see the possibility of independent microdistilleries becoming economically viable under more enlightened taxation and regulation.

The difference between column-still distillation and pot-still distillation in whiskey distilleries is the same as in brandy distilleries, already discussed in Chapter 7. (And I'll have more to say on column stills in Chapter 11, on ethanol.) But words, even in the most astute books on alcohol, can't substitute for touring a distillery.

Many whiskey lovers (as with brandy lovers) maintain that pot stills like the ones at Labrot & Graham make a better spirit than what can be obtained from a continuous column still. Such a claim won't go without challenge from the continuous column sect, of course, but one argument in favor of pot stills seems to make sense to me. Copper has a beneficial effect on the taste of whiskey: I think everybody more or less agrees with that statement. In a pot still, making relatively small batches of whiskey, the relatively small amount of vapor at any given moment moving relatively slowly through the distillation process has more of a chance to come into contact with the copper and more time to be affected by that contact than vapors in a column still.

The vapors leave the "wash" still, the first "pot" of the pot-still method, and then are condensed and re-evaporated in the second "pot," called the spirits still or doubler, and then pass on to the final condenser. Dials record every minute change in the alcohol, leaving very little to guesswork and chance. The first genuine Woodford Reserve out of its pot stills won't be available for drinking until the year 2002 or thereabouts, since it must age properly first. In the meantime, the distillery sells a Woodford Reserve that comes from the choicest barrels of Brown-Forman whiskey in its other warehouses. This whiskey is first-rate, but it is not yet real pot-still whiskey. The company has been criticized for this bit of duplicity, but our tour guide made that point clear.

The fermentation process that precedes distillation in modern distilleries is about the same in both column-still and pot-still distillation. First, the smaller quantity of yeast mash composed of malted barley and rye or wheat is prepared, much as Granddaddy did as described in Chapter 2, only the amounts are much larger. A bit of hops is often added, as one would to beer wort, which Granddaddy did not do. The larger quantity of grain mash to be mixed with the yeast mash is prepared separately, as Granddaddy did—mostly ground corn plus some ground rye or wheat. A hammer mill is the best tool for quantity grinding. In all commercial distilleries in the United States, "backset"—that is, mash from a previous fermentation—is saved and added to the new mash. That's why all bourbons are labeled "sour mash"—the "sour" comes from the backset. Backset speeds yeast action and maintains uniformity from one batch to the next. The amount of backset used relative to the new mash varies with the distillery.

The cooking of the yeast mash proceeds much as Granddaddy described, but, if hops are used, the water and hops are first boiled alone for about half an hour. The yeast mash is cooked for half an hour, cooled to 80°F, and the yeast added.

The regular mash and the backset have been cooking meanwhile, usually in huge carbon steel tubs that are mechanically agitated. The tubs have both steam injectors to keep the mash cooking and coils in the bottom to cool it down quickly. First the water and backset are heated, then the corn is added, and the mix boiled for half an hour. The temperature is then decreased to about 155°F, then the other grain or grains are added and the temperature is held there for ten minutes and then slowly lowered. When the mixture has cooled to 80°F, the yeast mash is added with lots of stirring or agitation. The actual process may vary a little from distiller to distiller.

Fermenting vats are usually huge wooden affairs made of cypress, although stainless steel vats are also used now. The mash is pumped into the vat with constant stirring, and, in three days or less, the mash starts to bubble and foam, and the smell of cereal begins to be replaced by the smell of alcohol. The mixture of these odors is lovely. Foam, like the head on beer, only darker and denser, froths up on top of the fermenting mash as the CO_2 bubbles out. Old-timers used to ladle out the thick foam and eat it for lunch. The temperature of the mash rises to about 90°F and slowly falls again to the mid-seventies. In a week or so, the bubbling simmers down, then quits, and the particles of grain fall to the bottom of the vat to become, along with the grain particles out of the wash pot, the distillers grains that make such good livestock feed, or which could be made into pastries and cereals for humans easily enough. On top of the grains is a watery-looking liquid that smells good: distillers beer. This liquid is pumped to the still for distillation.

Distillers wet or dried grains are an important by-product of making spirits. Before he retired from farming, my brother-in-law Bill Downs made regular trips to the distillery not far from his dairy farm to bring home "whiskey slop," as farmers call distillers wet grains. "It increases milk production significantly when fed with beet pulp or silage or hay," he told me. "The more liquid the slop, the more milk production per cow. I had a tank that held 20 barrels and had to pay only a nickel a barrel for the slop. A very inexpensive way to make milk. But sometimes you would have to wait half a day to get a load because so many farm trucks were lined up to get some." Added another brother-in-law, Paul, "Daddy fed slop when he could get it. He'd have us drive the slop truck to school and bring home a load. We were trucking beer slop then." Commented Bill, "Whiskey slop is a little better for making milk."

"Whiskey was really a by-product of grain production in the beginning," says Dave Scheurich, the manager at Labrot & Graham. "When farmers raised a surplus of grain, they made whiskey out of it. Then they found out that the mash left over was excellent feed. Feeding the spent mash to livestock became an integral part of the early distilleries. Now, though, it works out better in most cases to dry the spent mash and sell it to a wider market." (For more on distillers grains, see Chapter 11.)

Aging spirits in oak barrels is an art in itself, beginning with the cooper's skill at making the barrels. Only white oak may be used for bourbon. Not all white oak is created equal, however. There are slightly different strains within the species and even within the same strain, because the rate of growth can be different on different sites. "The oak's rate of growth affects the taste of the whiskey aged in it," Booker Noe explained. "The slower the tree grows, the better."

Barrels did not get their characteristic shape by accident. The bulging middle is a stroke of engineering genius. A barrel is easily maneuverable when full because only the middle touches the floor, which allows for easy pushing, balancing, and especially easy turning. The bulge also makes it easier to set the barrel to an upright position by first pushing down on one end and then letting up quickly. As the barrel falls back across the bulge, you can take advantage of the momentum to tip it up on its end or head. Moreover, we learned at Labrot & Graham that barrels placed on their sides on a set of rails, much like railroad tracks, will roll easily along and stay on the track. The bulge in the middle prevents them from running off.

After the barrels are put together at the Bluegrass Cooperage in

Louisville, Kentucky, the wood is steam-moistened and then heated or "toasted" very briefly to set the staves in their characteristic curved shape. But this practice does something else that seems to me a little magical. The starches in the wood start turning into sugars on the inside of the barrel. Then, when that inside surface is charred—literally set afire for a brief period—these wood sugars caramelize beneath the charred layer and form what the tour guide pointed out to us as the "red layer." This red layer is the main factor influencing the color, taste, and aroma of bourbon, as the whiskey expands into it and contracts out of it during temperature changes in storage.

The char layer that covers the red layer when the inside of the barrel is fired is prescribed by law, but the thickness of the char varies with distiller. The char layer absorbs impurities and lends its own flavoring to the whiskey. How did the practice get started? "There are many theories," says Scheurich. "The one I favor maintains that in the earliest days, when barrels were difficult to come by, pickle barrels were sometimes used for whiskey. But of course the brine in the wood had to be completely cleaned out. Burning off the inner layer of the barrel proved to be a fairly good solution. Then distillers discovered that the char remaining actually improved the taste of the whiskey."

During storage, heat and humidity vary in the warehouse: warmer and drier at the top, cooler and moister at the bottom. Some distilleries rotate the barrels from one rack to another for this reason. On the other hand, if you wanted the very best single-barrel or small-batch whiskey, you would keep barrels destined for this use in the most advantageous place in the warehouse. A little of the whiskey is lost from evaporation during aging, and the longer the aging, the more is lost. Traditionally, the loss is called "the angels' share," a bow to the realization that there is still something magical about a good barrel of whiskey. There is never absolute, mathematical, scientific assurance of what quality of liquor will pour forth when the barrel is opened. Lovely, I say.

*   *   *

Scotch whiskies have many things in common with American whiskeys. (Strange as it may seem, the plural of "whiskey" in America is "whiskeys"; the plural of "whisky" in Scotland, where the "e" is dropped, is "whiskies.") First of all, the magic is still the same, perhaps even more honored in Scotland. A common folktale in the Highlands says that distillers, when replacing a worn-out copper pot still, would hammer the same dents into the new one that existed in the old one, hopefully leaving nothing to chance in ensuring that the new still would perform exactly like the old one.

Scotch whiskies can be either "single malt" or blended, but the term "single malt" is even more rigidly defined than is single-barrel bourbon in Kentucky. A single-malt scotch is the product of one distillery, unmixed with any other distillery's whisky. By definition, that means a Scottish distillery. A single malt made in Japan (yep, there really is) cannot be called single-malt scotch. Only barley is used in making single-malt scotch; no other grain need apply. Blends use mixtures of single malt and whiskies made with other grains, distilled to a near neutral spirit. The more single malt is in the blend, the more expensive it will be.

The single-malt scotch industry is a wonderful demonstration of how a local economy matched to a local ecological agriculture can endure for centuries. Most of these distilleries (about one hundred in total) are small and still operate in the time-honored traditional manner. Some, such as Glenmorangie and Macallan, are still independent, that is, not completely owned by large corporations. Some of the single-malt distilleries are so small and local, in fact, that until recently their whisky was rarely heard of, much less consumed, outside the Highlands. The taste and character of single-malt scotches is so tied to its specific area and its specific climate, water, and varieties of barley that it would be difficult indeed to duplicate them anywhere else. And as the Scots themselves say, their climate is so nasty much of the time, it takes the good hard-bitten Scotch single malt, rough around the edges and tangy with peat smoke, to endure it.

Geographers would say that the climate of Scotland is particularly well suited for making barley whisky. But in fact that observation is sort of backward, environmentally speaking. A more accurate statement would be that barley whisky is particularly well suited to the Scottish climate. Centuries ago, canny Scots accepted nature as it was in their homeland and adapted their agriculture and their economy to it. Barley is one of the few grains stalwart enough to stand the growing season of the Highlands. Also, the cool, moist summers provide the perfect temperature and humidity for malting barley. The barley, after this wondrous single-malt spirit has been drawn from it, becomes grain concentrate for the cattle and sheep that adapt so well to the mountainous and uncultivatable heaths and pasturelands. Instead of concentrating on greenhouses so they could eat insipid tomatoes in March (as in Ohio), the Scots concentrated on malthouses so they could drink good spirits all year long. Good clear water flows through the mountains and into the lochs, often through peat bogs or over granite that give distinctive tastes and properties to the water that show up advantageously in the whisky. I am tempted again to use the word "magic," although the art of ecological food production only seems magical in a world where modern humanity has tried to supplant ecological artfulness with a brutal "scientific" technology bent on conquering nature rather than adapting to it. Peat was the most readily available and efficient fuel to fire the malt kilns in the earlier years, and again, "magically," peat smoke just so happened to give the Scotch whisky its unique taste.

Nor has the malting of barley been consolidated into its own big business to the extent that it has in the United States. Each small independent distillery used to, and often still does, make its own malt from its own preferred variety of barley. These might even be old varieties that do not yield as well as new ones, but are better acclimated to their soil or contribute something unique to the taste of that particular distillery's whisky.

Making malt progresses in the manner described in the chapter on beer. The barley will be piled to a depth of a foot or two, moistened to initiate sprouting, and then periodically turned so that molding or overheating does not occur. When the barley has sprouted to the precise degree described in Chapter 5, it is dried as quickly as possible. Drying used to be done wholly in peat-fired kilns, and even today, when other fuels are used, some peat smoke is wafted through the drying malt—a little or a lot, depending on how much of a peaty flavor the distillery wants to give its single malt. The sprout tips screened out of the malt after drying are important as a cattle feed on the distillery farm or nearby farms. So are the dried distillers grains left over after distillation, as in bourbon distilleries.

Fermentation and distillation are similar to that of American whiskeys, although for single malts, distillation must take place in copper pot stills. I haven't had the pleasure yet of journeying to Scotland, but from studying photographs, these gleaming, urnlike copper stills, like cognac stills, strike me as consummate works of sculptural art worthy of being admired in their own right. Some are squat and some are tall, and it is the latter, like the stills at Glenfiddich, that I find so visually appealing. Some distillers believe the shape of the still, squat or lean, imparts different qualities to the taste. Whether this is part of the fanciful, often overly romanticized promotion of single-malt scotches or a matter of fact is not something this wide-eyed wanderer in the world of whisky can say.

Another reason why single malts are usually more expensive than blended scotches is that they are almost always aged longer. By law, they must be aged three years, but almost all the single malts are aged much longer than that. The average of the more esteemed brands is around ten to twelve years, and sometimes twice that or more. In the past, aging was done exclusively in oak barrels used previously for sherry, and Macallan still uses nothing but sherry barrels. Used bourbon barrels are employed extensively today, which solves a problem for both the American whiskey makers, who must use new barrels for bourbon, and the Scotch, for whom sherry barrels in sufficient numbers have become very difficult to obtain. Even port and rum barrels may be used. Various single-malt scotch brands can be purchased as aged or finished in port wine barrels, or in sherry barrels, or in whiskey barrels. Single-malt scotch distillers are allowed to add a little caramel to their whiskies for coloring, but not all do.

There is wide variation in single malts—wider than in bourbon, I think—and, as with bourbon, you must study the labels to know exactly what is in the bottle. When you have a little extra money, you might want to experiment with one or two of the ultra-high-priced single malts. Try a Highland Park, twenty-five-year-old single malt from the Orkney Islands at only $150 a fifth. (There are Highland Parks of lesser age, still of premium taste, at half that price.) Or how about Old Fettercairn, a thirty-year-old single malt from the eastern Highlands, at only $200 a fifth. Or, if you won the lottery, how about celebrating with a bottle of Bowmore forty-year-old single malt, aged twenty years in a bourbon barrel and then twenty more in a sherry barrel, at $7,000 a fifth! That's right: 7-0-0-0.

But there are many good single malts at more affordable prices. Glenfiddich and Glenlivet are certainly not cheap, but fairly reasonable and usually available at your favorite bar. Glenfiddich doesn't have as heavy a peaty taste as Glenlivet, if heavier peatiness turns you off. Glenmorangie is the best-selling scotch in Scotland, for whatever that fact is worth. I favor Macallan, but I can't say if that's because of the taste or because the company has, at least so far, adhered to a policy of staying small and even old-timey and relying on sippers to appreciate the difference enough to pay for it.

There are smaller distilleries, even more faithful and pure to the old ways, like Springbank, but their single malts are not always available unless you go to Scotland or a very large liquor outlet. At a liquor outlet in Louisville, Kentucky, I spotted a fifth of thirty-year-old Springbank (in a locked case) priced at $225.

Great variation in quality and price is also characteristic of blended scotches. Some high-end blends, such as Johnny Walker

Gold and eighteen-year-old Chivas Regal, are moderately expensive and highly recommended if the unique individualism of single malts is not to your liking.

In Scotch whiskies, there is a third category, roughly between single malts and blends, called vatted malts. A "vatted malt" is a blend of single malts only, that is, without the addition of neutral grain alcohol or blended scotches. Chivas Brothers "The Century of Malts," which is a blend of "a hundred single malts from a hundred individual distilleries," is a recommended, newer example. Obviously, there could be almost as unlimited a variety of vatted malts as of conventional blends.

Not so incidentally, if you figure on buying good scotch cheaper in the British Isles, forget it. The tax situation is so punitive on spirits in the United Kingdom that you can actually buy your scotch cheaper in New York.

CHAPTER 10

The "White Whiskey" Mixers
& Other Popular Drinks

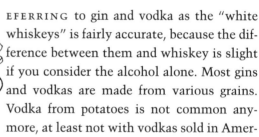EFERRING to gin and vodka as the "white whiskeys" is fairly accurate, because the difference between them and whiskey is slight if you consider the alcohol alone. Most gins and vodkas are made from various grains. Vodka from potatoes is not common anymore, at least not with vodkas sold in America, but Chopin vodka from Poland is still made entirely from fermented potatoes, and, indeed, from a specific variety of potato grown just for that purpose. The distillation method for gin and vodka from grain is the same as for whiskey. I don't know how to ferment potatoes and have found no one familiar with the process, but basically it would involve little more than chopping up the spuds and putting them in water to ferment. Gin and vodka are clear liquids because, unlike whiskey, they are not aged in wood. In fact they are not aged at all. Although all end up in the bottle at approximately the same range of alcohol content, gins and especially vodkas are first distilled to a higher alcohol content than whiskey, closer to that of a neutral grain spirit.

Because they are each more of a neutral spirit, gin and vodka contain less of the congeners that give whiskey its characteristic taste when aged. Expensive vodkas that are redistilled several times are close enough to pure alcohol to be considered "tasteless," yet they still contain enough of the congeners in distilled alcohol to impart some taste. Knowing when to stop saving the distillate for vodka or gin is as sharp a skill as knowing how to do the same with whiskey. Maybe more so, because the tolerance between some taste and no taste at all is closer. Good vodkas are scrupulously filtered, too, to give them a fine, smooth taste. Gin is flavored mainly with juniper berries, but also various other fruit and herb flavorings. Most eastern European vodka makers, as for instance Absolut and Stolichnaya, make fruit- and herb-flavored vodkas along with unflavored vodkas. Unflavored vodkas are the most popular spirit in America, because most sippers here prefer mixed drinks and vodka does not compete with the taste of the mix. However, some of the expensive vodkas now finding their way to America, like Belvedere, are good enough to stand alone, as in a very dry martini. You hardly ever hear a macho bourbon drinker anymore refer to vodka as "that commie drink."

In fact Ancient Age Distilleries in Frankfort, Kentucky is actually making an American vodka, and an *organic* vodka at that! Called "Rain," the new vodka is distilled four times, like the best eastern European brands. "Rain" boasts pure Kentucky limestone water and is filtered through charcoal and, would you believe, diamond dust!

Some of the better vodkas do come from once-Communist Russia and Poland, which reminds me that, even as I write this chapter (October of 1998), another campaign of regressive and repressive taxes against spirits is underway. The place this time is Russia; the target, naturally enough, is vodka. Russians drink an unbelievable 2.1 *billion* liters of vodka every year, twenty-eight bottles for every man, woman, and child in the country. And that doesn't count moonshine vodka. This shouldn't surprise anyone. *Vodka*, in Russian, means literally, or at least colloquially, "dear little water," underscoring the eastern Europeans' fondness for it. Wherever people were allowed to make it in earlier centuries, and even where they were not, winter breakfast often began with bread and vodka, and supper might end that way too. Vodka seems to have served in Russia about the same purpose coffee does in the United States.

The Russian government, strapped for cash largely because of its own past economic stupidity, has just announced even higher taxes on vodka, which are plenty high now. Boris Smirnoff, of the famous Smirnoff vodka family, is complaining in the papers that "the government already takes almost everything we make." History shows that the effect of more vodka tax will be negative. The higher prices that taxes will engender will spur the moonshine industry to more production, and much of the increase in taxes will have to be used to police the illicit trade. Meanwhile, the rest of us will be buying more Polish and Scandinavian vodka.

In most cases, the Russian government already has a controlling interest in the vodka business, because all 184 of its alcohol distilleries were nationalized during the Communist era (which proves that Communism is not inherently regressive to business—Smirnoff, Stolichnaya, etc., continued to make great vodka in spite of it). The actual situation, however, is a hybrid of private enterprise and nationalization. The distilleries make the pure alcohol, and, in many cases, the private vodka distillers buy the alcohol and use it to make their own unique vodkas, roughly parallel to what liqueur makers do.

But the seizure of the spirits industry by the powerful for the purpose of consolidating personal wealth did not begin in Russia with Communism, not by far. As early as the 1500s, Ivan the Terrible realized the enormous amount of money to be gained with control over spirits, and he established his own royal network of taverns, outlawing any he did not authorize. But he dispensed permits to nobles as political and economic favors. (Am I the only one who is reminded of the way U.S. bureaucrats issue permits to taverns here?) Later rulers tightened their monopoly on spirits. It is easy to see why an economic system as silly as Communism caught on in Russia, and why the people accepted the nationalization of its distilleries as well as of its farms. Communism was only another name for the monopolistic power that the Russian oligarchy had always exercised. Changing the politics of oligarchy did not change the powermongering. Its acceptance was practically bred into the Russian soul, be it under Ivan the Terrible or Stalin the Totally Horrible. Any genetic possibility of breeding anything else but a sheeplike flock mentality was quashed over the centuries by killing anyone who objected. Stalin finished off the genocide by slaughtering millions of Ukrainian farmers who didn't accept his terms of monopoly, extinguishing much of the gene pool of intelligent courage in Russia. I mean no disparagement of the Russian people, who, given a chance, are as resourceful as anyone, but I know as a shepherd that it will take a few more generations of breeding up and educating up the Russian mind before that country can hope to overcome its economic mess. Preying on one of the country's best chances to solve its problems, the vodka industry, is just more sheep psychology in action.

At the same time that Ivan the Terrible was monopolizing spirits in his country, King Jan Olbrect in Poland issued a decree allowing every Polish citizen the right to make vodka. A healthy distributive economy immediately ensued, and within a century there were forty-nine commercial distilleries in Posnan alone. Can't the rich ever learn that they will gain a more satisfying and enduring power in the long run by distributing the wealth rather than by consolidating it?

Ivan the Terrible, despite enacting the most severe and brutal penalties, could not stop illicit vodka distilling, nor will the present authorities in Russia. In earlier centuries, "moonshine" vodka was easy to get away with because distilling with heat had not yet come into vogue. Like pioneer New Englanders and their applejack, Russian peasants put their fermented grain beer out in the cold and drank what didn't freeze. It must have tasted terrible. But without the telltale smoke and distillation paraphernalia of the evaporation method, Ivan's agents had a much harder time detecting a vodka "distillery" in operation. Drinking ice-distilled liquor is dangerous from a health point of view, as pointed out earlier. Think of how desperately those early Russians must have craved alcohol. If caught, they could be subjected to cruel torture and death. If not caught, they would suffer the shakes and deliriums of "apple palsy" or, in this case, "grain palsy" from drinking the awful stuff. Again, I have to say: in the face of such dire compulsion, is it not better to educate people to drinking in a safer, saner manner rather than trying to stop them by physical or economic force from drinking at all?

The better vodkas are distilled as much as four times so that, despite the lesser cost involved by not having to age them, they are rather expensive, although seldom in the category with the longest-aged scotches or bourbons. Adding subtle flavorings cuts into the savings of not being aged, too. More mellowness (and cost) results from complex and scrupulous charcoal filtering. In earlier centuries, this filtering was done through woolen felt.

As in whiskey making, water is an important element in vodka, at least important to some distillers. Finlandia is a great vodka, perhaps because, as the distillery's advertisements suggest, the water used is "pure glacial spring water." Sounds good to me.

All gin and vodka labels I have read (except Chopin vodka) specify "from straight grain alcohol," or "100% neutral spirits from straight grain alcohol." Belvedere vodka is made entirely from rye; Alps vodka from wheat. Most are distilled from mixtures of grain. If the label doesn't say "from grain" or words to that effect, or doesn't spell out the source of the neutral spirits, such as potatoes, then you can't be sure. Neutral spirits, which are pure alcohol, could be made from anything that ferments. Some chemists argue that the source of the neutral spirit is not as important as most of us believe, since the result is the same—nearly pure alcohol. Ethyl alcohol is ethyl alcohol, so the argument goes, no matter where it comes from. If you go strictly by the numbers, it's hard to argue. Grain is used mostly because it is cheaper than other food sources of alcohol. I can imagine good gin or vodka coming from sugar beets as well as potatoes, but both would cost more to grow than grain. Pure neutral spirits could even be made from food garbage, but I am sure the cost of garbage collection and handling, plus all the regulations that would be necessary if the spirit were to be used in beverage alcohol, would make the garbage cost more than grain, too. Moonshine made from sugar alone and distilled three or four times makes a passable spirit for vodka or gin, but again, sugar is more expensive than grain.

Flavorings to gin and vodka are added in two different ways, the same as for liqueurs. Sometimes they go right into the mash during distillation. Or they may be suspended in mesh containers above the mash so that the vapors rise up through them. These processes are practically the same as described in the chapter on liqueurs, but the final spirit has a higher content of alcohol than most liqueurs.

Because high-proof vodka is considered the purest of all beverage alcohols, it is used in modern herbal medicine as an herb preservative. Herbs destined for teas are steeped in vodka to make herbal tinctures. Many herbalists think that vodka tinctures do a more effective job of preserving herbs than drying. When I suggested that the vodka might be the source of healthfulness, not the herb, an herbalist friend grinned and replied, "That might be a possibility, except for the fact that the vodka evaporates off the tea before you drink it."

Gin is gin because of the dominant flavoring of juniper berry oil in it. Gin would actually be a liqueur if sugar were added to sweeten it heavily. The fact that it is not sweetened is why it is referred to as "London dry," or "English dry," or "American dry." Oil of juniper berries is the most dominant flavoring in dry gin, but various other botanicals, such as cardamom, cassia bark, orange peel, coriander seed, angelica root, or most any other herb used in liqueurs, may be part of the mix. Obviously an infinite number of slightly different gins are possible. Gin was historically the first "liqueur" to be made with grain alcohol rather than from brandy. Grain alcohol was cheaper than fruit alcohol, even in the 1600s. The first grain alcohol from pot stills was harsh stuff without aging, and so flavorings were added to blunt the rough edges. In the case of gin, the "Dr. Sylvius" (his real name was Francescus de La Boie) credited with inventing it in Holland thought that the combination of juniper berries and grain alcohol would make a good diuretic for people with kidney problems. Since both alcohol and juniper berries are diuretics, he had a point there, except that his "gin" (from *geniver*, Dutch for "juniper") did not cure kidney problems as he had hoped. I asked one of my favorite doctors if martinis could help relieve an enlarged prostate as the modern folk belief would have it. He smiled and answered, "If martinis could do that, an awful lot of my patients wouldn't be coming to see me."

The first Dutch gin from grain alcohol was (and still is) heavier and more malty than today's dry gins—more like whiskey. When the continuous column still was invented, making the production of neutral grain spirit inexpensive, London or English dry gin—the kind we are more familiar with and drink almost exclusively in the United States—came on the scene. English gin today uses a set mixture of 75 percent wheat, 15 percent barley, and 10 percent other grains in the mash. It is distilled to a higher alcohol content than whiskey and then is cut to the desired bottle proof with water. It is very light, dry, and smooth. Recipes for the flavorings go back to the 1700s, so the distilleries say. American gin makers generally buy neutral grain spirits from other distilleries and add flavorings by redistillation as described in Chapter 7. The cheapest gins simply mix neutral spirit with extracts of botanicals, chiefly oil of juniper, without redistillation.

Gin can be enjoyed alone, but I don't know anyone who drinks it that way. Some very dry martinis come close, however, since extremely little vermouth is added. A few years ago, when a yuppie writer told me that the martini had become passé as a new generation of drinkers came along, I laughed loud enough to shatter all the martini glasses in the restaurant. A *good* martini will never go out of style, any more than Michelangelo's *Moses* will go out of style. Sure enough, in a few years' time the martini was "back" again, while all those awful wine coolers declined in popularity. No matter. The cycle will repeat itself as fickle human taste jumps from one fad to another.

I'm very partial to the martini my wife and her sister make, which is a far cry from just throwing gin and vermouth over some ice cubes. First of all, a good martini requires a good English dry gin such as Bombay or Tanqueray or maybe Beefeater. Boodles is good, but too perfumy for my taste. If you don't have a regular martini mixing glass, a wide-mouthed quart canning jar will do for mixing up martinis, even if it doesn't impress your cool executive friends. For two large martinis, put seven ice cubes (not six, not eight, says my very particular wife) in the jar or martini mixer, along with 5 jiggers of gin (let's go with Bombay Sapphire), not quite a fourth of a jigger of Martini & Rossi extra dry vermouth, and a couple of drops or maybe a third of a teaspoon of a good Scotch whisky. (You can vary the amount of extra dry vermouth to suit your taste, but leave the sweet vermouth for Manhattans.) Now, stir until the ice cubes melt just a little, perhaps for a minute, then put the jar in the freezer for two hours. Put the martini glasses in the freezer, too, so they get cold and frosty. While waiting, prepare the olives. Buy high-quality olives, the larger the better, and remove that awful red pimiento stuffing. Stuff the hollow olives with Roquefort cheese. If you don't have Roquefort, blue cheese will do, but it's not as good. At the end of two hours, pour the liquor, which is getting frosty cold in the freezer, into the frosted martini glasses, leaving the ice cubes behind. Put two or three olives in each glass. (We have a friend who is not crazy about martinis, but craves these stuffed olives soaked in gin. He may make up, or make my wife make up, a dozen such olives, which he dunks in his martini like a kid dunking cookies in milk.) Finally, put a pinch of salt into each martini. No, I don't know why that helps, but it does. Sip very slowly. Listen to the spirit gods sing.

I'm not afraid to say that our martini tastes better than the classic "Perfect Martini" served at the Rainbow Room in New York City, where Dale DeGroff, the Rainbow Room's famous mixmaster, uses Beefeater, puts a dash of sweet vermouth in his martini along with the dry vermouth, and skips the scotch and salt. Too bad. We call our martini the Perfect Matie after my sister-in-law's nickname, because, as far as we know, she perfected it.

Many people prefer vodka to gin in martinis but make them about the same way, with, perhaps, a twist of lemon or a pearl onion substituting for the olives. Incidentally, the drink maker should twist the little lemon strip to release some of the citrus oils in the peel into the drink. Really does make a difference. As with gin, I heartily recommend using a more expensive vodka; I think you will be able to taste the difference right away. If you are ordering in a restaurant, specify which vodka (or gin) you want in your martini. If you don't (and this is true when ordering mixed drinks with whiskey, too), you will get the "house brand," which invariably is a cheaper liquor. If you do specify a more expensive brand, expect to pay more for your drink. Skyy vodka, or Finlandia, are good choices and almost always available. Belvedere, a Polish vodka made completely from rye grain and distilled four times, is better in my opinion, but is only lately being publicized in the United States, and not all bars carry it. Ketel One is the latest rave, but I haven't tasted it and so can't pronounce judgment. I think even a novice will notice the difference between a Belvedere or Skyy martini and one made with a cheap vodka. Some drinkers will have a vodka martini with their workday lunch, believing it is not as noticeable on the breath as gin. Not true. My wife can smell vodka every bit as far away as she can smell gin.

Gin and tonic water is another classic mix very popular in the summertime. There's nothing better at the end of a hot day working in the fields or garden. You don't have to be so particular with this one. Pour one or two shots of gin into a tall glass of ice cubes, then fill with tonic water. A wedge of lime on top enhances the drink. A concoction of lemon juice, sugar syrup (or even 7UP or Sprite), and gin, which we call a Gin Buck, is also a nice hot-weather drink. Lemon and juniper berry tastes go together nicely on my tongue.

★   ★   ★

Mixing drinks is an absolutely endless subject. I hesitate to describe how we make martinis because only a novice sipper would try to impress others by saying such and such a method or recipe is the "only" way to make a certain drink. I don't know how many stars are in the firmament, but the number of mixed drinks can't be far behind. Lately, as the stock market brings unimagined and unforeseen paper wealth to investors (will that observation be outdated before this book gets into print?), one of the results of all the loose change jingling in upper-crust pockets is a readiness to experiment with new and expensive food and drink. That's why single-malt scotches and small-batch bourbons are such a rage. The same is true of mixed drinks, and of spending time at bars in general. There are bars in big cities where you must now make a reservation to belly up. Honest. Bartenders have taken on the aura of chefs. They have repertoires of hundreds of exotic drinks that they will be only too glad to whip up for you if you have the cash. You can hardly become inebriated because you will run out of money first. These New Age bartenders are often referred to as "mixmasters," which always makes me laugh because that is also the name of a well-known brand of milled cow feed. Even if society as a whole does suffer the much-rumored economic crash (which seems to me inevitable), the knowledge of mixmastering will not be lost, and we can all concoct our favorite drinks at home at a third of the cost of showing off at an expensive bar.

Here's a faint idea of what is going on in the world of mixed drinks, drawn from an advertising special in (where else?) *The New Yorker* magazine in 1998. For example, at a famous restaurant in New York called Pravda, the bartender will make you, using the tequila of your choice (there are scores of tequila brands, too), a red margarita with pomegranate juice. At the cigar bar in the Club Macanudo in New York, you can order a Macanudo martini, with your favorite brand of gin, Alizé (a liqueur) instead of vermouth, and cranberry juice, garnished with passion fruit. Or, high above the Macanudo Club in the Rainbow Room, how about a Cosmopolitan, composed of 1½ ounces of Absolut Citron, 1 ounce of Cointreau, and a dash of cranberry juice, shaken with ice, and poured into a chilled martini glass, with a twist of lemon.

A favorite at the China Grill on South Beach in Miami, Florida, is the Peach Sparkler, a mix of 1⅓ ounces Finlandia vodka, ½ ounce Peachtree Schnapps, 2 ounces orange juice, and 2 ounces Taitinger's champagne.

At the Biba restaurant in Boston, try a Purple Martin: 2½ ounces of Bombay Sapphire gin and ½ ounce of Elysium (a black muscat dessert wine) in lieu of vermouth. Chill, shake, and serve.

A famous drink in Los Angeles is the Butterfly's Kiss, composed of 2½ ounces of Skyy vodka and ½ ounce of Frangelico, an Italian liqueur, poured into a Pernod-coated glass with a lemon twist garnish. (Pernod is an anise-flavored liqueur. It is also a big company that now owns many spirits brands.)

If you get the Coco martini in Chicago's Narcisse, a salon on the River North, you get a string of faux pearls along with it. Harry's Velvet Room in Chicago serves forty kinds of martinis. The mixmaster at Jilly's in Chicago, Al Rohrssen, serves a Finlandia Dirty Gibson with Finlandia vodka, Spanish olive juice (ugh), two pearl onions, and an olive.

Many of the new drinks use vodkas infused with fruit juices, in much the same way I infused Hennessy brandy with blackberries to make what lesser souls out here in the flyover country call blackberry bounce. Thus a Red Martini in San Francisco's Red Room uses Skyy vodka infused with cranberries.

According to the special advertising section mentioned above, a group of high-rise sippers, fresh from jobs like hawking stocks on the New York Stock Exchange, regularly order a $250 quart of vodka or a $1,000 demijohn of champagne to go with their meal. Easy come, easy go. If we are not in the last days of another Gay Nineties before another Dirty Thirties, I'll even drink a couple of those Dirty Gibsons.

It is a desecration of good scotch or bourbon to mix anything with it, in my opinion. Scotch with a heavy peat-flavored smokiness especially does not mix well, except in very small amounts to accent other drinks. Besides, you can't duplicate with whiskey the amazing sight of a bar top full of gin or vodka martinis, all in different colors.

I suppose I'd make an exception for the Manhattan, a most popular American drink usually made with whiskey. Two and a half ounces of bourbon, a bit of *sweet* vermouth according to your taste, a half spoonful of orange bitters, and, if you want to honor tradition, a maraschino cherry. But if you substitute brandy for the whiskey in your Manhattan, I think you may never want to go back to whiskey. I like whiskey sours, a combination of any number of fruit juices, but especially orange and lemon juice, with whiskey, blended to your taste. But here again I think substituting brandy for whiskey makes a better drink.

If you can't find a place that sells orange bitters, essential to many mixed drinks, take a look at a recipe in *The Book of Bourbon*, previously cited, which contains lots of good recipes for mixed drinks with bourbon, if you don't mind ruining bourbon. Since some of the flavorings in orange bitters are found in good gins and sometimes vodkas, you might just steep half a pound of minced orange peel in ½ cup of gin and 1½ cups of a 100 proof vodka, along with ½ of sugar, and let the mixture stand for two weeks, shaking it once a day. The general procedure is not much different from making the lemon liqueur with vodka as described in Chapter 7, only orange bitters is more potent, to be used sparingly to flavor other drinks. A more practical solution to the bitters problem is to use Angostura bitters, which is almost always available from liquor stores.

About the only mixed drink that I think honors bourbon is the mint julep, and I have a hunch rum would work better, but I'm careful not to say that around my Kentucky-born wife. She proudly carries on the tradition of making mint juleps on Kentucky Derby Day, even though we live three hundred miles away from Churchill Downs.

There are various ways to make a mint julep, but the way she does it is a good introduction to learning how to get the hang of infusing any liqueur with an herb flavoring. Practice in bruising or macerating mint leaves for mint juleps can lead you to doing the same with basil for a basil julep, and then, well, the earth's the limit.

Mint grows wild in many places or is easy to start in your garden. In fact it is something of a nuisance weed. Ours is the common green spearmint, but peppermint and maybe other mints would work as well (but not pennyroyal, since it has been recently discovered that oil of pennyroyal contains toxic elements). My wife transferred our mint from where it grew wild around a side-hill spring near Granddaddy's barn, and which her family always used for making mint juleps in the dear long ago. (That spring still flows, by the way, but now it is in the backyard of a development house.) But with a start of that mint transplanted in our garden, and bourbon, we keep sacred the spirit of those times and the spirit of Granddaddy here in Ohio.

There is a reason for almost everything, even though the foibles of human behavior make that observation often doubtful. The reason mint juleps go so well with Derby Day is that both the right stage of mint for juleps and the Kentucky Derby occur at the same time, the first Saturday of May. It is then that the young mint plants have their highest transferable flavor. Has nothing to do with the bourbon, which is always at its highest transferable flavor. Carol picks the mint sprigs just before she makes the juleps, in the spirit of those who pick their sweet corn only seconds before boiling and eating it. Into an ample glass (yes, those Kentucky colonels like to use silver julep cups, but that is really putting on airs), she puts 2 teaspoons of powdered sugar (more or less to suit her taste) and several mint leaves. Then she bruises the leaves gently with the back of a spoon or any pestlelike tool. Bruising the mint to release the oil requires a little persistent work to get the powdered sugar liquefied without crushing the leaves too much. (She says it is easier to use concentrated simple syrup than trying to liquefy the powdered sugar. Simple syrup is made by heating equal parts of sugar and water till the sugar dissolves.) Too much bruising makes the mint oil a little bitter. When a spoonful of oil and powdered sugar liquefies in the bottom of the glass or julep cup, she fills the glass about two-thirds full of crushed ice. Now that almost everyone has an electric gadget to crush ice, this is no problem, but you can also put ice cubes in a cloth bag and whack them with the flat of an ax blade, as we do when making ice for homemade ice cream. Fill the glass with bourbon. The ounces of bourbon should be equal approximately to the ounces of crushed ice. Stir a little, stick a sprig or two of mint in the ice as a garnish, and let it set until the glass frosts up. Sip your julep slowly through a straw. Some people don't macerate the mint leaves, but simply put a big bouquet of mint in the ice and bourbon and sip with their nose buried in mint leaves.

Sometime, when no one from Kentucky is watching, substitute a light Bacardi rum for the bourbon. Better yet, substitute the rum into a Kentuckian's julep but don't tell her. Bet you a julep she won't notice the difference.

*   *   *

Rum is to the Caribbean what bourbon is to Kentucky and Tennessee. Rum is a difficult spirit to categorize, in that it may be clear, hardly aged at all for use in mixed drinks, or aged in wood to medium dark to dark amber color and used for mixes or sipped alone. But even that is a general statement of little value, because rum distillers are allowed to darken their products with caramelized sugar, both for flavoring and to make the liquor look as old as rum aged for many years in barrels. Rum is distilled like whiskeys and brandies, the darker type sometimes in pot stills, the clearer white or silver rums in continuous stills. Unless a vintage year is named on the label, you don't know how old the rum is. There are many, many brands, and some, like Bacardi, are offered in both dark and light liquors.

Rum is made from sugar cane juice, pressed from the stalks and then boiled to a molasses. This first process follows the way in which we northerners make sorghum molasses. I'm sure that a northern rum could be made from sweet sorghum, but I don't know anyone who does it. Fermenting molasses yields a weak alcoholic beer. Distilled, the beer yields raw rum equal in alcohol content to other distilled spirits.

*   *   *

No one in North America is likely to distill tequila in their back-yard even if it were legal, because the agave species that it is made from doesn't grow here. Tequila is more or less the national spirit of Mexico, and the agave used to make it is grown almost exclusively in the state of Jalisco. Tequila is made from distilling pulque, which is wine fermented from agave juice. There are many plants in the agave family, several of which can be used in making tequila. The usual species is appropriately called *Agave tequilana*, or on tequila bottles, "blue agave," and referred to colloquially as the tequila mescal plant. But in Mexico the two specific strains of agave used for tequila are called Agave-Azul and Agave-Xinguin. Don't ask me what that means; I just looked it up on the Internet. To be labeled tequila, the distillate must have come from at least 51 percent fermented Azul juice. Interestingly, the agave crop must grow and mature for about ten years before harvesting takes place, a fact that discourages moonshining.

No sipper's education is complete without enjoying a tequila margarita while listening to Jimmy Buffett music. Actually, the real education comes from listening to Jimmy Buffett fans trying to sing Jimmy Buffett's most famous song, "Margaritaville" while drinking margaritas. Buffett fans are a very strange lot, and they have a fondness for what they call the "lick, suck, and swallow" margarita. You put a pinch of salt on the back of your hand, where, if you have not yet downed too much tequila, you can keep it from falling off by holding your hand level. Then you must have a wedge of lime at the ready in your fingers (same hand) and a shot glass of tequila in the other hand, preferably Cuervo Gold. Okay. Lick the salt off your hand, immediately suck vigorously on your lime, and then quickly down your shot of Cuervo. I try to leave the party before this happens too often.

Tequilas, like whiskeys, may be blended or straight, but in the United States blends are much more generally available, which is similar to the status of scotch until just a few years ago. Tequilas vary greatly in price. Cuervo Gold is an expensive blend, and though I can't swallow a whole shot of it at once, it is great for sipping. As in the scotch and bourbon markets, there is a move on now to introduce the rarer and higher-quality tequilas, such as Casta Weber Azu or triple-distilled Porfidio Gold, to U.S. consumers. The distillation process at the more than thirty tequila distilleries in Mexico is similar to the distillation of other spirits. Extracting the juice from the agave plants and fermenting it is similar to the way in which sugar cane is turned into fermenting molasses for rum. There are dark and light tequilas, as with rums.

To make a margarita, you need tequila, of course, lime juice, and triple sec. Triple sec is an orange liqueur sold under several brand names. You can purchase a regular margarita mix instead of using fresh lime juice, and most people do. But I think it tastes better to make everything from scratch. Mix the ingredients to your own taste, but tequila ought to make up about two-thirds of the drink. Before pouring it into your glass, turn the glass upside down in a bowlful of coarse salt, so that the rim is coated. You can buy special margarita salt, which is quite coarse.

★   ★   ★

"Rice wine" or sake (sometimes spelled saki, and pronounced *SAH-kee*, with the accent on the first syllable) is no doubt the national spirit of Japan, although some is brewed in the United States. It is not a distilled beverage by definition. It barely fits into the category of a wine, however, being a little higher in alcohol content and being fermented and brewed more like beer than wine. It is clear and usually a little sweetish. Notice how I keep using the adverb "usually"? The reason is because there are some ten thousand different kinds of sake! That is why I say that there is no end to the discussion of the different kinds of alcoholic spirits in the world, so I might as well end this chapter here and leave the rest to your spirit of adventure.

CHAPTER 11

Fuel Alcohol: A Way to Make Untaxed Spirits Legally

THANOL is good spirits before it becomes automotive fuel. You can make it in exactly the same way you can make whiskey. You can't drink it only because the government dictates that the liquor distilled for fuel must be rendered unfit for human consumption by the addition of something dreadful. If Uncle did not so ordain, a hefty portion of the ethanol produced would never reach the gas pumps. However, most commercial ethanol today is made not with malt (although it very well could be) but with commercial enzymes, and is distilled and dried to a pure neutral spirit (200 proof), so that, even without the addition of gasoline, kerosene, or methyl isobutyl ketone, or whatever it takes to render it undrinkable, it would not taste nearly as good as good malt liquor.

Making ethanol is the only legal way I know to learn how to make distilled spirits without having to pay a small fortune in permit and bond fees. If you abide by the rules, the government is remarkably reasonable to small-scale ethanol producers. As long as you distill no more than 10,000 gallons (and the kind of producer I have in mind would produce only a fraction of that amount), it will cost you nothing in bond fees, mercy me. Nor will you have to pay any tax on your ethanol when you put it in your car or tractor tank. This amazing largesse came about during the so-called fuel shortage in the 1970s, when the government decided, in a rare moment of enlightenment, that it would be good for the country to let people at large turn their skills to developing alternative fuels.

Even though the backyard ethanol producer does not have to pay the government for the privilege of helping America solve its fuel problems, there are other strict regulations that must be followed, even in the smallest operation. You must first crawl to your nearest office of the Bureau of Alcohol, Tobacco, and Firearms, probably located in your state capital, bow subserviently, and request an application for a permit. This bowing and scraping has its advantages because it allows you to get acquainted with the people at ATF and assure them that you are not a moonshiner in disguise (even if you are). ATF workers can be downright human and nearly always helpful. They may not sound too enthusiastic, because they know, from past experience, that most applicants don't persevere in their enthusiasm for homemade fuel. Uncle doesn't realize just yet that the year 2000 is not the year 1975, and that a new generation of alternative fuel buffs just might want to get experience making ethanol in case gasoline prices climb, or in case the government someday becomes truly enlightened and allows us to distill homemade spirits without paying heavy fees and bonds. Also, because of advances made since the seventies, there are ideas around that might make ethanol production on a small scale practical right now.

Your request for a permit should include your address, of course, and the location of the planned alcohol plant. Also, you need to include a drawing or diagram of the premises upon which the still will be installed and the consent of the owner of that property if it is not yours. Supply a description of the still and the maximum capacity it will produce, plus the material(s) you will use to produce the alcohol. You will need to submit a description of the security measures to be used to protect your still and its production from thievery, and to protect others from the possibility of the highly volatile fuel blowing up. You are supposed to submit an environmental impact statement, too. Obviously, if you plan only a very small operation, say 500 gallons a year, some of these regulations aren't of crucial importance.

After you have submitted your request for a permit, you will receive notice of approval or disapproval in fifteen days, and, if the latter, you will be informed what you need to do to get approval. If you hear nothing in forty-five days, the regulations state that you can assume your permit has been approved and you can go ahead and start building or installing your still. After that, you will have to submit a record of the amount of ethanol you produce yearly, although this regulation too is not so crucial for very small operations, since you are not going to produce nearly enough to pay bond on it. But the government wants to be very sure that none of your production is being siphoned off (literally) for potable spirits.

To that end, you must provide information about what additive you plan to use to denature your alcohol to render it undrinkable. There are several alternatives, but the best for the small operation is a high-octane gasoline, at the rate of 5 gallons for every 100 gallons of ethanol. You may want to add more gasoline depending on your motor and circumstances (see below). But the government doesn't want any ethanol sitting around in its pure state, because the temptation to use it for vodka martinis might be just too great.

There is much information available about homemade ethanol that came out during the fuel scare of the 1970s, but most such books are out of print now—another sign either that the idea is a little more difficult than it first sounds, or, as I contend, that it was never pursued in any organized and concerted way on a small scale, as it is now being pursued in large-scale factories. The most necessary book you need should be available from libraries or through library loan: *Brown's Alcohol Motor Fuel Cookbook* by Michael H. Brown (Cornville, Arizona: Desert Publications, 1979; ISBN 0-87947-300-2.) I will try to encapsulate the basic knowledge of converting a motor to alcohol use later on, but Brown's book is the best detailed treatment of it that I have read. *Makin' It on the Farm: Alcohol Fuel Is the Road to Independence* by Micki Stout Nellis (Iridell, Texas, 1979) is also most helpful. So is Fred Stetson's *Making Your Own Motor Fuel*, already cited. *Prosperity*

Beckons: Dawn of the Alcohol Era by William J. Hale (originally published in 1936, and republished in 1979 by Rutan Publishing in Minneapolis) gives you the kind of historical perspective you need to understand the very real possibilities in ethanol. You can send for a government booklet called "Fuel from Farms—A Guide to Small Scale Ethanol Production," identified as "Report SERI/SP-451-519, U.S. Department of Energy, Feb. 1980." This is available from either the Superintendent of Documents, U.S. Government Printing Office, Washington, DC 20402, or from the National Technical Information Service (NTIS), U.S. Department of Commerce, 5285 Port Royal Road, Springfield, Virginia 22161. The government keeps all its bulletins in print nearly forever. There are new ideas in alcohol distillation since 1980, but nothing much has been written directly for the backyard ethanol producer.

Is backyard ethanol fuel production economically profitable? No, it is not, *presently*. Large-scale production is now going forward rapidly, but it is not economically profitable either without the subsidies that ethanol producers receive. But the oil industry gets lots of subsidies, too. As Vern Ader, president of Energy Integration Corporation in Mosinee, Wisconsin, and a longtime researcher in the field of alternative fuels, said to me, "If gasoline goes to five dollars a gallon, as it has in some parts of the world, the whole picture changes."

Presently, gasoline is so dirt cheap that, even where technology has dropped the amount of net energy needed to make a gallon of ethanol from 40,000 Btus to as low as 17,000 Btus, says Ader, alcohol still won't compete on a strictly dollar basis. He says that even with ethanol fuel cells, where the alcohol fuel is more than half water (a technology known and demonstrated since the 1930s), alcohol still doesn't compete. *Yet.*

It is not just a matter of cheap petroleum. We live in an extravagant oil culture, not a frugal alcohol culture. The infrastructure of motor vehicle goods and services in the United States is geared almost exclusively to petroleum fuel. To understand the enormous problem this makes for anyone trying to introduce a renewable fuel substitute for petroleum into our culture, consider a world that had never discovered petroleum. Contrary to what most people believe, the piston engine *preceded* gasoline. The first cars were made to run on alcohol (and on steam and electricity before that). The early Fords were alcohol-burners. The first diesel engines ran on rapeseed (canola) oil, not petroleum diesel. In some countries (Brazil, parts of Europe, and especially Cuba, where the people have no alternative but to burn alcohol from sugar cane), motors that run on ethanol are much more common than they are here. Some cars and tractors come out of the factory there ready to burn alcohol. Hitler ran his whole war machine on alcohol for the last two years of the Second World War, and the Germans remain very familiar, culturally, with alcohol for fuel today. In America the discovery of huge deposits of oil, right when automobiles were first coming into widespread use, meant that gasoline almost immediately displaced alcohol as a car and tractor fuel. America was swamped with oil. The culture of extravagant fuel use followed. People came to expect and then demand the huge quantities of gasoline they needed for unlimited travel and gas-guzzling, high-powered speed. Today the most asinine, whimsical, and unnecessary travel is considered a human right never to be denied or even questioned.

If we had remained an alcohol-fuel culture, railroads would have continued in heavy use for long-distance travel. Bicycles would have continued in common use for local travel, not just as toys for children. Auto engines would have been, by necessity and definition, of the low-mileage and lower-horsepower type, simply because biofuels could not and cannot be manufactured in large enough quantities at low enough prices to allow the kind of automotive idiocy we "enjoy" today. The quality of life today would be much better without gasoline. Those decades of pollution from leaded gasoline and the lingering excessive carbon monoxide pollution would have been altogether avoided.

Environmentalists often fear a "return" to alcohol for fuel because they believe it would mean cultivating every acre of ground a tractor won't fall off of to get the grain or biomass needed for the extravagant supply demanded. Studies by Marty Bender at the Land Institute in Kansas document the justification for such a fear. In fact, Bender suggests that any large-scale use of biofuels on the levels of gasoline and diesel use today, whatever the price of petroleum, would be ecologically inefficient and destructive of soil in the long run. But in an alternative-fuel culture—where some ethanol, some oilseed diesel fuel, some solar electric batteries, some train travel, some use of efficient blimp-type airships, and some change in the design of transport vehicles, coupled with a lifestyle of lower fuel consumption in general—small-scale use of ethanol might indeed be attractive ecologically. In any event, continued extravagant use of *any* fuel that would decrease food supplies would drive up the cost of both food and biofuel, so that a diminishing supply of oil or uses of other fuels like hydrogen would still compete ethanol out of the larger fuel picture. Humans, being remarkably adaptable, would quickly give up their powerful cars and long-range travel if the only alternative were starvation. If the rich tried to have both cheap food and fuel, there would be one soul-banging revolution.

If you decide upon a lifestyle spent mostly roundabout your home community, with a habit of travel not unlike the Amish, coupled with a small-scale, sustainable food production system relying mostly on your own labor, then a biofuels culture becomes quite practical. Getting by on 500 gallons of fuel per year, with fuel-efficient engines, is easier than you might think. During World War II, with gas rationing, we were allowed 3 gallons a week, and somehow we all survived quite well.

Many of the calculations used to show the impracticality of ethanol employ numbers and scenarios that don't apply to the very small farm or garden lifestyle. For example, debates on ethanol's "efficiency" usually assume that pure neutral spirits will be manufactured, which is what ethanol plants must produce if the fuel is to be used as a gasoline additive in today's conventional cars. But in a properly adjusted motor, you can burn alcohol as low as 140 proof, and 160 proof works fine. It is much cheaper to produce 160 proof alcohol than 200 proof, which requires not only more heat energy in the distillation process, but a drying operation to get the alcohol from 195 proof up to 200 proof. Pure alcohol is not possible from distillation alone. (If the technology of burning water and alcohol together, demonstrated as far back as the 1930s, is perfected, and it is being perfected in ethanol fuel cells, then the generation of electricity with alcohol becomes very attractive. See *Ethanol Fuel Cells for Rural Power Generation: Final Report, June 1994* from the Rural Electric Research National Rural Electric Cooperative Association, 1800 Massachusetts Avenue, N.W., Washington, D.C. 20036.)

Another significant difference in favor of very small operations when considering the definition of fuel efficiency requires a preliminary description of the by-products of ethanol production to appreciate. The reason ethanol fuel looks so promising is that the leftover mash makes an excellent protein feed for animals, as described earlier. It could make human food, too. A bushel of grain from which 2.5 gallons of alcohol have been extracted loses only the fat or energy value of the grain, and not necessarily all of that. About two-thirds of the volume of the bushel of grain is gone, but all the protein remains in a more concentrated, more easily digestible, and more economically transportable form. All the minerals are still there, too. That's why it is a little shrill when some environmentalists argue that using corn to make ethanol might take food out of the mouths of poor people. Using ecologically benign soybean inks could be viewed as taking food out of the mouths of poor people, too, but no environmentalist objects to that. If the grain mash from ethanol production is fed back to animals or humans, and if the animal (and human) manure is returned eventually to the soil, a limited production of ethanol strikes me as coming close to beating the so-called law of entropy.

What's more, points out Vern Ader, experiments demonstrate that when an on-farm distillation plant is operated in conjunction with an on-farm cheese plant, as could easily be the case in Wisconsin and other cheese-producing regions, the waste whey added to the grain will increase the alcohol yield to approximately 3.2 gallons per bushel. Waste whey now has other uses, but it is not hard to imagine that a small farm cheese plant would find its best use for whey as a mix with the grain to increase its alcohol plant's output. Also, points out Ader, the liquid stillage (whiskey slop) that remains after distillation can be used efficiently as drinking water for livestock, and, in the case of dairy cows, will increase milk supply. Furthermore, when the distillers grain, as the leftover mash is called, is fed to animals nearby, it does not have to be dried and bagged for faraway shipment. This is the most significant way that small on-farm alcohol operations can be more efficient than the giant alcohol plants now in operation. The giants must dry and ship their distillers grains to more distant markets. Ader says that when wet distillers grain is fed on the farm where the alcohol is being produced, there is a savings of approximately thirty-seven cents per gallon that goes directly into the farmer's pocket. "This is exactly why there is a need for more experimentation with farm-sized ethanol plants," he says.

However, even with on-farm alcohol plants, production is usually projected in the millions of gallons to make the plant commercially worthwhile. (Always in a capitalistic economy, quantity, not quality, is the way to profits.) Therefore, another problem looms. Even at 10 million gallons, which is considered a small plant, the amount of grain mash left over from distillation requires a larger number of animals to consume it than the normal-size farm can handle. So, again, the conclusion is that ethanol is not practical on a typical farm. But a plant producing only 500 to 1,000 gallons is, of course, a very different situation. It would have no problem feeding the wet mash to a smaller farm's normal number of livestock.

Carbon dioxide is also produced in the distillation process. The same bushel of corn that yields 2.5 gallons of ethanol and 18 pounds of high-protein feed also produces 18 pounds of carbon dioxide as the grain ferments. In large plants this CO_2 can be sold to industry, although at present this avenue has not been pursued as much as the dried distillers grain. In a small backyard plant, that

CO_2 could be piped off to a nearby greenhouse and used to good effect.

The biggest problem with a small alcohol plant is that it is labor-intensive. (A pain in the ass, in other words.) Although producing 1,000 gallons is not a really big job, it takes about as much time and botheration as producing 10,000 gallons, often when there is other compelling farmwork to be done. This is generally the reason why all the people who embraced backyard alcohol in the seventies quit. Gasoline was just so much easier and didn't require tinkering with motors. Take away easy gasoline, and project motors made for ethanol, and a lot of those people would still be producing alcohol and would have by now found new ways to do it, with much more efficiency and ease.

Almost everyone with experience in biofuel production tells me that an alcohol plant or a biodiesel plant (I don't address the latter because it is beyond the scope of this book, but biodiesel might become more practical a fuel than ethanol), whether it is tiny, small, big, or gigantic, is only practical if it is operated cooperatively by a group of interested people. The large plants, successful now as long as they have the government subsidy, are mostly farmer-owned cooperatives in which the farmers have invested their money. Hired help, often highly paid hired help, runs the plant, which of course adds to the cost. To do the same thing on a very small scale and much more cheaply per gallon, five neighborhood small farmers, for example, each needing 1,000 gallons of fuel, could come together and build a 5,000-gallon still and take turns operating it. If they each wanted 5,000 gallons, then they'd put together a 25,000-gallon plant, still very small by industry standards.

Currently, 200 proof ethanol is being produced to be used as a 10 percent mixture with gasoline, in which case no adjustments need to be made on standard engines. In fact the ethanol in the mix will clean the carbon off the motor and reduce carbon monoxide emissions. The contention that the ethanol causes poor engine performance is apparently nonsense. But a 10 percent mix with gasoline is of interest only to the grain industry, which sees it as a way to get rid of surplus corn. A small farmer or backyarder would use so little fuel that a mere 10 percent addition of alcohol to his gasoline would be insignificant, except in terms of lowering pollution a little. So the real interest among alternative-fuel buffs is in the 85 percent alcohol, 15 percent gasoline mix that automakers are now turning out a few cars to use, or alcohol-and-water fuel, as in 160 to 190 proof alcohol. The latter is just as practical as the 85 to 15 mix. Racing cars today often run on pure alcohol. The more complete combustion possible with alcohol means greater speed if the motor is adjusted to handle the fuel properly.

Converting an existing engine to using 85 or 100 percent ethanol is not difficult, but is a job for someone knowledgeable about carburetion and fuel injection. Essentially, you have to enlarge the opening in the carburetor jets or fuel injection nozzles to allow more alcohol into the manifold than is required for gasoline. Brown's book, cited above, advises boring out the jets to a size 40 percent larger than for gasoline, and the book tells you precisely how to do that. Then in most cases you have to advance the spark a little, again as discussed in Brown's book. Any good mechanic can do the conversion. In earlier motors, fuel flow into the carburetor could be adjusted by valves so that, with these motors, reboring should not be necessary. In almost all early cars, advancing the spark could be done by a flick of the wrist on the spark lever. Alcohol-fueled motors won't necessarily start easily in cold weather, and some engines converted to alcohol have dual fuel tanks and even dual carburetors. After the engine warms up, the operator switches from gasoline to alcohol, much like in early tractors that ran on kerosene after the engine was started and warmed up on gasoline. Also, alcohol tanks can be equipped with heaters to warm up the alcohol for easier starting in winter. If cars and tractors were built for alcohol, any problems of poor starting would long ago have been eliminated. In the early days of diesel fuel, poor starting was a problem, too, but no longer. Finally, in many cases, increasing the compression of an engine makes it perform better on alcohol. This usually requires a slightly different design of the engine.

You can use a moonshine still to make ethanol, but it would benefit greatly from the addition of a taller (4-foot) stripping column and/or reflux column above the evaporator. This allows the alcohol vapors a longer time to rise through the plates or marbles in the columns, and therefore more opportunity to condense and revaporize over and over again, as described in earlier chapters. The alcohol vapors coming out of the top of the column then have a better chance of reaching a high proof in one pass, avoiding the necessity of redistillation. Some on-farm ethanol producers have used electric fence porcelain insulators in the stripping column rather than marbles or plates. Others weld in steel plate strainers. The books mentioned above illustrate stills you can use for models, and these books will lead you to scads more information. So will the Internet. In the early days of *Mother Earth News*, the magazine sold some very detailed plans for a small ethanol still, and these plans might still be available.

The technology of the distillation process is constantly undergoing changes that appear to make alcohol more practical. For example, a new yeast has been discovered at Purdue University that will feed on almost any kind of plant material and turn its starches into sugars for ethanol production. With this new yeast, ethanol plants can make use of almost any plant waste or crop residue, such as rice hulls, rain-ruined hay, grass clippings, sawdust, etc. This yeast could lower production costs to under $1.40 a gallon, say its champions. The lignin left over from distillation (rather than grain mash in the usual process) is then burned as part or all of the distillation fuel. Also, a new enzyme has been developed through gene splicing that reportedly can accomplish the same feats as the new yeast. Its proponents claim they can produce seven gallons of ethanol for every one gallon of oil or ethanol that is burned in distilling it.

While I find these kinds of development more frightening than reassuring, since they suggest ways to turn all plant life into fuel for a gas-guzzling, travel-mad society and then burn the leftover fiber rather than returning it to the land as organic matter, I can see only a very limited use of traditional ethanol on small farms as something positive. Let us imagine in a society of the future: five small neighboring farm families living a lifestyle that technologically would resemble an Amish community somewhat. They would use small tractors and small engines like those on chainsaws and lawnmowers, as many Amish do, along with their own manual labor and perhaps some draft horses. These families would use cars for local travel and perhaps an occasional trip. All the motors, whether for tractor or tools or car, would be superefficient in terms of fuel usage. Let's say such a small garden farm would require 700 gallons of fuel per year. A bushel of corn yields 2.5 gallons of ethanol, and so for 700 gallons, and with corn at the average yield of 120 bushels per acre, only 2.3 acres would be devoted annually to fuel production. For all five families sharing a still to produce 3,500 gallons, the total acreage of corn for fuel would be around 15.

The five families would take turns operating the still and share all expenses. The wet distillers grain would be equally shared by each farm, or sold to other nearby farms or made into baked goods, if there was a surplus of it. Since every bushel of corn or wheat is still worth half a bushel in nutritional value for animal (or human) feed after distillation, only 7.5 acres, or 1.5 per farm, would be actually devoted to fuel. Moreover, because the farms are contiguous or nearly so, animals would be close to the distillery, and the wet distillers grain could be hauled to the animals at a low cost per farmer and at a great savings over having to dry the distillers grain. The manure from the livestock would go back on the land from which the corn was harvested.

That still leaves the energy problem, which is the real reason that alcohol (or gasoline for that matter) might never be truly efficient. It takes lots of heat to distill the alcohol or refine the petroleum. Vern Ader (and of course many others) has an answer for that, too. With a little ethanol plant integrated into the operation of the farm, an anaerobic digester, using proven technologies, could be installed to make methane gas from the manure before the manure is finally returned to the fields as organic matter. The methane gas would then be used to heat the still. There could even be surplus energy from which to generate electricity. Ader calls it a "Farm Ethanol/Feed System Integrated with an Anaerobic Digester/Manure Management System."

And of course, under a more enlightened government, you could draw a little of that fresh alcohol off the still, put it in an oak barrel, and have yourself some fine spirits in a few years. O Entropy, where is thy victory? O Entropy, where is thy sting?

CHAPTER 12

"Not Necessarily:"
The Slightly Fictional Story of
a Stubborn Winemaker

Inspired by reading about the Williams Brothers Somersetshire
Cidery in England and visiting Mike Wineberg at his winery near
Mount Vernon, Ohio, and by conversation with my friend, Ed
Fackler, the contrariest orchardist of all.

AUL CREEL did not utter a single word in the classroom until he was halfway through third grade. In a more modern era, he would have been quickly enrolled in the schooling professionals' favorite special class of the moment and bombarded with tests for autism, or hearing impairment, or dyslexia, or agoraphobia, after which teachers would have concluded what Paul's classmates already knew: he was just plain bullheaded. Passive resistance was the only defense available to him to protest the fact that he did not want to be in school. He hated school, hated teachers, hated standing in lines two by two, hated chanting the Pledge of Allegiance, hated just about everything that forced him to act like a lamb in a flock of sheep. The supreme power of the United States said he had to go to school, but no power on Earth could make him speak there.

Even in his own habitat on his father's farm, or on the playground, where he outshone everyone in sports, he was quiet and reserved. He never made quarterback on the high school football team only because he was too soft-spoken to yell out the signals.

Though it seemed not particularly significant at the time, his first words in the classroom came after his teacher, who had an urban background and felt ill at ease in the rural environment of Fowler Village, observed rather shrilly that if more farmers went to college, as she hoped all her students would, they would be more successful in the modern world.

"Not necessarily," quavered a soft little voice, seeming to issue out of the overhead lights in the general vicinity of where Paul sat.

The teacher halted in doctrinal midstream, her verbal oar poised and dripping tentatively over her desk. "Please?" she said, eyes widening as she realized who had spoken. "Please?"

"Not necessarily," the soft voice repeated, now a little louder. If any doubts were left as to whose mouth the words had slipped from, they vanished as Paul's face turned a violent crimson.

"And why do you say that?" Teacher asked, also softly, not wanting to scare away the first sign of intellectual life she had observed in the boy.

But the boy had made his point, and in his mind nothing more needed to be said. If Teacher didn't understand his objection, if she did not know that there were scores of farmers all around Fowler Village who were quite successful without going to college, then she was the one who needed more education.

The second time he spoke out in public was in his senior year at Fowler High, on the occasion of the last football game of the season. Fowler was losing 21 to 0 to a larger school, and as Paul trotted past the opposing team's rooting section on his way to the locker room at halftime, a taunting voice jeered at him. "You boys mighten as well come out for the second half. Yer gonna get the shit kicked out of ya if ya do." Paul stopped, looked at the crowd, trying to spy out the source of the remark, and, in a fairly loud voice, made more ominous by its characteristic softness, he replied, "Not necessarily."

In the second half, he scored four touchdowns and tackled so violently on defense that the opposing star player had to limp out of the game several times. Fowler won 28 to 21.

The third time he spoke loud enough to be heard more than ten feet away was on Omaha Beach when his company was pinned down by heavy German machine-gun fire. One of his men starting crying, helpless to stop the moist spread of urine through the crotch of his pants. "We're all going to die," the soldier wailed in abject panic. "We're all going to die!" Paul rolled over beside him in the sand, grabbed him with the hand not clenching his rifle, stuck his face into the crazed, weeping boy's tears, and said, still rather softly, but plain to hear under the scream of overhead shells, "Not necessarily." And then, considering his usual subdued manner, Paul practically screamed twice more: "NOT NECESSARILY." Having delivered what was for him a lengthy speech, he rolled away, pulled the pin on a hand grenade, stood up into the teeth of raking gunfire, and, just as he had many times thrown a runner out unerringly from center field, hurled the grenade straight into the machine-gun nest that held his men prostrate. He raced then to the shelter of boulders up at the head of the beach, his men following him, bleating and pissing, as they ran crouched over, exactly like a flock of sheep following their shepherd.

Through the Battle of Normandy and on across southern France, Paul shepherded his company with what sometimes seemed an infallible ability to avoid casualties. Otherwise he rarely spoke to his men or associated with them during lulls in battle or periods of rest and recreation away from the front. While they drank themselves to oblivion on the cognac they liberated along the way, or roostered around with the older and fatter and coarser women that the officers had passed over, Paul pored over the farm magazines and horticultural books his mother sent him. Whenever possible, he walked through the countryside, ignoring churches and castles and sometimes mortar shells to observe closely the small, meticulously kept farms that so fascinated him, and the village inns that served the food that the farms provided. He wrote in his journal a terse observation: "Not even war can completely starve out people who are self-subsistent. A lesson here." Occasionally his men heard him comment out loud, though not to them, as when he gazed upon a magnificent but bombed-out stone barn and muttered over and over, "Stupid, stupid, goddamn stupid!" He spent hours loitering around Normandy gardens, neat and orderly, every plot an outdoor pantry of survival food. He drew diagrams of the garden designs and got the gardeners to write the names of the plants in his notebook. When he found a garden with a bomb hole in it, he would clench his teeth, shake his head, and growl, "Stupid goddamn war."

The day he found the winery with two walls blown out, he sat down and began to cry. A Frenchman, watching from the shadows of the crumbling building, approached him hesitantly, stood silently staring at him, and finally spoke in perfect English: "This was my life, my living. My father's living. His father's living."

They studied each other in silence, sharing sorrow. When he spoke, Paul as usual did not waste words. "Where are your grapevines?"

The man smiled. "Not grapes. Apples. This is Calvados country."

When Paul did not show the recognition that the word would have inspired in someone knowledgeable about spirits, the Frenchman explained. "We make, or at least used to make, the best apple brandy in the world. And we think the best French cider wine, too. You just came through part of what was once our orchard before the last tank battle."

Paul's eyes glowed with an intensity no one in the army or any teacher in school had ever witnessed. Out came his notebook. Had any of his men been present, they would have been amazed at the way the words now tumbled from his tongue. "Will you show me how you make your wine and brandy? What apple varieties do you use? How many acres does it take to make a living from apple wine?" He fired questions so fast that the Frenchman threw up his hands and, smiling, beckoned Paul to follow him.

He led the American around the side of the shattered barn, paused only a moment as he looked around for prying eyes, making a final decision. Something about Paul exuded trustworthiness. The French farmer began to scrape aside dirt and debris to reveal a cellar door not quite flat to the ground. Down steep steps they descended, then into a large and ancient vaultlike room with stone walls that curved to form a roof over their heads. In a row, 50-gallon wooden barrels sat on their sides on a low stone shelf, a spigot sticking out of each barrel end like a sink faucet. "The bastard Germans never found it," he said with a triumphant gleam in his eyes, "and neither have the Yanks, you understand." Paul nodded. The Frenchman just seemed to know that he was addressing a man who could make the Sphinx seem talkative, who would keep the cellar a secret.

He produced two glasses seemingly from nowhere, and drew amber liquid from one of the spigots. The room immediately bloomed with the aroma of apples, yet so pure and light a smell as to seem to be only the soul of apple, which indeed it was. Paul put his lips to the glass, and the fragrance rose even more intensely into his nose until it seemed to penetrate his very brain. Paul drank and looked abruptly at the farmer with surprise. "Apple wine," the Frenchman said. "Apple wine as good as grape wine, though few vintners will admit it. No sugar in it as in most apple wines. Only a few apple varieties in the best of years are up to it. This is 1936 vintage from Dabinett, Reinette de Champagne, Rambour d'Hiver, Pomme du Rhin, and a little wild crab added. Thirty-six was a perfect apple year for us."

"This is not like any cider I've ever tasted," Paul explained, "much better than what my father makes by adding sugar and raisins."

"Now try this," the Frenchman said, drawing from a barrel on the other side of the cellar. When Paul raised the glass to his lips and let the liquid flow over his tongue, it seemed to explode in a vaporous fire that did not burn but only warmed. He straightened up, startled. Never had he tasted anything like it. The Frenchman smiled.

"Brandy. The best Calvados," he said. "Also from thirty-six. With brandy and wine you can save the perfect year in a cask until another perfect year comes along."

Out came Paul's notebook again, and for an hour the two farmers talked animatedly about fruit and wine and brandy, and finally on all things agricultural, Paul intently asking question after question. This was the first French farmer he had met who could speak English, and he aimed to make the most of it. Studying his notes in a foxhole a few days later, Paul noticed that what he had written down was mostly details of what oak wood could do to apple juice fermenting slowly in a cool cave, and what it would do for brandy over years of aging.

Two weeks later Paul's luck ran out. The sixth sense that seemed to tell him in some mysterious way when to move and when to stand still under fire abandoned him, and a mortar shell tore a gaping hole in his thigh. By the time the medics got to him, he had lost so much blood that they shook their heads.

"He's going to cash it in," one of them said, thinking Paul unconscious.

"Not necessarily," the bleeding man grunted through clenched teeth.

Back in England, Paul realized that he had not been so unlucky after all. His wound had delivered him from the battlefield just a few weeks before the Battle of the Bulge, and as he followed the news through those awful winter days, he learned that nearly his entire company had been wiped out. Overwhelmed with sorrow and anger, he would close his eyes, sleep fitfully, and dream the dream that had kept him alive: his little farm in a valley far from the sounds of exploding gunfire and screaming boys. The sun came up at one end of a valley and set on the other end, and no one could enter without his say-so. The house on the farmstead and the barns and outbuildings were all white with green roofs. When he awoke he often wondered why these colors, but he could see them so clearly in his mind that he was sure the farm existed somewhere.

In January the doctors said that he would walk only with a crutch and only slowly for the rest of his life.

"Not necessarily," said Paul.

By March he was hobbling around, his teeth biting his lips in pain, the crutch left behind in his room. In April he could walk assisted only by a cane over the English countryside. Life became for him more promising and beautiful than he had ever dared believe possible. The hospital where he was recuperating was in Somersetshire, in the west of England in a region of pastoral plenty he would never have believed possible, growing up as he did with the idea that all England looked like the aftermath of industrialism as in the movie *How Green Was My Valley*. He spent his time in horticultural and agricultural libraries, amazed to find that the English had forgotten more about farming than Americans yet knew. Away from the libraries, he roamed the sheep downs and orchards of Somerset, always observing, always taking notes. One day, expanding his horizons with a bicycle, deliberately forcing his leg to work whether it wanted to or not, he came upon an orchard, so snowy white with blossoms that it seemed to have been caught in a sudden Corn Belt snow squall.

But it was the aroma of the blooms that caught his attention, a more intense smell, somehow, than what he had normally associated with apple blossoms before. Leaving his bicycle, he hobbled into the orchard. The trees seemed to spread endlessly in front of him, enveloping him in a wondrous world of blooms, bees, and birds. Surely a garden of paradise. Presently he found himself facing a farmer, peering through the blossoms at him.

"Am I still on Earth?" he asked the man, who after a few moments responded with a knowing smile.

"Just barely," the Englishman answered. "It is bloody beautiful, isn't it?"

"Beauty's the reason we farmers keep on farming," Paul remarked, thereby conveying the reason he was trespassing. "But tell me. What kind of apples are these? I know about corn, not apples, but I swear the fragrance of these trees is different."

The Englishman stared at him, obviously a bit surprised. "Yes, you are right. Not many notice. These are rare, old varieties. Yarlington Mill, Michelin, and Kingston Black mostly." He waved his hand to convey the message that there were others. He did not know how interested a Yank on the mend might be, even a Yank who was a farmer. "These varieties were developed a century and more ago, when apple cider was a much more popular drink and making it was a respected art."

Paul pulled his notepad out and began asking questions. The Englishman waved his hand to stop him. "Come," he said, "I will show you something." He said the word "something" with an edge of immense but quiet pride.

Down through the aisles of apple blossoms the English farmer, whom Paul would come to know as Tom Billiams, led the way, slowly, to accommodate the soldier's hobble, the slowness building a kind of suspense. At last they emerged from the orchard to look down into a valley at the most beautiful little farmstead Paul had ever set eyes on. A sharp cry of pleasure sprang from his lips. Dairy cows loitered inside a gray stone wall enclosing the east side of a gray stone barn. A stone cottage sat a bit above the barn and close enough to it for humans inside to hear any animal that might cry out in need during the night. Sheep grazed among the apple trees on the opposite hill. In the lowlands, spreading out up valley and down away from the farmstead, were little fields of hay and grain. At the top end of the valley, on the highest hills, forest rose up thick with oak trees.

The Englishman started down the hill but Paul did not immediately follow. He just continued to stare at the landscape, repeating over and over, softly, so that only he could hear: "This is it. This is it. The only thing missing is the green roofs."

For the rest of his recuperation, Paul spent almost all his time at the Billiams farm, healing faster now, hardening his muscles at farmwork, mucking out the barn, milking the cows, learning how to prune and graft, observing how Billiams had reduced his orchard insect control program to only three sprays. But most of all he observed the way that Billiams made the cider he was famous for all over the region. The apples were squeezed in the largest press Paul had ever seen: "We found it in Germany," said Billiams. The juice flowed directly into a huge wooden barrel, one larger than Paul had imagined could be coopered together. "Holds four hundred gallons," said Billiams. "They ain' no oak trees big enough for barrel staves like that anymore." In the vault, the temperature stayed around 55 degrees, cool enough for slow fermentation. "That's part of the secret, cold fermentation," Billiams explained. But he would not tell the whole secret of why his cider was famous throughout the neighborhood. He said that he used no wine yeast or sugar in his cider making. But he would not say exactly what specific gravity and alcohol content the cider had to reach before it was pumped out into smaller oak barrels that had been used previously for sherry. "If I told it all," he grinned, "how could I say there is a secret to the process?"

"Might part of the secret be in fermenting such a large amount all at once in oak wood?" Paul asked, trying to break the code. "Could sheer volume and a large area of contact with the wood help?"

"Maybe. Having the cider ferment right over a large amount of lees in the bottom of that big barrel probably helps more than anything," Billiams offered, as if he were not sure himself.

"Since, like grape wine makers, you don't use sugar, does that influence the taste?"

"Sugar increases the alcohol content. Don't tell anyone, but apple wine should not be as alcoholic as grape. The alcohol can obscure the delicate apple taste."

"How much alcohol?"

Billiams smiled. "Now there you go again. Can't I have my little secrets?"

Although he longed for the war's end and going back home, when Paul was finally mustered out, he found himself so attached to the Billiams farm that leave-taking was difficult. "If sometime in the future I manage to have a farm like yours, Tom, would you send me cuttings from your cider trees?"

"Of course. Little enough pay for all the work you've done for me."

"I owe you," said Paul. "This farm has been my real recovery hospital."

The desire to go home again gives home an allure that the actual return soon reveals as overly romantic. For Paul, the good of his homeland was still there, but so was the bad of it: the narrow view of the world that homelife so often produces, that part of home that his homesick mind had so easily ignored when away. But intent as he now was on following a plan he had thought through in foxhole and hospital bed, even after the euphoria of coming home had passed, southern Indiana kept on seeming like heaven to him, warts and all.

"These damn knob hills is no place for a farm," sniffed his father, who had farmed there all his life and lived comfortably enough, but somehow felt he had to apologize for it. "The future here is somewhere else."

"Not necessarily."

"Well, I'm doing you a favor by not selling you that land you think you want," said Uncle George. "It's good only for rich people's houses someday."

"Not necessarily."

"Well hell, Paul. Why in the world would you want to pay good money for that damned knob hill? That ground's so steep you could stand it on end and plant both sides of it and still not get but half a crop. All you got there is an overgrown, worm-eaten old orchard that won't even make good firewood."

"Not necessarily."

Eventually Paul wore his uncle down. While George complained that there was no money to be made in any kind of farming in Floyd County, despite the fact that he had gotten fairly rich farming there himself, he sold the hillside farm and rundown house and barn to Paul "reasonable."

To the mind ordained to farming, there can be no thrill as keen and challenging as taking possession of a neglected acreage and putting it to comely, productive farmland again. Paul set out with boundless energy and a sharp chainsaw, working dawn to dusk and often into the night by lantern light. The thirty acres of orchard lay mostly on a cold northern slope, which Uncle George thought an accident of stupidity on the part of the original orchardist, but which Paul knew to be deliberate. On a north slope, blossoming would be delayed until the fitful days of warm and cold in early spring has passed. Nor would the sun on a warmish winter day seduce the buds to start to swell, as it would on a south-facing slope, so that they might freeze when the nighttime temperature plunged. And because the hillside was so steep, air currents would move up and down the slope enough to keep the temperature a few degrees above freezing on cold nights and save the blossoms.

Paul also knew from old courthouse maps, which often showed the location of pioneer orchards, that the trees had been planted about 1840, when cider was still king of the popular alcoholic beverages, and he felt sure many of the varieties would be old-fashioned cider apples. The man who had planted the orchard had come from New England, where his family had grown apple trees even before the Revolution. The fact that these trees were still mostly alive, although hopelessly overgrown with suckers and dense top growth that had encouraged much deadwood lower down, meant that the varieties were also acclimated to the place, and had reached some kind of equilibrium with both fungus and bug.

The first thing Paul did was to clear the brush from an area of the lower fields and plant apple seeds in rows. Many of them, to Uncle George's surprise, germinated and grew two feet tall in the first year. In the second spring he grafted scions from the old trees onto the whips. He also grafted on scions from Tom Billiams's Yarlington Mill and Kingston Black trees. Uncle George, who had made his tidy fortune in dairying, found this apple work mysterious, but Paul offered no explanation.

Paul went slow on pruning the old trees. It would hurt them to prune back the heavy top growth all in one year, he knew. He cut the deadwood out first, then the limbs that formed too acute and weak an angle with the larger limbs they were growing on. All prunings over two inches in diameter he carefully sawed into woodstove length. Along the road in front of the house he put up a sign: "Aromatic applewood / green or dried / for fireplace and meat smoker." He arranged the wood in tied neat bundles that were easy to carry and priced them at a dollar a bundle. Uncle George guffawed. "Nobody'll pay that much, especially for them twigs," he said. "You're wastin' your time."

"Not necessarily."

To Uncle George's amazement, the wood sold about as fast as Paul could cut it, the fireplace wood to weekend drivers from the tri-city area of Louisville, Jeffersonville, and New Albany, and the green "twigs" to hill farmers who knew about apple-smoked bacon. Eventually wood-carvers stopped by, too, willing to pay five dollars for a block of apple at least ten inches square. Uncle George mumbled under his breath about "damn fool city people."

In the second year, Paul lopped off most of the top growth to expose the lower part of the trees to sunlight. The trees too far gone to be saved he now cut down, assured that scions from them were growing on the seedlings in the nursery. By the third year, all that was left to remove were clusters of water sprouts and a few larger limbs lower down that he could now see were crossing and competing with other limbs.

In the meantime, Paul repaired the buildings and mowed away the brush in the low fields at the foot of his knob hill farm with a rotary mower as the first step in returning them to plots of pasture and cultivated field. Frequent mowing and a little lime was all this land needed to return as if by magic to bluegrass and white clover. What the buildings needed mostly was roof repair, here and there a little foundation work, new window and door framing, a few new siding boards, and lots of paint. This gave retired Uncle George something to do, and sometimes his father, too, when he was not busy on his own farm. Both father and uncle had by now developed a theory that Paul's mind was a little shell-shocked from the war and that working his little farm, however silly his labors seemed to be to them, was healthful. The boy would come to his senses in due time. Paul had them paint all the buildings white with green roofs.

Even by the second year, the apple trees started coming back into production. By the third year, a complete transformation had taken place. "I swan, I can't believe it," Uncle George said. "Those trees was on their last legs, but look at 'em. As healthy as the ones over to Hargen's Orchard."

Paul also paid attention to the cutover woodland above and to the side of the orchard. Here a few ancient white oak trees had survived fire, pasturing, and lumbering, but were now being challenged by an army of saplings fighting for the available moisture. He cut down some of the competing trees, many of them locusts big enough for fence posts, and in general cleared away the brush to release to the sun a few smaller white oak trees that were trying to get established.

"Whatchya messin' around up there in that bresh for?" Uncle George asked, beady-eyed.

"You wouldn't believe me if I told you," Paul said good-naturedly.

Paul had gone to day work across the Ohio River in Louisville at the Blue Grass Cooperage Company shortly after he had bought the farm. His father and Uncle George thought it strange that anyone would travel that far to find work, but at least the boy would earn some cash money at higher city wages to make his land payments. Only a few weeks after he started to work, he also cut down the five huge white oaks up on the high side of the knob and had them hauled to the sawmill. Both father and uncle were pleased to see that Paul had found a source of cash on the farm that they had overlooked. But Paul did not sell the logs. Soon they came back from the mill in stout three-by-six inch planks, as long as the individual logs would allow, eight feet and more. Paul carefully stacked and stickered them in the barn to dry and ignored all questions from his elders as to what he intended. They did not try to press him: by now they knew that when Paul decided not to talk, there was no way to make him.

The truth was that Paul was working at the cooperage to learn the craft. The white oak stacked in the barn he intended to turn into barrels for his cider wine. The wood needed to dry for a year naturally and then in a kiln for a month, so said his notes from

France and England. Paul was soon so well liked at Blue Grass for his hard work that he was given permission to make staves from his wood on the machinery in the plant if he did the work when the plant's own production line was idle.

"White oak from farther north makes better barrels than white oak from southern Indiana, you understand," one of the old coopers warned him.

"Not necessarily," said Paul. "If the trees grow far up on the knobs where the land is so poor they grow real slow, I think the wood would be about the same." The cooper stared at him, thought a little, and agreed he might be correct. It seemed to Paul as good a time as any to broach the crucial question. Could the cooperage's machinery turn out a barrel eight feet tall or a little more, something that would hold around four hundred gallons?

The cooper looked at him quizzically and then stared at the other workers who had gathered around to listen, turning the possibility over in his mind and theirs. "I expect so," he finally said while the others nodded agreement. "You might have trouble with leaks in a barrel that big though."

"Not necessarily."

When Paul brought three giant barrels home, one at a time in his pickup truck, Uncle George's jaw dropped till it almost bounced off his potbelly. Paul immediately ran water through them until the wood swelled them shut, closing off all leaks.

"I see now. I see," his father said, realization and then embarrassment flooding over him. "You've had this all figured out from the beginning, haven't you? Every last thing you've done for three years has been following a plan."

Paul grinned. "Not necessarily. I didn't know about the cooperage in Lousiville when I first came home. I thought I was going to have to make barrels on my own."

Having understood that perhaps Paul was not suffering from battle fatigue of some kind, his father and Uncle George did not so much as lift an eyebrow when Paul started digging what looked like a cave in the side of a steep hill on the farm. In fact they helped, waiting to be told what the cave was for.

"Probably a root cellar," Uncle George opined.

"Nope. This thing's getting too big for a root cellar."

"Maybe an icehouse."

"Naw. I'm thinkin' it's one of those bomb shelters everyone's buildin'. In case of atomic bomb attack. Paul, you know, would be thinkin' hard about bombs after what he's been through."

Paul said nothing, but kept digging. The excavation, however, was not totally underground, but exposed to the sky, ruling out the bomb shelter theory. As he dug into the hill, he built walls of sixteen-inch-wide cement blocks on either side of the excavation, and filled the blocks with concrete as the wall rose. On the outside of the walls went drain tile, just like for a cellar. At twenty feet into the hill, he stopped and built the rear wall, forming a space about thirty-five feet wide by twenty feet. deep, divided by a wall down the middle into two rooms of the same size. Over it all, above ground, went a low gabled roof with flooring over the rafters. He then filled the entire atticlike space with sawdust.

"Yep, a root cellar for sure," his father said, and George concurred.

"Nope, it's a wine cellar," said Paul, doing his best not to grin.

"Well, I'll be damned," his father said.

"Well, I'll be damned too," said his uncle.

On a shelf dug out of the slope above the wine cellar and directly to the rear of it, Paul next built a smaller building to house the apple grinder and huge old press he had found in Vermont. Apple juice could then flow by gravity from the press house down into the big wooden barrels positioned at the rear of the cellar. Next he gouged a sidehill lane along the slope from the orchard to the press house to facilitate hauling the fruit.

Four years from the time he bought the farm, Paul was selling cider the likes of which, his father declared, had never before been tasted in the Ohio River valley. True to Paul's hunch, the first fermentation in the huge oak barrels produced a particularly mellow, rich cider that could be bottled sweet right out of the big barrels or racked into smaller, used whiskey barrels (which he bought at the cooperage) and sold as a somewhat harder cider. Uncle George, to no one's surprise, discovered that he had an affinity for what he called "the publicity department," and in a year or two Paul's Knob Hill Farm Cider was known and revered throughout the region.

Paul, however, seemed hardly interested in the cider, and was glad that Uncle George was more than willing to take over the selling as well as the publicity. The younger man turned his attention almost entirely to a row of small casks in the corner of the wine cellar next to a table that he referred to as his "laboratory." On the table and the shelves above it were test tubes, hydrometers, Brix testers, and a stack of wine-making manuals. "Everything in the world is written down somewhere," Paul often said, mostly to himself.

At first he needed sugar to boost the alcohol content high enough to turn the cider into real wine. Only after five years could he test enough of his old varieties, some of which even the horticulturists at Purdue could not identify, to come up with a wine taste that began to satisfy him. And only after the Billiams's scions had begun to bear fruit did he finally succeed in producing the sugarless wine he was after.

"But you can't sell wine without paying out more money in permit fees than the stuff is worth," his father reminded him.

"Not necessarily," said Paul, who had been talking with people in the wine industry and knew that political plans were underway to allow family farms to make and sell wine at more reasonable fees. Sure enough, by the time he was ready to produce apple wines that were equal in quality to the grape wines also being produced in the Ohio River valley, the law had changed to favor both kinds of wineries.

"You knew that was going to happen, didn't you?" his father remarked, again full of amazement about his son.

"Not necessarily," Paul said with a smile. "Just a hunch."

Eventually, Knob Hill Farm Apple Wine was known and revered throughout the region, and Paul Creel was much in demand at winemaker conventions. Of course he never actually gave a speech, but sometimes he would appear on panels at wine seminars, where his most frequent answer to all questions was, of course, "Not necessarily."

In 1990, after two sons and a daughter had entered into the business with him, his wife asked Paul if he didn't think it was a good idea for him to retire. "And don't say, 'Not necessarily,'" she added.

Paul smiled. "No, dearest, I am not going to retire. I have one more big goal to accomplish."

"What's that?"

"I want to see if I can make apple brandy as good as the finest Calvados."

"But we've been through this before. The government is never going to reduce permit and bonding fees to make small farm distilleries feasible," she reminded him. "Only big companies can afford it."

He looked out over his orchard, over all the years of his life so far, and a certain, almost mischievous gleam flashed in his eyes.

"Not necessarily."

BIBLIOGRAPHY

Carl E. Feather, *Mountain People in a Flat Land* (Athens, Ohio: Ohio University Press, 1998).

Charles Allen Smart, *RFD* (Athens, Ohio: Ohio University Press, 1998). A great book for "forward-to-the-landers," with a few wonderful asides about art and good whiskey and the enjoyment of life in the country.

Tom Stevenson, *The New Sotheby's Wine Encyclopedia* (London: DK Publishing, 1997). The winemaker's and wine drinker's bible. Contains absolutely everything you could ever want to know about locating wineries around the world.

Oscar Getz, *Whiskey* (New York: David McKay Co., 1978).

Dwight L. Smith and Roay Swick, eds. *A Journey through the West*, (Athens, Ohio: Ohio University Press, 1998).

Harriette Simpson Arnow, *Seedtime on the Cumberland* (Lincoln: University of Nebraska Press, 1995).

"Michael Barleycorn," *The Moonshiner's Manual* (Willits, Calif.: Oliver Press, 1975). A most curious piece of ephemera and the only source of step-by-step information on how to make moonshine that I have found. As the author says, "It is not against the law to read this book."

Stephen Morris, *The Great Beer Trek*, revised edition (New York: Stephen Greene Press/Pelham Books, 1990). The joy of beer, by Chelsea Green's own publisher.

Fred Stetson, *Making Your Own Motor Fuel* (Charlotte, Vt.: Garden Way Publishing, 1980). This book and the following one are the best I've found to tell how to make ethanol and convert motors to its use.

Michael H. Brown, *Brown's Alcohol Motor Fuel Cookbook* (Cornville, Ariz.: Desert Publications, 1979).

Micki Stout Nellis, *Makin' It on the Farm: Alcohol Fuel Is the Road to Independence* (Iridell, Tex.: 1979).

William J. Hale, *Prosperity Beckons: Dawn of the Alcohol Era* (Minneapolis: Rutan Publishing, 1979). Originally published in 1936, this is an extraordinarily visionary book that I think everyone should read (even if it seems a little bit naive) for a solid basis in the history of automotive fuel.

Ethanol Fuel Cells for Rural Power Generation: Final Report (Rural Electric Research National Rural Electric Cooperative Association, 1994).

"Fuel from Farms—A Guide to Small Scale Ethanol Production," Report SERI/SP-451-519, U.S. Department of Energy, February, 1980.

Kermit Lynch, *Adventures on the Wine Route* (New York: Farrar, Straus and Giroux, 1998). An excellent book on wine to make you appreciate the artistry, skill, and respect for nature that goes into the very best wines.

Steve Semken, *Moving with the Elements* (North Liberty, Ohio: Ice Cube Press, 1998). Although Mr. Semken doesn't discuss his wild fruit wines in this book, his approach to nature here is unique and poetic and weird and wonderful, and was for me a joy to read.

Hurst Hannum and Robert S. Blumberg, *Brandies and Liqueurs of the World* (New York: Doubleday, 1976). A very thorough coverage of the topic. I highly recommend it as background for brandy and liqueurs specifically, but also for good details about the distillation process.

Gary Regan and Mardee Haidin Regan, *The Book of Bourbon* (Shelburne, Vt.: Chapters Publishing, 1995). Anyone interested in anything about bourbon will want this book for their library. It is the best source of information on where the bourbon distilleries are located, and which give tours and which don't. I believe this book has been updated since the 1995 edition. Since the bourbon business is enjoying dynamic growth, get the latest edition available for the most up-to-date information.

The Farmer's Wife, or, The Complete Country Housewife (Nantucket, Mass.: Longship Press, 1976). Originally published about 1770. There's a section on making wines as it was done back into the late Middle Ages. Amazing how basically the same the process has always been.

Paul Correnty, *The Art of Cidermaking* (Boulder, Colo.: Brewers Publications, 1995).

Joe Fisher and Dennis Fisher, *The Homebrewer's Garden* (Pownal, Vt.: Storey Publishing, 1998).

Dave Miller, *The Complete Handbook of Home Brewing* (Pownal, Vt.: Garden Way Publishing, 1988).

David Ruggiero, "Homebrew: Making Your Own Distinctive Beers is Easier than You Think." *Fine Cooking Magazine*, February/March 1994, pp.60–64.

Frank Browning, *Apples* (New York: North Point Press, 1998). A good book for unusual details about apples and cider wine.

Vrest Orton, *The American Cider Book* (New York: North Point Press, 1995).

Annie Proulx and Lew Nichols, *Cider: Making, Using and Enjoying Sweet and Hard Cider* (Pownal, Vt.: Storey Publishing, 1997). My favorite cider book, particularly because it includes details of making apple brandy by the easy stovetop method.

INDEX

CHELSEA GREEN

Sustainable living has many facets. Chelsea Green's celebration of the sustainable arts has led us to publish trend-setting books about organic gardening, solar electricity and renewable energy, innovative building techniques, regenerative forestry, local and bioregional democracy, and whole foods. The company's published works, while intensely practical, are also entertaining and inspirational, demonstrating that an ecological approach to life is consistent with producing beautiful, eloquent, and useful books, videos, and audio cassettes.

For more information about Chelsea Green, or to request a free catalog, call toll-free (800) 639-4099, or write to us at P.O. Box 428, White River Junction, Vermont 05001. Visit our Web site at www.chelseagreen.com.

Chelsea Green's titles include:

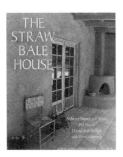  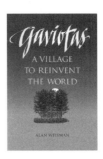

The Straw Bale House
The New Independent Home
Independent Builder:
   Designing & Building a
   House Your Own Way
The Rammed Earth House
The Passive Solar House
The Earth-Sheltered House
The Sauna
Wind Energy Basics
The Solar Living Sourcebook
A Shelter Sketchbook
Mortgage-Free!
Hammer. Nail. Wood.
Stone Circles

Four-Season Harvest
Passport to Gardening
The Flower Farmer
The Apple Grower
The New Organic Grower
Straight-Ahead Organic
Solar Gardening
The Contrary Farmer
The Contrary Farmer's
   Invitation to Gardening
Whole Foods Companion
Simple Food for the
   Good Life
The Bread Builders
Good Spirits

Gaviotas: A Village to
   Reinvent the World
Who Owns the Sun?
Global Spin:
   The Corporate Assault
   on Environmentalism
Hemp Horizons
Believing Cassandra
Beyond the Limits
Loving and Leaving the
   Good Life
The Man Who Planted Trees
The Northern Forest
Seeing Nature
Believing Cassandra

Cook 50 pounds of meal in a
barrell half full of water 212 F with
steam. until boiling

leave sit 8 or 10
hours
then
cool
to
80 F
Then Put in Yea

10 lbs of malt - this sweetens.
Dont use sugar it makes
whiskey burn the throat.

Malt is
sprouted
barley, dried
and ground.

white wash
inside

Low Wines

Wiskey

During Prohibition and the Depression
I made about two gallons a day -
sold it for $15.00 a gallon.